Desire of the Analysts

SUNY series in Psychoanalysis and Culture
Henry Sussman, editor

Desire of the Analysts

Psychoanalysis and Cultural Criticism

Edited by
Greg Forter
and
Paul Allen Miller

STATE UNIVERSITY OF NEW YORK PRESS

Published by
State University of New York Press, Albany

© 2008 State University of New York

For information, contact State University of New York Press, Albany, NY
www.sunypress.edu

Production by Judith Block and Eileen Meehan
Marketing by Michael Campochiaro

Cover image: Atussa Hatami, "the other." Courtesy of the artist.

Library of Congress Cataloging-in-Publication Data

Desire of the analysts : psychoanalysis and cultural criticism / edited by Greg
Forter, Paul Allen Miller.
    p. cm. — (SUNY series in psychoanalysis and culture)
  Includes bibliographical references and index.
  ISBN 978-0-7914-7299-6 (hardcover : alk. paper) — ISBN 978-0-7914-7300-9
(pbk. : alk. paper) 1. Psychoanalysis and culture   I. Forter, Greg.   II. Miller,
Paul Allen, 1959–

BF175.4.C84D47   2007
150.19'5—dc22
                                                                2007016659

10 9 8 7 6 5 4 3 2 1

Contents

Part Three
Psychoanalysis and the Author

Part Four
Psychoanalysis and Sexuality

Acknowledgments

This volume grew out of a conference that took place at the University of South Carolina in February 2003: the fifth annual University of South Carolina Comparative Literature Conference, organized by the editors and entitled "The Desire of the Analysts: Psychoanalysis and Cultural Criticism in the New Millennium." We wish to thank all the conference participants for making it an unusually stimulating event. The South Carolina Humanities Council and the following units at the University of South Carolina provided generous support: the College of Liberal Arts, South Carolina Honors College, the Department of Languages, Literatures, and Cultures, the English Department, the Women Studies Program, and the Philosophy Department. We also wish to thank Noreen Doughty and Paulette Jiménez for their adminstrative assistance, as well as the following graduate students in Comparative Literature: Mandy Bayer, Kay Clowney, Atussa Hatami, Georg Schwartzman.

Portions of Paul Allen Miller's chapter (chapter 1) will appear in altered form as "L'espace littéraire, la pensée du dehors, et l'objet sublime," in *La Littérature a-t-elle un espace?*, edited by Pierre Zoberman (Paris: Presses Universitaires de Vincennes, 2006). A shorter version of Greg Forter's chapter on Fitzgerald (chapter 6) appeared in *American Literature* 78.2 (June 2006): 293–323. We are grateful to that journal's editors for permission to reprint.

Introduction

GREG FORTER AND PAUL ALLEN MILLER

Why do we—or at least some of us—continue to desire psychoanalysis? How might that desire contribute to the project of interpreting, perhaps even changing, the world in which we find ourselves at the dawn of a new millennium? What, finally, is the relationship between the desire for psychoanalysis and the domain of expressive culture, a relationship that the title of this collection assumes in its yoking of "psychoanalysis" with the enterprise of "cultural criticism"?

These questions in part reflect longstanding concerns among cultural critics, but they have a special urgency in the current intellectual climate, for there has recently been much talk of the death or irrelevance of psychoanalysis. The proclamation has come from many quarters. Psychiatrists have trumpeted new discoveries in biochemistry that they say render quaint such concepts as repression, displacement, transference, unconscious motivation, and even the mind itself (as opposed to the brain). They contend that we must confine our discussions of mental activity to empirically verifiable facts, implying that the intangible quality of "the psyche" renders it no more than a metaphysical leftover of religious belief in the soul. Perhaps most damningly, these critics point to the development of powerful psychotropic drugs, especially for the treatment of depression, as proof of the obsolescence of Freud and his followers. For if depression is simply the effect of a genetically influenced chemical imbalance, and if this imbalance can be redressed through the diligent application of Zoloft, who needs talk therapy of any kind, let alone of the kind that can take years and perhaps cost thousands of dollars?[1]

A similar form of skepticism has come to prevail in the humanities and social sciences. In the latter field, the criticisms leveled are closely related to those in psychiatry. Freudian thought is disreputable, on this view, because the existence of unconscious processes cannot be empirically verified.

Or else—and sometimes the two criticisms are paired—the problem is with the non-falsifiability and testability of psychoanalytic claims, with the fact that the hypothesis of unconscious intentionality means that no instance of human behavior remains insusceptible to psychoanalytic interpretation (Grunbaum; Salter). As in the case of psychiatry, both complaints reveal a strong empiricist bias. What "is" here is what can be seen, measured, quantified, manipulated; whatever cannot be (seen, measured, etc.), by definition, does not exist. Ironically, this ontology excludes "conscious" every bit as much as "unconscious" intentions. Empiricist arguments against the unconscious are therefore self-refuting.

Moreover, the emphasis on "testability" in such contexts refers, above all, to the production of quantifiable, repeatable results. These are good things if one wants, for example, to launch a rocket or measure recidivism rates for juvenile offenders. But the psychology presupposed by such requirements is of necessity normative, since the aim of science and social science is to produce models that are as widely applicable as possible. This is the psychology of institutional normalization, industrial management, and criminology. It is, in short, the reified psychology of the subject as object of taxonomical knowledge. In this sense, it is by definition at odds with the methods of the talking cure. Free association, the interpretation of dreams as described by Freud, and the practice of the case history are tied to the unrepeatability of the signifying chain as enunciated by a specific speaking subject. In the last analysis, this logic of the signifier, its irreducible particularity and structure of difference, precludes the talking cure's results from being reduced to the repeatable, and thus from becoming the basis of a normative science or social science.

The ebullience with which humanists from the sixties to the eighties turned to psychoanalysis as a tool for exploring the intersections between individual experience and large social forces has also dampened considerably. But the reasons for this are more complex than in the case of the "hard" and social sciences. In part, they have to do with the extravagance of critics' initial investments in Freud. One is often struck, for example, by the similarity in tone of a critic like Frederick Crews, who has made an entire second career out of his hostility to Freud, and those ex-Communists or fellow travelers whom we now associate with the God-that-Failed syndrome.[2] For these critics, psychoanalysis was indeed like a religion; having once ferociously idealized it, they were led by the revelation of cracks in its edifice to denounce it with the zeal of the convert. They are in this sense perhaps best seen as disillusioned apostates, as thinkers for whom the discovery of frailty in a God they had trusted led (for psychoanalytically explicable reasons) to that God's unequivocal repudiation.[3]

The reasons for the initial "overestimation" of psychoanalysis are, however, worth exploring. They were inextricably tied to the radical project of the sixties (a "decade" that, of course, lasted into the seventies), and in particular, with the feminist insistence that "the personal is the political." Psychoanalysis provided adherents of this view with an exhilarating method of investigation that promised to reveal how domination was internalized and lived at the deepest subjective level, and thus to make the self and body central sites for political struggle. Many of the earliest inquiries of this sort were politically and theoretically naïve; they were also often based on questionable interpretations of Freud. Others, however, were extremely sophisticated and politically fruitful. In the American context, the latter included Herbert Marcuse's *Eros and Civilization* (1955), Norman O. Brown's *Life Against Death* (1959),[4] and such radical feminist interventions as Nancy Chodorow's *The Reproduction of Mothering* (1978) and Dorothy Dinnerstein's *The Mermaid and the Minotaur: Sexual Arrangements and Human Malaise* (1976). Britain witnessed, in roughly the same years, the emergence of a sophisticated Marxist psychoanalysis at the film journal *Screen* as well as the publication of Juliet Mitchell's groundbreaking *Psychoanalysis and Feminism* (1974). And in France, too, as Sherry Turkle has shown (chap. 3), a highly idiosyncratic, Lacanian-inflected discourse of militant intersubjectivity was central to the euphoria that gripped participants of the student uprising in May 68—and that seemed for a brief, incantatory moment to prophesy the surmounting of destructive social differences. (Lacan himself expressed reservations about the uprising, in a manner consistent with what Joseph Valente has called his "notorious allergy to institutionalized political commitments" [153].)

This joining of psychoanalysis with radical politics had, of course, a distinguished history, despite Freud's own political conservatism and his pessimism about projects of human liberation.[5] In the United States in the early twentieth century, for example, those most receptive to "the new psychology" were as often political and cultural radicals as they were doctors or clinicians.[6] These included cultural critic Walter Lippmann, heterodox socialist writers and editors Max Eastman and Floyd Dell, feminist activist Mabel Dodge, and anarchist Emma Goldman (Goldman enthusiastically attended Freud's lectures at Clark University in 1909).[7] All found in Freud the prophet of a revolt against bourgeois sexual repression; all saw this revolt as a crucial part of the broader social revolution, which promised both the liberation of personality and the making of an equitable social order.

The more recent turn toward psychoanalysis had, we are suggesting, similar roots. It expressed in part that radical optimism accompanying the widespread sense in the sixties that the world was being born anew—and born in such a way as to shatter all barriers to personal fulfillment and social solidarity. That many have come to see this aspiration as hopelessly "utopian" is a measure both of the movement's frailty and of the almost unimaginable power of the forces ranged against it. In light of that power, it's perhaps unsurprising that some turned away from the psychoanalytic enterprise, as they did from the political one, with the violence peculiar to the disappointment of hopes that were once so central to one's way of being that losing belief in their fulfillment leads one to scorn those very hopes.[8]

The failure of sixties radicalism is important for another reason as well. As many commentators have noted, it led to the displacement of political hopes into the realm of discourse—to an emphasis on discursive interventions and the disruption of linguistic hegemonies—and to an academic writing increasingly divorced from concrete political struggles. This is emphatically *not* to say that "theory" or academic work more generally always marks a retreat from politics. Our point is rather the opposite of this. Many humanists turned to theory and to academic pursuits as a way of trying to understand the forces that had thwarted their political projects, and so to build a sturdier basis for political intervention.

Perhaps the most formidable challenge to psychoanalysis emerged from this self-scrutiny, and that is the challenge of historicism. For if there is one thing that most humanists who came to resist psychoanalysis share, it's a critique of the insufficiently historical character of psychoanalytic methodologies. Psychoanalysis, they argue, ignores historical determinations; it sees historical phenomena as the straightforward effect of psychic processes; it attributes those processes to the social "organism" as if that organism *were* a person; it fails to take account of the historically specific character of the data on which Freud's hypotheses were based; and therefore, it at once universalizes and transhistoricizes such phenomena as the Oedipus complex, the castration complex, repression, and the contents of the unconscious—or in a more Lacanian vocabulary, alienation into the Symbolic, symbolic castration, the mirror stage, the Real, and so on.

The post-sixties version of this critique was most trenchantly developed in two quite different institutional contexts. The first was the Center for Contemporary Cultural Studies at Birmingham during Stuart Hall's tenure. The outlook of Hall and his colleagues was explicitly socialist; their project was animated by a need to integrate semiotic and psychoanalytic approaches into a critique of contemporary culture, while (1) refusing to hypostatize that culture into an irresistible monolith, and therefore (2) leaving open a space for individual agency and for subcultural reinscription of dominant meanings. Much of the felt urgency for this project came from what the Center saw as the growing hegemony of Lacanian theory (sometimes in its Althusserian form) in cultural politics on the Left—and in particular, at *Screen*.[9] The journal had developed a powerful analysis of Hollywood's "cinematic apparatus"; its contributors saw that apparatus as a dominant mechanism for the subject's captation in the Imaginary, which they tended (at this early stage) to associate unproblematically with dominant ideology. (That is, ideology was for them a function of the illusion of plenitude that came from disavowing lack.) Normative sexual difference, heterosexual identity, and nationalist ideology were all enforced through the formal codes of a narrative cinema that had its origin in D. W. Griffith: through the cuts and seamless edits that hid the mechanism of filmic production from view while suturing the (implicitly male) viewer into the position, not so much of a central male character, as of the cinematic apparatus itself. This act of suturing turned the viewer into the unseen seer and master of a universe over which he retained omnipotent (if Imaginary) control. It engorged him with an Imaginary plenitude that depended on the cinematically-facilitated disavowal of Symbolic castration, emblematized by the invisibility of the *cuts* in Hollywood film.

What Hall and his colleagues found objectionable in this theory was its perceived abstraction and structural determinism.[10] *Screen* theorists, they argued, had little interest in the actual subjectivity or experience of real viewers; "the viewer" was a purely structural position into which each and every viewer could not but be sutured. This conceptualization made it difficult to imagine a *resistant* reader of film—a viewer who wasn't fully "interpellated" by the film's effort at ideological induction. Short of a successful and total disruption of the Hollywood system itself, then—short of its supplanting by an experimental cinema that would be equally, if oppositely, deterministic in foreclosing Imaginary disavowal[11]—there seemed to be no possible progressive response to film, no chance even of an internally conflicted response, and indeed, in some sense, no spectatorial interiority at all (since viewers were "positions" rather than people).

Furthermore, the equation of ideology with the Imaginary and with the disavowal of Symbolic castration appeared to render the *content* of ideological belief largely irrelevant. All ideology was on this view subtended by, if not equivalent to, an illusory sense of plenitude; the formal mechanisms producing this sense could seem at times more important than the substance of the ideologies elaborated by a given film. The logical telos of

Screen's position was thus that even films with politically progressive content were reactionary if their style was conservative. A perspective that critics from the Frankfurt School to Jameson had used to legitimate formal experimentation against the conservative instincts of Lukács and orthodox Marxism had become a repressive mandate that ignored both the concrete experience of the viewer and the semantic richness of the filmic text (Lukács; Jameson, *Marxism and Form*; Adorno, "Commitment"). Since, moreover, the ideological content of any film invariably had Symbolic components—i.e., it was articulated in visual and verbal language—the question of *which* Symbolic order the *Screen* theorists urged one not to disavow became urgent. It made little sense to overcome disavowal and "accept" induction into the Symbolic if the Symbolic in question was entirely patriarchal and fully implicated in consumer capitalism.

The second context in which a sophisticated historicist critique of psychoanalysis developed after the sixties was that of French philosophy in the seventies and eighties—in particular, the strand of historically based philosophical inquiry initiated by Michel Foucault. Here, the critique was aimed less at the determinism of psychoanalytic theories of subject formation than at the pretension of psychoanalysis to have discovered (rather than produced) a truth about human beings. Foucault, that is, attacked what he called the "repressive hypothesis" proposed by Freud. He argued in *The History of Sexuality* that human beings are not in fact constituted by a sexuality they have repressed; it's rather the case that, at a specifiable moment in time, a range of social practices that included psychoanalysis led people to develop a sense of themselves as having deep subjective realms by encouraging them to talk incessantly about the sex they were said to have repressed. Such a critique called into question the transhistorical reality of human sexuality by insisting on its discursive production. The discursive production functioned, in turn, to facilitate social control. By encouraging patients to talk about their hidden sexual secrets, and by disseminating throughout the culture an elaborate vocabulary for doing so, psychoanalysis furthered what Foucault considered the quintessential project of modernity: the project of colonizing individual selves with an impersonal discursive power, whose incitement to speech merely guaranteed conformity to the new "common sense" that our true selves are our deep selves, which are in turn our sexual selves.

Psychoanalysis was thus for Foucault, or at least for a strand of his late thought, at once an institutionalized self-delusion and a technique (or ruse) of power. It not only mistook for ontologically real what it had in fact invented—a deep subjectivity whose "truth" is sex; in doing so, it also helped naturalize and render opaque the modern self's "voluntary" docility, its self-subjection to the emergent regime of (sexual) knowledge, and thus its conformity to norms that, because of this self-subjection, no longer required external coercion (*Sexuality*, Part Two).

Both these critiques seem to us important and in some respects persuasive. The acceptance of neither one of them *requires* us to repudiate psychoanalysis altogether, however much the Foucauldian critique has sometimes been read in that way.[12] Their effects on this side of the Atlantic, however, have not always been benign. A striking irony of both traditions is how much of a *historical* character has been lost in the process of their migration. The Birmingham position made its way to the States in the form of "cultural studies," and in particular, in the virtual domination of American Studies programs by an historicist, antitheoretical, and even antimethodological method. Birmingham's critique of psychoanalytic abstraction in the name of reclaiming the agency of cultural "decoders" has turned into a suspicion of theory as alien to those decoders' lives—and thus, as reactionary elitism. The result has been a mode of analysis that declines to universalize psychic processes, to be sure, but at the cost of rigorously avoiding the question of how historical, cultural, and psychic determinants *interact* in the encoding and decoding of discrete cultural forms. Indeed, the result has been too often to discard altogether any usable theory of the subject and consequently of the social determinants of subjective experience.

The fate of the Foucauldian critique in the United States has proceeded in a different but parallel fashion. This critique migrated largely into literature departments by way of the University of California at Berkeley (where Foucault taught in 1975 and then again in 1983–1984), and became what would later be called the New Historicism.[13] The cultural analyses produced under this banner, like those of Foucault in his archeological and genealogical periods,[14] have tended to be studiously "synchronic" and thus evasive of problems of historical causation. They have also been mostly uninterested in the psyche as a domain with even a relative autonomy from others: all domains are equally "discourse," and all serve power equally, so that individual psyches become mere conduits for a carceral force that functions in the modern episteme to produce the illusion of that psyche's freedom. Finally, though not as adverse to abstract thought as the proponents of cultural studies, the neo-Foucauldians' suspicion of narratives of liberation has led them to avoid any serious engagement with the powerfully historical and utopian versions of psychoanalysis developed by such figures as Adorno, Marcuse, and Jameson.[15] A great deal of potential value for cultural criticism has been lost in the process.

It is worth remarking here that Foucault's texts as a whole exhibit a much greater ambivalence toward psychoanalysis than his American followers allow. *Les mots et les choses* argues, for example, that psychoanalysis is not one of the human sciences (and thus not merely a mechanism for the exercise of power/knowledge), but rather a mode of inquiry into those sciences' condition of possibility (385–86). Similarly, at the time of Lacan's death, Foucault declared that what Lacan had "sought was not a process of normalization, but a theory of the subject" (*Dits et Ecrits* 4 204).[16] And in his 1982 course at the Collège de France, he directly stated that only two twentieth-century thinkers had anticipated his inquiry into the relation between the subject and truth: Heidegger and Lacan (*Herméneutique* 180–82). On the basis of these and other comments, Christopher Lane has persuasively shown that Foucault's engagement with psychoanalysis was, while undoubtedly conflicted, serious and sustained in ways the New Historicist position consistently (though not uniformly) ignores.

These institutional critiques of psychoanalysis have been accompanied by a widespread consensus about the depthless character of contemporary, postmodern experience. The terms of that consensus are well-known. Postmodern culture, we are told, is characterized by the obsolescence of narrative as a meaningful way of organizing experience; by a corollary liberation of self from "depth" and from the claims of history (both personal and social); by fragmentation as a self-dispersive and wholly surface phenomenon; and by a knowing affirmation of identity as itself a series of recycled quotations, simulations without originals, bits of borrowed and flattened materials that neither "express" interiority nor bear any relationship to a lived past. That the triumph of such a view has coincided with intellectuals' renewed suspicion of psychoanalysis should, we believe, give us pause. For though the political implications of postmodern culture are no doubt multivalent, it seems to us undeniable that such a culture works to produce modes of subjectivity that, in their sociopathic lack of affect,[17] are hospitable to the work of global capitalism. As Fredric Jameson has noted:

> The new or postmodern development . . . remains progressive to the degree to which it dispels any last illusions as to the autonomy of thought, even though the dissipation of those illusions may reveal a wholly positivist landscape from which the negative has evaporated altogether, beneath the steady clarity of what has been identified as "cynical reason." (Jameson, *Postmodernism* 323, see also 12)

The price of postmodern demystification, in other words, is the capitulation to a consumer culture in which one knows oneself to be implicated—

from which one knows thought has no "autonomy"—but whose negation becomes inconceivable once one grants this implication.[18] The depthlessness of postmodern culture is merely a symptom of this general effacement: the eradication of any space, whether psychic, cultural, or political, from which one might articulate opposition to the current social order.[19] To dispel the illusory transcendence of the given is thus to sanction a cynical (because knowing) cooperation with the coercions of late capitalism.

The hostility to the psyche among intellectuals risks, in this context, lending authority to an amnesiac culture of depthlessness whose disavowed condition is the machiadora and the literally "projected" sweatshops of the third world. As Derrida writes in his meditation on Marx, "no progress permits us to ignore the fact that there has never on earth been a time when, in absolute numbers, so many men, women and children, have ever been enslaved, starved, or exterminated" (*Spectres de Marx* 141, our translation). For this reason alone, it appears to us worth trying to reclaim the critical power of a mode of thought that honors the materiality of psychic suffering in the name of enriching our expressive projects and our material analyses of culture.

The need for this reclamation is rendered especially urgent by recent history. The conference on which this volume is based was conceived before September 11, 2001, but the events of that day and the U.S. response to them have created a moral and political climate that cries out for psychoanalytic understanding. This is perhaps most evident with respect to the torture of Iraqi prisoners by U.S. soldiers at Abu Ghraib. In a grotesque inversion of the libratory psychoanalysis discussed earlier, that torture seems to have been based on a "psychological" understanding of Arab beliefs and practices. The Pentagon, the military, and neoconservatives close to the Bush administration circulated Raphael Patai's *The Arab Mind* in the months leading up to the invasion. This book is, according to one source, "probably the single most popular and widely read book on the Arabs in the U.S. military."[20] The lessons it teaches are crudely racist and psychologically dehumanizing. Seymour Hersh has called attention to two ideas that especially impressed and influenced U.S. policymakers: that Arabs are responsive only to violence, not to rational discourse; and that they have a special vulnerability where matters of sex are concerned, since they have been taught to think of nudity and sexual activity as sources of shame (38–39). With these views in mind, and with the hysterically reiterated cry of a "war on terror" in one's ears, it's a very short step to exploiting the vulnerability of "the Arab mind" for the sake of "national security," as well as to chronicling the sexualized torture in photographs that can be used as blackmail in the gathering of "information" ("If you tell us what we need to know, we won't show the pictures to anyone else"). The question of links in the chain of command becomes almost irrelevant in such a climate. By denigrating earlier concerns over prisoner mistreatment as "isolated pockets of international hyperventilation" (Hersh 17), Secretary of Defense Donald Rumsfeld transmitted, in public and therefore to our troops, precisely the message privately conveyed in Administration memos dismissing the Geneva Conventions as "quaint" and suggesting that any strictures against torture would impinge upon the president's boundless authority as Commander in Chief.[21]

The questions raised by such a scenario are of an urgently psychoanalytic kind. They include the question of where the psychic sanction for humiliating the Other comes from; how that authority is transmitted (if not by direct order); on what cultural understandings the authority is based; the pleasure involved in instrumentalizing and torturing others; how this pleasure might be related, not merely to the Imaginary jubilation that comes from mirroring one's leaders dominative wishes, but to the much more terrible sense that in this mirroring something gets lost, some vital ideal of the nation dies; and how these largely *psychic* questions relate to such *social* ones as the invasion's imperialist motivations, its world-hegemonic and economic implications, the problems of a "volunteer" army that disproportionately conscripts minorities and the poor, and the relationship between masculinist violence and the increasing militarization of our society.

Finally, the example of Iraq is useful in suggesting how a genuinely social psychoanalysis may sometimes find it fruitful to pursue the most apparently asocial of Freud's concepts. In a speech delivered at the signing of a $417 billion defense bill, George W. Bush made the following slip: "Our enemies are innovative and resourceful, and so are we . . . They never stop thinking about new ways to harm our country and our people, and neither do we."[22] The President's difficulty with his native tongue is sufficiently well-known that it might seem fruitless to belabor it. And yet this slip is unusually alarming. To take it seriously *as* a slip is to conclude that, in a postcold war, post-bipolar world, a world as complex as the one we now live in, the pursuit of a doctrine of preemptive war that's rooted in theological paranoia (you're "with us or against us") may be a displaced expression of the death drive. The very weapons whose purchase the speech honors are perhaps the instruments of our own destruction. They are weapons deployed for our own protection that will instead rebound upon us, since the objectification of an "enemy" against whom missiles must be launched secures the anger of those already impoverished and rendered desperate by our foreign policy, and whom we then purport to "free" with Apache helicopters and F-16s. If the Freudian death drive means anything it is this: there are many ways to commit suicide, and a nation that must have enemies to strike is perhaps after all not without remorse for its historical crimes. The president's slip reveals, however, that the inner-directed destructiveness of remorse (i.e., the guilt and self-beratement) is in this case unconscious; it reveals itself only in parataxis because it is usually deflected outward onto an Other whose aggression our president solicits as punishment for our national crimes, while simultaneously believing himself an unwilling victim of the Arab people's dark, inscrutable hatreds.

The importance of reclaiming a psychoanalytic method that is fully social and culturally critical should be clear from these examples. And yet there is a curious sense in which that reclamation has already begun—or in which psychoanalytic thought has never been fully stifled. We have only to look around us, indeed, to find that assumptions derived from Freud continue to exert a peculiar fascination in nearly every corner of our culture. A psychoanalytic psychotherapy serves as a central, organizing principle for the HBO hit *The Sopranos*. The culture of TV advertising, for all its reliance on nonnarrative techniques and its cult of the reified image, betrays everywhere its belief in an unconscious to be solicited and ideologically bound through images of phallic potency and sexual satisfaction.[23] And the "virtual war" that seemed at first to take place on TV and so to implicate neither minds nor bodies has given way to wrenching stories about the trauma of battle, the radicalization of American families through the psychic suffering caused by war, and the devastating results for veterans of having been granted license to kill by a society that institutionally disowns the damage inflicted upon them when they exercise that license.[24] In a world where videotaped beheadings, performed in the name of a transcendental father, are among the most frequently visited sites on the Internet; where reality television stages spectacles of sexuality, abjection, and sadism for a global audience; and where the appeal to unconscious, inchoate fears and desires constitutes the express stock and trade of advertising executives and political consultants alike: might not psychoanalysis constitute the untranscendable horizon of our current predicament?

The media's concern with psychic suffering and the continued appeal to unconscious desire are, of course, as often exploitative and sensational as they are culturally critical. The same cannot be said for the persistence of psychoanalytic thought in intellectual circles. For here, too, rumors of Freud's death turn out to have been greatly exaggerated. One could in fact persuasively argue that, throughout the period of psychoanalysis's ill-repute, our *most* influential critics and theorists have made an engagement with

Freud, Lacan, Klein, and others indispensable to their inquiries. In the humanities, what serious work is done today that does not, at least tacitly, assume the existence and centrality of a concept of the unconscious, of repression, of desire, and of the sexed subject? Judith Butler, Kaja Silverman, Slavoj Žižek, Toril Moi, Leo Bersani, Jacqueline Rose, Fredric Jameson, Gayatri Spivak, Edward Said, Homi Bhabha—these have been among the most significant contributors to a vibrant intellectual life in the United States over the last two decades. None of them employs psychoanalytic categories dogmatically. Many profess other, perhaps more personally significant intellectual allegiances, and some have offered detailed critiques or modifications of psychoanalytic concepts. And yet the work of each is inconceivable without psychoanalysis itself, with which each has engaged in a persistently fruitful dialogue. Furthermore, each of these thinkers has embarked on that engagement in the name of anatomizing historically specific cultural and social institutions, deploying psychoanalytic theory with the critical audacity necessary to cultivating radical forms of dissent. A psychoanalytic cultural criticism has remained in this way central to intellectual discourse even as the trends we have described have worked in part to marginalize it. There is perhaps no greater confirmation that the radical possibilities unearthed by the talking cure remain relevant for us today than this intellectually inexpugnable residue (of those radical potentials.

Thus do we desire analysis, and as (cultural) analysts, we desire. The pun in our title—the desire both of and for analysts/analysis—comes from Jacques Lacan, who for the thinkers just mentioned is the pivotal, inescapable figure. (This is true even for those who, like Bersani, can in no sense be called "Lacanians.") One could point to any number of reasons for this centrality. These range from the undoubted appeal of Lacan's anarchic intellectual omnivorousness to the suggestion that Lacan has offered the most serious effort to "return" to Freud by revising him, emphasizing those aspects of Freudian thought that have turned out to resonate in our intellectual moment. For us, however, the most persuasive reason remains that offered by Jameson in the seventies ("Imaginary and Symbolic"). Jameson argued that at a moment when Freud had been all but fully domesticated by a revisionary ego-psychology in American psychoanalytic circles—at a moment, too, when psychoanalytically inclined humanists had become frustrated by Freud's political pessimism and transhistorisicm—the Lacanian emphasis on induction into language as the condition of human subjectivity promised a psychoanalytic theory that was fully social, and therefore political. For what could be more social than language? Is language not by definition "communal," the very medium of intersubjective relations? If one could then trace the formation of human subjects to the process by which a language that's necessarily "other" and prior to those subjects is internalized *by* them, one might begin to understand how an entire set of social meanings concerning gender, race, and class position were consented to and claimed as one's own. One might start to see how linguistically encoded social ideologies are inscribed at the deepest levels of the self, precisely inasmuch as each one of us internalizes the "desire of the Other" in and through the Other's *language*—a language we did not choose, yet to whose protocols we must accede if we are to participate in the symbolic exchanges so central to any community of rational, "sane" human beings.

Lacan's work has of course been criticized—not least by Jameson himself—for failing to make good on this promise of a psychoanalysis that was fully social and politically critical. A central impulse of this volume is to recover and reactivate the promise itself. The essays that follow do so largely by engaging and seeking to extend the ethico-political dimensions of Lacan's thinking. We want, therefore, to trace in brief the lineaments of this dimension. To do so, it is crucial to indicate that, for the Lacan most centrally concerned with ethics, the emphasis on language as a realm of socio-symbolic exchange is inseparable from the concept of *desire*.

Lacan codified both the vitality of the talking cure (as exemplary symbolic exchange) and the potential dangers of that cure in the concept of "the desire of the analyst," a term in which, as is often the case in Lacan, the genitive is both objective and subjective. This concept, while directly aimed at the practicing analyst, as all of Lacan's teaching was, has clear implications for the cultural critic as well, and it will repay our time if we linger a moment over the details of his formulation. In the analytic situation as formulated by Freud and Breuer in their initial *Studies on Hysteria*, the analyst both becomes the object of desire, and his or her desire is also necessarily solicited. This is the phenomenon known as transference and countertransference. Lacan formulated this concept in his reading of Plato's *Symposium*, which opened the seminar on *Le Transfert* (VIII). It is not coincidental that this seminar followed immediately after that on *L'Éthique de la psychanalyse* (VII): the talking cure is centered on the double demand that characterizes the transferential relationship; and the ethics (as well as the politics) of analysis is necessarily implicated in this complex interplay between the desire for the analyst and the analyst's desire (Chaitin 180–84). Indeed, the analytic situation is precisely the moment in which our own, individual ideological and libidinal investments come face to face with those of the other whom we seek to understand, to liberate, and ultimately to aid to realize his or her desire in a way that must fundamentally speak to our own (otherwise, why would we become analysts at all?) without becoming our Imaginary double. The ethics of analysis and the ethics of interpretation, then, whether clinical or cultural, demand a radical openness to the desire of the other and a simultaneous refusal of a false objectivity, of a disavowal of our own inescapable demand.

More precisely, in the analytic situation, the analysand, through transference, metaphorizes the analyst into the place of his or her desire. The analyst comes to occupy the position of that desire, and his or her refusal to comment directly on the associative chain of the analysand serves as the surface on which the analysand in turn comes to recognize the nature of his or her own desire. The danger comes precisely in the possibility—indeed the necessity—of countertransference, that is, in the process whereby the analyst's own desires are solicited by the discourse of the analysand. Like Socrates in his relation with Alcibiades in Plato's *Symposium*, the moment the analyst yields to these solicitations, the analytic situation is reversed and the doctor becomes the patient, the beloved the lover, and the chain of association is short-circuited. By the same token, the moment the analyst refuses the countertransference, the moment Socrates refuses the affective relationship, then all hope of Alcibiades' pursuit of the good per se is lost, the transferential relationship is broken (Lacan, *Séminaire* VIII 185–86).

It is thus only through a profound knowledge of the nature of his or her own desire that the analyst can serve as the mirror for the analysand and that the countertransference can be turned into a means of investigating, rather than satisfying or frustrating, the desire of the other. It is only through an understanding of the fundamentally empty nature of his or her desire that the analyst can serve in this role (Lacan, *Séminaire* VII 347–51; *Séminaire* VIII 127). That emptiness, however, is not a void or absence, but a refusal of every fetish, a fundamental openness: the recognition of desire per se (Žižek 131; Gurewich 369; Freiberger 225–26). As Diotima teaches Socrates in the *Symposium*, Eros (Desire) can never be any specific good (beauty, wisdom, wealth, happiness), but can only be the process of the pursuit of the good per se. Transference, metaphoricity, and substitution are thus not means to an end, but the nature of desire itself (Julien 120). Suffering is the product of a refusal to accept this pursuit or of its fixation on a single object that in the end can only disappoint. Like Socrates, the analyst must be able to lie on the couch with Alcibiades and arise in the morning unstained.

On the level of cultural criticism, the desire of the analysts is precisely the attempt to collectivize this process. It is the refusal of the authoritarian discourse of the master and ultimately of the didactic discourse of the university as well. It is a commitment to a radical democracy that refuses all reified fetishes (the flag, the party, the constitution, capitalism, the class struggle), but at the same time recognizes that metaphorizations and fetishes are inevitable and necessary, that desire must be solicited and concretized both personally and socially in order to be realized. The transference, the search for a subject supposed to know, cannot be escaped (Žižek 168). The analyst is always desired and always desiring. But the cultural analyst must respond with a relentless and ascetic negativity[25] that reveals the illusory nature of each fetishistic substitution, each neurotic displacement, without yielding to the temptation of countertransference, of imposing one's own fetishes, one's own object of desire, as a totalizing discourse of mastery.

Analysis is both the product of and an answer to suffering. It demands an ethics of care (Silverman 29–50) and listening, a loving Socratic asceticism, and a relentless criticism of all attempts to arrest the discourse of desire, to normalize it, to cede on the possibility of its realization by accepting the decreed range of acceptable social goods as the definition of our being. It is for this reason that we continue to desire analysis. The essays in this volume all demonstrate this level of care, criticism, and analytic rigor. They refuse the mantle of mastery even as they insist on their desire as a desire of and for the desire of the others. Each essay represents an open-ended commitment to hear the suffering that lies at the heart of the analytic situation and to make articulate its desire in a world that seeks to silence the demand of the other, whether through violence or intellectual, political, and cultural terrorism.

Part One, "Psychoanalysis and the Future of Cultural Criticism," addresses a question that arises organically from the interdisciplinary character of psychoanalytic criticism: why study *this particular* object or practice, the domain of "culture" at all? If the phenomena one finds in this process are after all *psychic* phenomena, why introduce a mediating object in the first place—why not simply study the mind? To legitimize this move by saying that literature, for example, is a product of the mind and that it therefore repays psychoanalytic attention is merely to restate the problem. For such a response risks reducing literary texts to the psychic phenomena they "contain" or "express" or (in a more contemporary vernacular) "expose," "enact," and "perform." The specificity of literary representation then becomes epi-phenomenal in ways that repeat the epistemological error characterizing the hunt for sexual symbols among an earlier generation of psychoanalytic critics.

To justify what we do as *cultural* critics, then, especially as we move into a new millennium whose "common sense" includes a suspicion of

psychoanalysis and of humanistic inquiry, we need a more nuanced understanding of what cultural texts do that other texts do not. Paul Allen
Miller's "Sartre, Politics, and Psychoanalysis: It Don't Mean a Thing if It
Ain't Got *das Ding*" provides one version of such an understanding. Drawing on Sartre's well-known question, *"Qu'est-ce que la littérature?,"* Miller
challenges the caricature of Sartre so common among contemporary intellectuals, in which his "literature of engagement" becomes a euphemism
for literature as propaganda. According to this caricature, Sartre's call for
a literature that's "engaged" is understood as the demand for a linguistically unambiguous indictment of the dominant social order. Miller focuses
instead on Sartre's insistence that literature is an *act* that entails the *unveiling* of a fundamentally new object. Attending to the Heideggerian
echoes in this formulation, he links it to the Lacanian concept of the Real,
suggesting that what literature does is to enact the unveiling of a Real "object" beyond yet subtending the historically particular Symbolic order in
which the literary text is produced and consumed. The exposure of this
nonsymbolic object takes place paradoxically *through* language; it is the effect of a linguistic concentration peculiar to literary representation, in
which the deepest recesses of a language are mined for the internal contradictions whose repression and radical forgetting make possible a culture's symbolic universe.

These contradictions are, in Miller's view, what author and reader
collaborate to "unveil" in any literary engagement. The political value of
Sartre's call-to-arms resides for him less in its appeal to action than in its
insistence on the critical capacity of literature as what Miller calls a "practice of the letter": a linguistic practice that reveals what that very practice
has had to negate and deny in order to be comprehensible within the system of dominant meanings in which it participates. Miller demonstrates
this theoretical argument through exemplary readings of four literary texts:
Juvenile's *Satire* 1, Stéphane Mallarmé's "Sonnet en—yx," Mark Leyner's
"The Young American Poets," and Sartre's own *Les chemins de la liberté*. He
asks us to hold in dialectical tension the concrete historical instances in
which these texts were produced, on one hand, and their intervention in
the transcendental, interlocking registers of Symbolic, Imaginary, and
Real, on the other. One of the essay's most suggestive contributions is in
this sense to distinguish between these registers' historical *persistence* with
respect to the *form* of their interaction and their historical *variability* with
respect to their social "content."

In "Psychoanalysis, Religion, and Cultural Criticism at the New Millennium," Henry Sussman, most squarely of all our writers, responds to the

twin questions that motivated this volume: why do we continue to desire psychoanalysis, and what should its role be in the cultural criticism of the new millennium? Sussman's wide-ranging essay offers a tour de force overview of many of the most immediate challenges facing both analytic thought and contemporary culture. He contends that the most basic categories of the analytic clinic—"recapitulation, *revenant*, reproach, resolve, revelation, apology, complaint, complicity, manipulation, transference, projection, and fragmentary and always provisional healing"—remain central to all contemporary forms of cultural analysis, so central that we no longer even recognize their nature or their provenance. We desire analysis, Sussman persuasively argues, because it is the condition of possibility for clarity and comprehension of the very fabric of our existence. These terms represent not only the all but Kantian categories of our tortured individual psyches but also the working assumptions of our collective institutions "whether defined by kinship, ethnicity, religion, or occupation and class." The condensation, displacement, and return of repressed desire is now the explicit fabric of our complex, interrelated, and discontinuous postmodern existence.

Therefore, the role of psychoanalysis in the cultural criticism of the new millennium, Sussman contends, should be to provide for a great communal transference, a kind of collective metaphorization, clarification, and in the last instance (but as Althusser reminds us, the last instance never comes) realization of our desires. Cultural analysis is to offer a means of reflection, a series of feedback loops and interventions. One specific area that Sussman proposes for analytic intervention is that of religion. In a world of competitive fundamentalisms, of projection and disavowal in the name of an all-powerful, castrating father, we must ask what psychoanalysis can contribute to our religious understanding, beyond impotent denunciations of the future of an illusion. Psychoanalysis, Sussman argues, must take religious speech and religious desire seriously if it is to have a role in fashioning a meaningful collective discourse in the new millennium, if it is not to capitulate to the "official religion" of commodified intolerance and self-satisfied moralizing. Sussman closes with a finely nuanced reading of the film *Far from Heaven*, showing how the psychoanalytic critic is able to offer a carefully calibrated response to the latter's dramatization of the racism, homophobia, and anticommunist hysteria that constituted the official religion of classical postwar American culture.

The essays in Part Two, "Psychoanalysis and Collectivity," focus on what Freud once named "group-psychological" processes: the psychic forces that bind human beings together into groups, as well as those that thwart or undermine—or even destroy—group formations. Among Freud's most influential accounts of these forces is that of *Civilization and Its Discontents* (1930).[26] There he focused on what we might call the intrapsychic legacy of group-psychological dynamics. He argued that the very condition of human groups—of civilization itself—is the renunciation of innate aggression and the sublimation of directly sexual Eros into "brotherly love." The problem, in his view, is that the aggression renounced toward others is redirected toward the self, in the form of guilt and through the agency of the now-internalized authority figure, the super-ego. The price of civilized relations is thus a permanent and ever-intensifying unhappiness: the more one refrains from acts of aggression, the more intensely one wishes to commit them; and the more intense the wish, the more severely does the super-ego punish the psychic impulse toward renounced acts.

The essays in Part Two draw upon Freud's discussion of these matters while seeking to resist his political pessimism. In "Lacan's Four Discourses: A Political Reading," Slavoj Žižek traces the lineaments of a new kind of political community based upon the collectivizing of the analytic relation. The desire of the analyst, as Žižek notes, is in fact a fundamental historical fact, discerned by Lacan in figures ranging from Socrates to Hegel. It is not an illusion, not something that can be set aside in the name of either a specious scientific objectivity or an opiated spiritual quietism. For this reason, as Žižek notes, psychoanalysis is the enemy of all forms of new age Buddhism[27] and pseudo-spirituality that, through the discourse of the master, seek to put aside or quench the passions. Psychoanalysis, rather, seeks to rouse them, to incite us to insist on our desire and not to settle for any substitutes. It "asserts a violent passion to introduce a Difference, a gap in the order of being."

Such a position has direct political and personal consequences. If, as Žižek contends, the "climax of analytic treatment is a momentous insight into the abyss of the Real," which nonetheless leaves us to return us to our established social roles the next morning, then we must ask: is the talking cure just a one-night stand, or does it raise issues of deeper collective significance? Žižek's answer to his self-posed question is an emphatic affirmation of the political significance of analysis, and he proposes to demonstrate the nature of this significance through a reading of Lacan's four discourses: those of the master, the university, the hysteric, and the analyst. Lacan's goal, he argues, is to produce an analytic collective whose discourse is not sustained by any claims of mastery or authority but by the very surplus of enjoyment that figures the *objet a*'s relation to the Real. The four discourses thus come to map the "properly LENINIST moment of Lacan."

Žižek undertakes his reading of the four discourses as a strategy of collective action through an examination of Seminar XVII, *L'envers de la psychanalyse*, which constituted Lacan's response to the events of May 1968. In this seminar, Lacan was concerned primarily with "the passage from the discourse of the Master" to that of the "University as the hegemonic discourse" of capitalist modernity. This discursive shift signaled a move from ecclesiastical and monarchical forms of domination based on sovereignty to new forms founded on scientific and technical reason. Lacan's analysis here anticipates Foucault's analytics of power in Volume One of the *History of Sexuality*. But the analyst, unlike the priest and his heir, the therapist, does not seek confession and does not offer empathy; rather, through his specific discourse he offers the *objet a* to the split subject ($) by means of his originary signifier (S^1), which in turn engenders the signifying chain (S^2), by means of which the analysand traverses the fantasy screen and encounters the Real. As Žižek summarizes in *Looking Awry:*

> The *discourse of the analyst* is the inverse of that of the master. The analyst occupies the place of the surplus object [*objet a*]; he identifies himself directly with the leftover of the discursive network. Which is why the discourse of the analyst is far more paradoxical than it may appear at first sight: it attempts to knit a discourse starting precisely from the element that escapes the discursive network, that "falls out" from it, that is produced as its "excrement." (131)

To collectivize the desire of the analyst, then, is precisely to collectivize this ec-centric discourse as a form of political practice.

Deneen Senasi's "Signs of Desire: Nationalism, War, and Rape in *Titus Andronicus, Savior,* and *Calling the Ghosts*" expands the inquiry into collective psychic processes by focusing on the relations among nationalism, trauma, and gender. Senasi juxtaposes two debates that have rarely been brought together: the debate surrounding the definition and dating of nationalism, and the debate about trauma and witnessing, especially in relation to the problem of historical (as opposed to purely personal) trauma. The first of these allows her to address the "transnational" and transhistorical features of nationalism. Drawing on recent historians who have challenged the equation of nationalism with modernity, Senasi argues that nationalistic enterprises both predate the modern period and have a theorizable consistency. They are based in aspirations toward cultural homogeneity that emerge (paradoxically) in response to perceived threats to that homogeneity. Furthermore, the aspiration toward homogeneity has historically entailed the symbolic appropriation of women as tokens in the narrative of nationalist identity. This appropriation robs women of linguistic agency, diminishing their capacity for self-narration in direct proportion to the increase of their value in masculine narratives of the state. Since, moreover, the demand for cultural homogeneity requires that women incubate and transmit the seed of a given "nationality," the woman's body becomes a central battleground on which the nation is preserved or sullied. For an ethnic "other" to rape "my" woman is for him to engage in an act of violation that, though aimed principally at my "nation," threatens the structures of patriarchy as well, while making the woman an abjected instrument in a battle fought principally between men.

Senasi's innovation in the debate about trauma emerges from her analysis of nationalism. The centrality of *witnessing* in recent trauma theory, she argues, works at the expense of the *victims* of trauma. For while it may be true that a dispassionate facilitator is necessary to enable women victimized by nationalist violence to narrate the tales of their violation, Shoshana Felman and (especially) Dori Laub have tended to see the witness herself as a heroic figure through whom alone the victim's narrative is able to take form. In this sense, the theory of witnessing instrumentalizes the female victim of trauma in the name of the witness's aggrandizement. Senasi's essay derives this critique from an analysis of Mandy Jacobson and Karmen Jelini's documentary *Calling the Ghosts* (1996)—a film about women raped in the Omarska concentration camp during the Bosnian war. One of these women, Jadranka Cigeli, is a striking antithesis to Laub's model of the victim as someone without memories and with no will to speak on her own. "While Jadranka considers remaining silent, she ultimately makes another choice. . . . Moreover, [this] decision . . . is entirely her own; it is not mediated by a listener but instead appears to come directly from her own memories and cognizance of the trauma she has survived. In this way, the film implicitly emphasizes the agency of the survivor and her sense of self-possession in both the decision to speak and the account she narrates." The documentarian's act of witnessing becomes, in this context, a collaborative act, one that subordinates the project of bearing witness to the desire and knowledge of its female subjects.

Part Three focuses on the recently renewed question of "Psychoanalysis and the Author." This question has been reopened on the "other side," so to speak, of poststructuralism, by critics and theorists concerned to reground their analyses in complex forms of human sentience. Those engaged in this regrounding neither abandon the poststructuralist critique of an internally coherent subjectivity nor ignore the social and discursive forces that decenter that subjectivity. Rather, they argue that the critique of subjectivity can and should be enriched by an attention to subjective particularity: to the ways in which such decentering forces as "language" or "heteronormativity" are always lived from a specific location that inflects and embodies and particularizes these general, structural effects. A description of the bereavements induced in all of us by a language that severs us from Being, for example, cannot alone account for the specific *relation* to language that each of us develops—or for the indelibly unique characteristics of a given author's linguistic innovations. The best kinds of cultural analysis will thus acknowledge that writers and visual artists are neither wholly spoken by the discourses that shape them nor fully "outside" of or in control of those discourses. They are, instead, simultaneously captives of predetermined meanings *and* agents of new meanings, the novelty of which has everything to do with the authors' psychic and social histories.

Kaja Silverman's "Moving Beyond the Politics of Blame: *Let Us Now Praise Famous Men*" explores these matters through a reading of James Agee and Walker Evans's documentary modernism. Paying particular attention to Agee's text, Silverman suggests that the book is in part a meditation on its own procedures. It asks, that is, "How can I (Agee) represent the poor sharecroppers whose plight I have been commissioned to record, without either condescending to them from a superior class position, pretending to see them 'objectively,' or romanticizing and prettifying their poverty?" To elaborate Agee's answers to this question, Silverman develops a psychoanalytic phenomenology that not only highlights the Heideggerian component of Lacan's thinking but brings the two thinkers explicitly into dialogue. From Heidegger, she takes the concept of "care": a form of responding to objects in the world that refuses to instrumentalize them or constrain them within preconceived categories, but rather responds to their sensuous appeal to be known in their particularity. In Lacan, Silverman finds a vocabulary for describing how care becomes psychologically possible. She extrapolates from his theory a language with which to challenge our conventional understanding of desire as appropriative of external objects, suggesting instead that the condition of Heideggerian care is a mode of desire that Lacan has theorized as imbuing external objects with libidinal investments that illuminate those objects as they "are." Agee, then, on Silverman's reading, displays Heideggerian care by deploying desire in this irradiating way.

The key Lacanian formulation in this context is that of "raising the object to the status of *das Ding*." This statement describes the process by which we come to "value" and "invest in" objects *without* assimilating and thereby destroying them (i.e., absorbing them into the cognitive parameters of the ego). We do this by putting them "in the place" of the Thing, which is for

Lacan the primordially lost Real object—that is, at the intrapsychic level, the mother prior to one's differentiation from her. It's only by hooking new objects up to this lost one that those objects can become meaningful for us. They become radiant and palpitant with significance inasmuch as they trigger memories of the Thing and thereby solicit our desire. The danger, of course, is that we will then *mistake* the new object for *das Ding*, abrogating the distance necessary to keeping the object alive through the play of signification—choosing, indeed, to halt that play through the narcissistic appropriation of the object as one that will *in fact* make us whole (again). For Silverman, negotiating this difficulty defines the particular form of agency that each of us has as desiring beings. That agency takes place within constraints: for each of us, only some objects (and not others) will be capable of being raised to the status of the Thing. But one of Silverman's central claims is that the aim of expressive culture is to expand and broaden this range, making previously maligned "objects" available to an irradiating and social desire.

Greg Forter's essay approaches the problem of the author from a related angle. In "F. Scott Fitzgerald, Psychobiography, and the Fin-de-Siècle Crisis in Masculinity," he seeks to bridge the growing chasm between historical and psychological methodologies in literary studies, noting that scholars have tended to focus on historical forces and determinants to the exclusion of psychic ones—or vice versa. The result of this exclusiveness has been that either the meaning of historical processes are treated as immanent to the literature, in ways that obscure the psychic mediations between such processes and literary texts; or else psychological factors are granted an explanatory power that occludes their embeddedness in historical structures.

Mindful of these difficulties, Forter offers a reading of Fitzgerald's gender formation that places psychic and historical forces in dialectical relation to each other. This project, he argues, requires the reclamation of that much-maligned mode of inquiry, psychobiography, but a psychobiography that's fully alert to the historical factors impinging upon the formation of a given psyche. The crucial, mediating link in this process is that of the bourgeois family. For the family stands as the institution through which, during those crucial and relatively secluded years of early childhood, larger social meanings and ways of "assuming" those meanings are transmitted to the child. It is the place where the "objective" possibilities for gender in a given era become *subjectively* possible and calibrated to individual yearnings. Forter, therefore, develops an account not just of the social forces that produced a crisis in masculine identity between 1890 and 1920, but of the way this crisis was mediated for Fitzgerald by the specific pre-Oedipal dynamics of his relationship to his mother, on one hand, and by his father's particular forms of "castration" as an Oedipal object, on the other. In light of these factors, Forter shows how Fitzgerald developed a deep *ambivalence* toward modern masculinity that shaped the two key events of his adulthood: his marriage to Zelda and his choice of writing as a vocation. Especially crucial in the latter regard is the gendered ambivalence of Fitzgerald's formal practice, which at once embraced and repudiated the injunction to aesthetic "hardness" and detachment that characterized mainstream U.S. modernism.

The essays in Part Four of this volume explore in novel ways the question of "Psychoanalysis and Sexuality." Central to each is the problem of sexuality's relation to the death drive. On one hand, the essays examine the complex dynamic of sadomasochism, both within and beyond the bedroom; on the other, they pursue the hypothesis of death as an expression of desire's intrinsic finitude, suggesting that the existential fact of death responds to an impulse within desire itself, rather than standing outside of and "opposing" sexual desire. Finally, the essays in this section are linked by their common concern with how the expressive texts on which they focus—far from passively "reflecting" the dialectic of sexual desire and death—solicit the reader's (or viewer's) collaboration in that disturbing dialectic.

In "Desiring Death: Masochism, Temporality, and the Intermittence of Forms," Domietta Torlasco offers perhaps the most vivid account of this collaboration. Torlasco interprets the voyeuristic sadomasochism of Nazism in Liliana Cavani's *The Night Porter* in two related theoretical contexts. First, she articulates the "loop" through which the (scopic) drive emerges in Lacan's *Four Fundamental Concepts*. That is, she shows how subjectivity is constituted through a movement of the drive profoundly at odds with our common-sense distinction between subject and object, active and passive, seeing and being seen. To "locate" oneself as a subject of the look who actively engages the visual field, one must pass through a prior identification with the passive object of vision, so that "underneath" the self's stability is a confusion between itself and the world whose disavowal is the condition of any visual mastery. The second theoretical paradigm links this problematic of vision and agency to masochism through the work of Kaja Silverman and Leo Bersani. Just as the subject achieves visual mastery through a disavowed identification with the object of vision, so, too, according to these theorists, does the sadist achieve the psychic distance necessary to the project of cruelty by way of a disavowed identification with the other person's pain.

Torlasco unfolds the bewildering temporality that emerges when these disavowals are undone. Through detailed close readings of the flashbacks in Cavani's film, she shows how they work to thwart the narrative teleology of sadism, rendering the scopic and sadistic drives "reflexive" by turning them back upon themselves. The narrative of Nazi violence whose logical conclusion is death becomes suspended in a "future anterior": a moment at once already past and deferred into an indefinite future. This suspension goes hand in hand with an insistent blurring of the distinction between Max, the Nazi voyeur and sadist, and Lucia, the object of his sadistic voyeurism. By yoking this blurring to the disturbance of chronology, the film asks its viewers to embrace and sustain a violence that does not come to conclusion, and that does not do so because it fails to locate both an object on which it might realize its violence and a subject from which that violence emanates. The ethical urgency of such an argument lies here: it is only by sustaining the *fantasmatic* tension of a violence in which our identifications remain mobile—in which we oscillate incessantly between active and passive, subject and object, seer and seen—that we can resist the real violence made possible by choosing the masterful position through which to bring the fantasy to fruition.

Our last two papers are set in seventeenth- and eighteenth-century France. They represent a sustained psychoanalytic investigation of the territory first mapped by Foucault's *History of Sexuality*: the historical construction of sexual identity. Sharon Diane Nell begins by continuing the dialogue on sadomasochism initiated by Torlasco. Her "Sadistic and Masochistic Contracts in Voltaire's *La pucelle d'Orléans* and Graffigny's *Lettres d'une Péruvienne*; or, What Does the Hymen Want?," does more than project the same sadomasochistic template back in time. It addresses a notable lacuna in Foucault's history, by addressing the issues of female sexuality and virginity as they were understood in the literary, medical, and judicial discourses of the period. More particularly, it examines highly stylized depictions of sadomasochistic practices in two literary works of the period, in which they function as a series of contracts or conventions that seek to regulate, and in some cases are regulated by, the hymen. The hymen, then, names less a quasi-anatomical feature portrayed in the discourse of the period than a discursive space in which issues of libidinal economy as well as sexual and gender domination are negotiated. It names a membrane regulating the commerce between two or more subjects and their respective attempts to impose an order on the power and the pleasure that flow through, and threaten to obliterate, that membrane.

In the case of Voltaire's *La pucelle d'Orleans*, the text itself establishes a sadistic contract in which Jeanne d'Arc (Joan of Arc), the virgin on whose hymen the destiny of a nation rides (sometimes literally) is subjected to repeated attempted rapes and deflowerings as the condition of the French triumph over the English invaders. The result is a picaresque mock epic in which Sadean violence is visited upon the virile maid, and yet, just as described in Bakhtin's romance chronotope, nothing ever happens. Jeanne emerges each time ready for fresh assaults. Her hymen remains miraculously intact, and the French eventually triumph. Yet, if this version of the narrative were left to stand unmodified, then in fact the power would be all on the side of young amazon virgins who resist penetration and submission, the object of sadistic violence. This obviously cannot be. Instead, in a meta-narrative moment, we find out that the actual result of the conflict had been determined by a verse-writing contest in heaven. The hymen, then, is both what allows the narrative and political commerce of the poem to be transacted, and the vanishing mediator that is allowed no positive presence, no desire of its own.

In *Lettres d'une Péruvienne*, again we find the convention of the romance chronotope: a series of attempted ravishments, actual kidnappings, and harrowing adventures spanning both sides of the Atlantic. But in the end nothing really happens. The basic relations governing the characters, their bodies, and their sexuality remain essentially unchanged. This time, however, the logic of their narrative and sexual commerce is essentially masochistic. Déterville, the French suitor of the Incan princess, Zilia, abases and enslaves himself but at the same time agrees not to approach her too closely, even though he claims that he so desires. The maintenance of her hymen is in fact the condition of his desire, and he can only cross the membrane of enjoyment if it remains intact.

With Pierre Zoberman's "Queer(ing) Pleasure: Having a Gay Old Time in the Culture of Early-Modern France," we move beyond the world of sadomasochistic enclosure, while staying firmly in the realm of the history of sexuality. Zoberman's paper poses the problem of the relation of pleasure specifically to homoeroticism and more generally to being and acting "queer" in the court of Louis XIV. It focuses on the person of Monsieur, the king's brother, who became known as the "magnificent sodomite." Zoberman proposes that the most salient category under which we can examine Monsieur is that of "desire." Rather than seeing an opposition between queer theory and psychoanalysis, Zoberman argues persuasively that psychoanalysis in its most unadulterated form has always been queer. Taking off from Lacan's seventh seminar, *The Ethics of Psychoanalysis*, Zoberman argues that Monsieur in his pursuit of all forms of pleasure—not just those of the boudoir, but also those of the ballroom and buffet—ultimately should be read in a fashion analogous to Lacan's famous reading of Antigone, that is, as one who does not cede on his or her desire. Monsieur, by pursuing pleasure beyond the recognized forms sanctioned by the pleasure and reality principles operative in seventeenth-century France, comes to rejoin the tragic heroine on the stage of his own theatrical life.

Zoberman's archeology of Monsieur's passions ranges across a vast range of primary texts from the period. On one hand, he accepts the essential correctness of Foucault's position that we do not find liberation from the regime of sexual identity by saying yes to "sex," but rather in a rigorous examination of bodies and pleasures. On the other, he argues that an historically informed psychoanalysis is best equipped to do this. Zoberman's project is in fact not merely of antiquarian interest but an urgent task. His paper compels us, through this genealogy of pleasure in the court of the Sun King, to ask what it means to be and act queer both in the seventeenth century and in the new millennium. Ironically, for the historicists, Zoberman shows that it is only through the transhistorical languages of psychoanalytic "desire" and "pleasure" that we can begin to trace the true historical significance of Monsieur's *being* queer.

NOTES

1. Torrey's book is unusually frank about the politically reactionary impulse animating much of the recent anti-Freudianism. One of its central contentions is that, among the "malignant effects" of Freud's theory, perhaps the most crucial is the conceptual armature it gives to radicals seeking to question the current (gendered, class, racial) order by insisting on environmental rather than biological determinants to human behavior. At the same time, it's worth noting that not all proponents of pharmaceutical treatment are conservative or hostile to psychoanalysis. Julia Kristeva, for example, does not deny the beneficial effects of pharmacology but notes that the effects and manifestations of depression cannot be rigorously accounted for without examining them on the level of the subject's speech as well as that of the neuron (*Black Sun* 10).

2 See especially Crews, *Skeptical.* Crews's *Sins of the Fathers* was among the first and most influential early examples of psychoanalytic literary criticism in the United States.

3. As in the case of communism, those who followed this route are legion. Among the most interesting is Mikkel Borch-Jacobsen, who published in 1988 one of the very best deconstructively inspired reinterpretation of Freud (*Freudian Subject*), but who within little more than a decade began a crusade to discredit psychoanalysis that barely differs from Crews's own (see his *Remembering Anna O*). For a brilliant discussion of the transferential dynamics entailed in this loss of faith among psychoanalysts, see Roustang.

4. Marcuse's and Brown's books were published in the fifties, but they had their first significant impact on the New Left in the sixties.

5. On psychoanalysis and Left politics, see especially Robinson and Abramson. The earliest fully elaborated attempt at a conceptual fusion of Freud and Marx appears to have been Wilhelm Reich's *Dialektischer Materialismus und Psychoanalyse* (1929). An especially incisive and influential celebration of the conservative, pessimistic Freud is Rieff.

6. Hale offers the most detailed account of Americans' reception of psychoanalysis. Also useful are the essays on psychoanalysis in Heler and Rudnick.

7. On Lippmann, Eastman, Dodge, and Dell, see *1915*, 27–47, 69–115. Buhle's first chapter offers an interesting account of the relations between first-wave feminism and psychoanalysis, including the place of Goldman in that encounter.

8. Eagleton discusses both the turn toward theory in the wake of the sixties and the aggression directed in some of that theory toward the political aspirations that many radicals perceived to have failed.

9. Prominent theorists and critics who published and/or were editors at *Screen* during these years include Christian Metz, Laura Mulvey, Peter Wollen, Jacqueline Rose, and Stephen Heath.

10. See especially Hall and Morley. The Birmingham School's critique of psychoanalysis, though motivated by a historically specific problematic, reflected and extended a long-standing lack of curiosity among British cultural materialists toward psychoanalysis and the Marxist–Freudian tradition.

11. Several *Screen* editors and contributors—most notably Mulvey and Wollen—did in fact make experimental films that sought this kind of subversion.

12. Leo Bersani is a critic who has consistently managed to take both psychoanalysis and Foucauldian thought seriously, without either conceptual confusion or any explicit defense of this tendency. Judith Butler's work, in contrast, can be seen in part as an explicit and extended attempt at reconciling the two theoretical positions.

13. The founding text of New Historicism was of course Greenblatt. See also Seltzer and D. A. Miller. Miller's book is unusual both in the brilliance of its execution and in the way his investment in the novels he examines troubles the New Historicist paradigm with a pleasure in the textures of writing that is not fully containable by the "power" his text anatomizes.

14. On Foucault's synchronic historicism, see P. A. Miller, "Suppression of the Negative" and "Post-Foucauldian Theory." On the three periods of Foucault's work, the genealogical, the archeological, and the ethical, see Davidson.

15. One link between the Foucauldian and Birmingham traditions is their shared antipathy to Althusser—see, in the New Historicist context, D. A. Miller, 65n.

16. All translations from foreign-language editions are our own.

17. The recent movie version of Brett Easton Ellis's *American Psycho* is particularly brilliant at bringing this out.

18. Jameson has, of course, been the most persuasive analyst of postmodernism as "the cultural logic of late capitalism." See his book of that title, as well as his fascinating short essay "Cognitive Mapping."

19. The American neo-Foucauldians are especially fond of stressing this impossibility of transcendence. "What exactly [does] it mean," asks Walter Benn Michaels, "to think of [Theodore] Dreiser as approving (or disapproving) consumer culture. . . ? It . . . seems wrong to think of the culture you live in as the object of your affections: you don't like or dislike it, you exist in it, and the things you like and dislike exist in it too." "What [is] wrong," he continues, "with the project of assessing Dreiser's attitude toward capitalism" is that "it depend[s] on imagining a Dreiser outside capitalism who could then be said to have attitudes toward it." The radical immanentism of such formulations is designed to make oppositional politics seem sentimental, quaint, insufficiently knowing—a naïve projection of contemporary critics back onto the objects of their analysis. The use of Dreiser to make this point is especially perverse. Michaels needs to discount in advance the author's explicit and conscious anticapitalism. He does this not in the name of uncovering a (personal or political) unconscious that contradicts Dreiser's official position. His point, rather, is that culture is a homogeneous discursive field that "speaks" its literary texts unbidden, without the complications and mediations of subjectivities fraught with internal conflicts and therefore affirming aspects of their culture while actively resisting others. Each text produced in a culture, on this model, necessarily "exemplifies" that culture. Each expresses a dominant ideology that is the discursive equivalent of air: something at once pervasive and irresistible, incapable of becoming an object of reflection and insusceptible of being challenged (what sense would it make to be against air?), for which writers serve as passive media, regardless of what a given author thinks he or she is saying. See *Gold Standard* 18, 19.

20. Quoted in Whitaker and attributed to a "professor at a U.S. military college."

21. The *Washington Post* has published a link to the most incriminating of these memos. See U.S. Department of Justice, "Memorandum for Alberto Gonzales, Counsel to the President."

22. Bush gave this speech on 5 August 2004. See "Bush's Campaign Gaffe."

23. The most common examples of this con are those commercials in which men ignore their girlfriends or wives in sexy lingerie until the women call out seductively "I've got some Bud Lite!"—at which point the men come running. A more recent ad for Miller Genuine Draft takes this "concept" a step further: in it, the bottle of beer actually *is* the "other woman," so that the guy is "cheating" by drinking it instead of his usual brand.

24. Michael Moore's documentary *Fahrenheit 9/11* offers a devastating account of how one conservative Democratic family, which initially supported the invasion, was radicalized by its son's death. Baum's "Price of Valor" documents the

Veteran's Association complete disavowal of the psychic price of killing, as well as the remarkable dearth of studies about this price.

25. In the sense of Adorno in *Negative Dialectics*.

26. *Civilization* marks, in fact, the culmination of a line of thought extending throughout the final phase of Freud's thinking—a phase that can indeed be seen as an extended inquiry into the problem of how human beings manage to live together at all. In *Beyond the Pleasure Principle* (1920), Freud laid out the problem at an abstract, theoretical level: while Eros, he argued, works toward the binding of individuals into small groups (couples, families) and of small groups into ever greater unities (nations, the world community), the death drive counters this binding work with a destructive unbinding (regression to prior states as well as concrete acts of aggression) that threatens all units and bonds and even identities with dissolution. The following year, in *Group Psychology and the Analysis of the Ego*, he traced the concrete workings of Eros and death drive in an analysis of the army and the Church. He argued that these are exemplary groups in that they are organizations in which a sufficient number of people have "agreed" to renounce their aggressive impulses toward each other in the name of retaining the love of a commonly held "father." This process raises the leader (who can of course be an abstraction, such as "the nation," as well as an actual person) to the status of a collective ego ideal, which one loves because it reflects back an image of self that each of us *is not*, but would like to be. The problem, for Freud, is that the aggression renounced in this process threatens to return, as internecine warfare, whenever the distance between ideal and actual object (leader, nation) becomes too starkly visible.

27. Žižek does not seem to have classical Buddhist texts in mind. They firmly insist on the ineradicable nature of desire. Even Nirvana, in the Mahayana tradition, is ultimately the recognition of *dukkha* as the condition of existence (*samsara*) and the renunciation of all substitute satisfactions (i.e., the "realization of desire"). Indeed, it is hard to see how Bodhidharma's ripping off his eyelids so that he would not fall asleep during his nine years meditating before a wall or how the self-immolating monks of the Vietnam conflict could represent "Indifference." Žižek's description fits much better the life of the comfortable middle-class seeker of spiritual narcosis than it does Basho, Dogen, or even Siddartha himself.

WORKS CITED

Adorno, Theodor. "Commitment." *The Essential Frankfurt School Reader*. Eds. Andrew Arato and Eike Gebhardt. Oxford: Blackwell, 1978. 300–18.

———. *Negative Dialectics*. Trans. E. B. Ashton. New York: Seabury, 1973.

Abramson, Jeffrey. *Liberation and Its Limits: The Moral and Political Thought of Freud*. New York: Simon & Schuster, 1984.

Baum, Dan. "The Price of Valor." *The New Yorker*, 12 and 19 July 2004: 44–52.

Borch-Jacobsen, Mikkel. *The Freudian Subject*. Trans. Catherine Porter. Stanford, CA: Stanford UP, 1988.

———. *Remembering Anna O.: A Century of Mystification*. Trans. Kirby Olson and Xavier Callahan. New York: Routledge, 1996.

Buhle, Mari Jo. *Feminism and Its Discontents: A Century of Struggle with Psychoanalysis*. Cambridge, MA: Harvard UP, 1998.

"Bush's Campaign Trail Gaffe." *The Guardian Unlimited*, 6 August 2004. http://www.guardian.co.uk/uselections2004/story/0,13918,1277552,00.html

Chaitin, Gilbert D. *Rhetoric and Culture in Lacan*. Cambridge: Cambridge UP, 1996.

Crews, Frederick C. *Skeptical Engagements*. New York: Oxford UP, 1986.

———. *The Sins of the Fathers: Hawthorne's Psychological Themes*. New York: Oxford UP, 1966.

Davidson, Arnold. "Ethics as Ascetics: Foucault, the History of Ethics, and Ancient Thought." *The Cambridge Companion to Foucault*. Ed. Gary Gutting. Cambridge: Cambridge UP, 1994. 115–40.

Derrida, Jacques. *Spectres de Marx*. Paris: Galilèe, 1993.

Dreyfus, Hubert. *Being-in-the-World: A Commentary on Heidegger's* Being and Time, *Division I*. Cambridge, MA: MIT Press, 1991.

Eagleton, Terry. *After Theory*. New York: Basic, 2003.

Feher-Gurewich, Judith. "A Lacanian Approach to the Logic of Perversion." *The Cambridge Companion to Lacan*. Ed. Jean-Michel Rabaté. Cambridge: Cambridge UP, 2003. 191–207.

Foucault, Michel. *The History of Sexuality, Volume I: An Introduction*. Trans. Robert Hurley. 1976. New York: Vintage, 1980.

———. *Dits et écrits: 1954–1988*. Vol. 4. Eds. Daniel Defert and Francois Ewalt. Paris: Gallimard, 1994.

———. *Les Mots et les choses*. Paris: Gallimard, 1966.

———. *Herméneutique du sujet: Cours au Collège de France*. 1981–1882. Ed. Frédéric Gros. Paris: Gallimard/Seuil, 2001.

Freiberger, Erich D. "'Heads I Win, Tails You Lose': Wittgenstein, Plato and the Role of Construction and Deconstruction in Psychoanalysis and Ethics." *Lacan in America*. Ed. Jean Michel Rabaté. New York: The Other Press, 2000. 223–46.

Freud, Sigmund. *Beyond the Pleasure Principle. The Standard Edition of the Complete Psychological Works of Sigmund Freud*. Vol. 18. London: Hogarth, 1955. 7–64.

———. *Civilization and Its Discontents. The Standard Edition*. Vol. 21. London: Hogarth, 1961. 64–145.

————. *Group Psychology and the Analysis of the Ego. The Standard Edition.* Vol. 18. London: Hogarth, 1955. 69–143.

Greenblatt, Stephen. *Renaissance Self-Fashioning: More to Shakespeare.* Chicago: U of Chicago P, 1980.

Grunbaum, Adolph. *The Foundations of Psychoanalysis: A Philosophical Critique.* Berkeley: U of California P, 1985.

Hale, Nathan. *Freud in America.* 2 vols. New York: Oxford UP, 1971–1995.

Hall, Stuart. "Encoding/Decoding." *Culture, Media, Language: Working Papers in Cultural Studies, 1972–79.* London: Routledge, 1996. 128–38.

Heler, Adele, and Lois Rudnick. *1915, The Cultural Moment: The New Politics, the New Woman, the New Psychology, the New Art, and the New Theater in America.* New Brunswick, NJ: Rutgers UP, 1991.

Hersh, Seymour M. *Chain of Command: The Road from 9/11 to Abu Ghraib.* New York: HarperCollins, 2004.

Jameson, Fredric. "Cognitive Mapping." *Marxism and the Interpretation of Culture.* Eds. Cary Nelson and Lawrence Grossburg. Urbana: U of Illinois P, 1988. 347–60.

————. "Imaginary and Symbolic in Lacan." *Literature and Psychoanalysis: The Question of Reading, Otherwise.* Ed. Shoshana Felman. New Haven, CT: Yale French Studies, 1977.

————. *Marxism and Form: Twentieth Century Dialectical Theories of Literature.* Princeton, NJ: Princeton UP, 1971.

————. *Postmodernism, or, The Cultural Logic of Late Capitalism.* Durham, NC: Duke UP, 1991.

Julien, Phillipe. *Pour lire Jacques Lacan.* 2nd ed. Paris: E. P. E. L, 1990.

Kristeva, Julia. *Black Sun: Depression and Melancholia.* New York: Columbia UP, 1989.

Lacan, Jacques. *Le Séminaire. Livre VII: L'Éthique de la psychanalyse.* Ed. Jacques-Alain Miller. Paris: Seuil, 1986.

————. *Le Séminaire. Livre VIII: Le transfert.* Ed. Jacques-Alain Miller. Paris: Seuil, 1991.

Lane, Christopher. "The Experience of the Outside: Foucault and Psychoanalysis." *Lacan in America.* Ed. Jean-Michel Rabaté. New York: Other, 2000. 309–47.

Laqueur, Thomas. *Making Sex: Body and Gender from The Greeks to Freud.* Cambridge, MA: Harvard UP, 1990.

Lukács, Georg. "The Ideology of Modernism." *The Meaning of Contemporary Realism.* Trans. John and Necke Mander. London: Merlin, 1963.

Michaels, Walter Benn. *The Gold Standard and the Logic of Naturalism: American Literature at the Turn of the Century*. Berkeley: U of California P, 1987.

Miller, D. A. *The Novel and the Police*. Berkeley: U of California P, 1988.

Miller, P. A. "The Suppression of the Negative in Foucault's *History of Sexuality*." *Cultural History After Foucault*. Ed. John Neubauer. New York: Aldine de Gruyter, 1999. 185–208.

———. "Towards a Post-Foucauldian Theory of Discursive Practices." *Configurations* 7 (1999): 211–25.

Morley, Dave. "Texts, Readers, Subjects." *Culture, Media, Language: Working Papers in Cultural Studies, 1972–79*. London: Routledge, 1996. 128–38, 163–73.

Rieff, Philip. *Freud: The Mind of the Moralist*. New York: Viking, 1959.

Robinson, Paul A. *The Freudian Left: Wilhelm Reich, Geza Roheim, Herbert Marcuse*. New York: Harper & Row, 1969.

Roustang, François. *Dire Mastery: Discipleship from Freud to Lacan*. Trans. Ned Lukacher. Baltimore, MD: Johns Hopkins UP, 1982.

Salter, Andrew. *The Case Against Psychoanalysis*. New York: Harper & Row, 1972.

Seltzer, Mark. *Henry James and the Art of Power*. Ithaca, NY: Cornell UP, 1984.

Silverman, Kaja. *World Spectators*. Stanford, CA: Stanford UP, 2000.

Torrey, E. Fuller. *Freudian Fraud: The Malignant Effect of Freud's Theory on American Thought and Culture*. New York: HarperCollins, 1992.

Turkle, Sherry. *Psychoanalytic Politics: Freud's French Revolution*. New York: Basic, 1978.

U.S. Department of Justice. "Memorandum for Albert Gonzales, Counsel to the President." http://www.washingtonpost.com/wp-srv/nation/documents/dojinterrogationmemo20020801.pdf.

Valente, Joseph. "Lacan's Marxism, Marxism's Lacan (From Žižek to Althusser)." *The Cambridge Companion to Lacan*. Ed. Jean-Michel Rabaté. Cambridge: Cambridge UP, 2003.

Whitaker, Brian. "Its Best Use Is as a Doorstop." *The Guardian Unlimited*, 24 May 2004. http://www.guardian.co.uk/elsewhere/journalist/story/0,7792,1223525,00.html.

Žižek, Slavoj. *Looking Awry: An Introduction to Jacques Lacan through Popular Culture*. Cambridge, MA: MIT Press, 1991.

Part One

Psychoanalysis and the
Future of Cultural Criticism

1

Sartre, Politics, and Psychoanalysis

It Don't Mean a Thing if It Ain't Got *das Ding*

Paul Allen Miller

In *Qu'est-ce que la littérature*, Sartre argues that literature is neither an exercise in pure aesthetics nor a mere reflection of pre-existing conditions but always an intentional act directed toward a specific audience. He challenges the writer to take responsibility for both the act and the audience to which it is addressed. In this way, Sartre proposes that we produce a *littérature* that is both *engagée* and existentially authentic. His position is in fact more nuanced than has often been recognized. He does not call for a mere "Literature of Ideas," in Nabokov's dismissive phrase,[1] nor does he demand the production of endless *romans à these*, as is often alleged (Contat and Idt x). Rather, for Sartre, the author simultaneously creates and unveils an object (*Qu'est-ce que la littérature?* 55) that in turn constitutes an invitation to the reader to participate in, and make possible, this unique moment of unveiling. "Ecrire, c'est faire appel au lecteur pour qu'il fasse passer à l'existence objective le dévoilement que j'ai entrepris par le moyen du langage" ["To write is to make an appeal to the reader that he make enter into objective existence the act of unveiling that I have undertaken by the means of language"] (*Qu'est-ce que la littérature?* 59).[2] The literary moment is not that of simple communication in which a pre-existing message is passed from one speaker to another, nor that of free play in which a fundamentally non-ideological, floating world is created. It is rather a moment of creation between author, reader, and text in which a brand new object is called into existence through an act of profoundly situated and yet transcendent unveiling: transcendent precisely in so far as the act of unveiling does not exhaust itself in the moment (*Qu'est-ce que la littérature?* 74–75).

Engagement, then, is not something willed or refused; it is a fact of the creative act. In calling into being an object that is fundamentally new, the literary work has changed the world from what it was prior to the conjoined acts of creation and reception that constitute it. This is true as much for mimetic forms as for more formalist ventures since there is no attempt to present an image of the world through language that is not also the creation of a parallel world (*Qu'est-ce que la littérature?* 29) or, in more contemporary terms, a world of difference. In choosing therefore to call into being one object rather than another, one is necessarily responsible for the invitation to a specific act of unveiling that constitutes one's creation. This is not a claim of authorial responsibility in the naïve sense that every act someone commits upon reading your text can be laid to your moral or ethical account or that you are somehow fully self-present in the moment of creation; instead, the claim is in the precise philosophical sense that responsibility has been understood from Socrates to Bakhtin (i.e., you owe a response to the questions your act elicits). For whom, then, are you writing, for what purpose, and why did you call into being this act of unveiling rather than another (*Qu'est-ce que la littérature?* 29–30)? The answers you give in turn open up the possibility of a deeper dialogue leading to further symbolic, creative, and responsive acts, thus revealing either a willingness to pursue the implications of one's actions to their end (authenticity) or a refusal to acknowledge them in their finality (*mauvaise foi, L'être et le néant* 84–85). "Ecrire, c'est donc à la fois dévoiler le monde et le proposer comme une tâche à la générosité du lecteur" ["To write is thus both to unveil the world and to propose it as a task to the reader's generosity"] (*Qu'est-ce que la littérature?* 76).

Although to the jaded ears of postmodernism the jargon of authenticity, transcendence, engagement, bad faith, and the concept of language as a means manipulated by the subject rather than as the ground of the subject's constitution may sound *dépassé* (*Qu'est-ce que la littérature?* 18), the challenge of Sartre's question remains fundamental. As writers, students, and consumers of literature, how do we justify this pursuit? More fundamentally, what is this pursuit? How can we give an account of it that neither degenerates into "the dead-end of formalist criticism" (de Man) nor produces yet another, more sophisticated positivism (reception theory, new historicism, and too much of what passes for cultural studies)? In short, what is literature? It would be naïve to assume that Sartre's postwar text is the last word on the subject. But might it not be the first?

Terry Eagleton's response to Sartre's question, in *Literary Theory: An Introduction*, that literature does not exist—only cultural semiotic systems do—is both typical and oddly metaphysical. It must assume the possibility of the existence of such an entity in order to deny it, and in doing so it violates the very materialist pragmatics on which its assertion is based. To say that there is no such thing as literature because there is no single external object that corresponds to a consistent descriptive definition of it is to assume that objects exist outside the systems that describe them and render them visible as objects of knowledge. This is classic idealism and, as a reader of Althusser and Lacan, Eagleton knows better. By this same logic, neither history nor society exist since no one consistent instantiation of the object exists separate from the set of theoretical protocols that calls them into existence as an object of study. All sciences construct their own objects.

Eagleton in both the first and second editions of this seminal study proposes to replace literary theory with rhetorical and cultural studies (*Literary Theory* 169–89). But, cultural studies can offer no reason why literary studies should not become a branch of sociology. Cultural studies cannot explain why we should teach and read poetry, novels, romances, or plays as opposed to newspapers, greeting cards, royal land grants, and contract law.[3] This is a position that puts the very existence of the discipline of literary study into question. In short, Eagleton's move is self-defeating as a position in literary studies, and it is contradictory in its own basic assumptions that literature does not exist but culture does. It is an ideological gambit that seeks to exert the hegemony of its own protocols and, in Sartrean fashion, to create and unveil its own object of study. To that extent I accept and applaud it. Cultural studies as a movement has in many ways been salutary. It has successfully dethroned the narrow, stifling formalism that dominated Anglo-American literary criticism and theory from the time of Leavis and New Criticism to the last gasps of American deconstruction. But it has hardly answered, let alone disposed of, Sartre's nagging question. The fact of the matter is that most of us still consider ourselves teachers of literature, even if we no longer know what that is.

In this essay, then, I will take up Sartre's challenge, but I propose to move beyond the Marxian and existential terms in which he framed the question toward a post-Freudian definition founded on the works of Slavoj Žižek, Julia Kristeva, and Jacques Lacan. This is not as strange as it seems: for, the Sartrean notion of authenticity and good faith is ultimately based on a concept of desire as *manque à l'être*. It is this lack at the heart of being which propels us forward in the project of our existence (*L'être et le néant* 624–25). Such a vocabulary is central to post-Freudian analysis as well, as is exemplified in Lacan's deliberate echoing of Sartre's terminology (Lacan, *Séminaire* VII 229; *Séminaire* XI 341; Ragland-Sullivan 43), and their common Hegelian and Heideggerian heritage (Butler, *Subjects of Desire*). But where for Sartre this lack at the heart of being is ontological, for post-Freudian analysis it is a fact of language: our lack is an effect of the castration we suffer upon entrance into the world of the Symbolic, that is, of the a priori renunciation of plenitude all human beings undergo when we enter into the world of difference that makes articulated thought, and thus subjectivity, possible (Kristeva, "Temps des femmes" 11; Moi 99–100; Žižek, *Enjoy Your Symptom!* 270). It is for this reason, I would argue, that post-Freudian psychoanalysis escapes the Sartrean strictures on the logical impossibility of repression. So long as the unconscious is seen as substance in which ideas arise and are censored before they can come to consciousness, then the only way they can be censored is if they are already fully formed and known to exist by the subject. The subject thus becomes split against itself and can only engage in repression through a deliberate, knowing act of bad faith (*L'être et le néant* 85–90, 616–23). Such objections, however, hold no purchase on a conception of the unconscious as an effect of language. In the post-Freudian view, the unconscious is not a seething pit within but precisely that portion of enjoyment that haunts the institution of the subject itself. It is the voice of the Other, that is, the meanings and significations that constitute our unique subject positions in relation to the pre-existing world and thus escape our conscious control even as they are the fabric out of which consciousness itself is made (Lacan, *Séminaire* VII 42; *Séminaire* XI 142, 167; Žižek in Hanlon 842; Ragland-Sullivan 221).

Yet, my purpose in writing this text is not to call for a reconciliation of the Sartrean and Lacanian projects, both of which are now well over half a century old and, in their own terms, no longer of burning contemporary relevance. It is to advance a psychoanalytic concept of the literary object that can meet the demands of Sartre's question, which at the beginning of a new millennium still goes unanswered. In this context, I will argue that what we refer to when we say that we study the literary is a set of texts that problematize the dominant Symbolic system through a self-conscious manipulation of its own founding contradictions. Literature is thus a practice of the letter that, through a concentration of signifying effects, points to a beyond of the Symbolic, to the irrational kernel of our enjoyment. In Kristevan terms, the literary is that form of writing that "by means of the polyvalence of sign and symbol, which unsettles naming and, by building up a plurality of connotations around the sign, affords the subject a chance to imagine the nonmeaning, or the true meaning of the Thing" (97). The Thing, here, refers to a concept first outlined by Lacan in his *Ethics of Psychoanalysis*, *das Ding*. By *das Ding*, Lacan means, "le hors-signifié. C'est en fonction de cet hors-signifié, et d'un rapport pathétique à lui, que le sujet conserve sa distance, et se constitue dans un mode de rapport, d'affect primaire, antérieure à tout refoulement" (*Séminaire* VII 67) ["the beyond-of-the-signified. It is as a function of this beyond-of-the-signified and of an emotional relationship to it that the subject keeps its distance and is constituted in a kind of relationship characterized by primary affect, prior to any repression" (*Seminar* VII 54)]. *Das Ding* is, then, the pre-object. It is that piece of the Real that is both in us and beyond us, that is the ground of desire (Silverman 16; Žižek, *Sublime Object* 208–09; Žižek, *Looking Awry* 169). The literary, on this view, is thus the unveiling through language of a fundamentally new object that, in the moment of its unveiling, points to a beyond of the very situated nature that its fundamentally linguistic and hence Symbolic character necessitates (Žižek, *Enjoy Your Symptom!* 169–70).

This definition, I contend, is not essentializing because every formation of the Symbolic is unique, as is every point of insertion in it, and thus every relationship to its beyond (Ragland-Sullivan 230–31, 299–305; Clément 16). The Imaginary, the Symbolic, and the Real are not reified things but a set of logical relations presumed by the existence of the speaking subject (Julien 213–14; Mitchell and Rose 171n.6). Hence, the speaking subject exists only to the extent that it exists in language—defined as the total set of codes and syntagmatic relations that make articulated meaning possible—that is to say, to the extent that it exists in the Symbolic (Althusser 72; Julien 176; Moxey 990). It is only a subject to the extent that it can project an image of itself, by means of which it can come to identify with the meanings into which it is born: this realm of projection and identification is the Imaginary (Julien 48–49; Roudinesco 216). And finally that subject is only finite (i.e., not god) to the extent that neither its self-projection nor the codes against which it projects itself constitute the sum total of existence—that is to say, to the extent that the Real exists as that which is beyond the Imaginary and the Symbolic (Ragland-Sullivan 188; Lacan, *Séminaire* XX 85). No one of these logical relations, however, has any necessary or prescribed content in and of itself. Moreover, this definition of the literary as "a practice of the letter that, through a concentration of signifying effects, points to a beyond of the Symbolic" is fully historicizeable (Žižek, *Sublime Object* 135), equally applicable across all genres of composition, and politically engaged in so far as the Symbolic system of any given social formation represents the dominant codes, syntaxes, and rules of substitution operative therein (Lacan, *Séminaire* VII 114–19, 128–29; *Seminar* VII 95–100, 107).

It may be objected that virtually any text may be read in this way, as in Eagleton's famous of example of the drunk pondering the metaphysical implications of the sign "dogs must be carried on the escalator" (6). This is quite true on one level. As Sartre was among the first to point out, literature is at least as much an act of reading as an act of writing. One *can* read the phonebook or subway signs as literature. But simply because such materials can be read as literature does not mean that all materials equally repay a literary reading. Eagleton exhausts the possibilities of his subway sign more quickly than he would either a Shakespearean sonnet or a speech by Macaulay. In the same fashion, virtually anything may become the object of a sociological analysis, but it is not clear that all objects equally repay the effort expended or yield as rich an experience. They do not all represent practices of the letter that produce in a sustained fashion the "sublime object."

The sublime object, to which, according to the Seminar on the *Ethics of Psychoanalysis*, the phenomenon of beauty[4] is intrinsically related, is that which is raised to the level of the Thing (Lacan, *Séminaire* VII 133; *Seminar* VII 112). The Beautiful and the Sublime, then, become two aspects of the same Thing: the first representing the beyond of representation and the second representing the impossibility of that representation:

> although the suprasensible Idea/Thing cannot be represented in a direct, immediate way, one can represent the Idea "symbolically," in the guise of beauty (in other words, the beautiful is a way to represent ourselves "analogically" the good in the phenomenal world); what the chaotic shapelessness of the sublime phenomena renders visible, on the contrary, is the very impossibility of representing the suprasensible Idea/Thing. (Žižek, *Enjoy Your Symptom!* 164)

The sublime object is not that which is caught up in the endless substitutions of Symbolic exchange, but occupies a place beyond the quotidian satisfactions of the pleasure and reality principles and as such is cognate with perversion. (Lacan, *Séminaire* VII 131; *Seminar* VII 109–10).[5]

The Thing is, in Lacan's memorable phrase, that aspect of the Real that "suffers from the signifier." It appears within discourse as the place of "flocculation," the point of attraction to which shards of meaning, elements of signification, are attracted, where they are gathered into strands and chains (Lacan, *Séminaire* VII 142; *Seminar* VII 118). It does not appear directly but only through the representation of representations, the *Vorstellungsrepräsentanzen*. It is then the no-thing, the unrepresentable, that nonetheless attracts the representation and its means.

The sublime object, therefore, is not that which is searched for within the existing protocols of knowledge, but that which is "found" or "created," while nonetheless inhering in the Symbolic as a necessary moment of its own self-betrayal. It is worth quoting from the *Séminaire* at some length on this difficult point:

We come once again upon a fundamental structure, which allows us to articulate the fact that the Thing in question is, by virtue of its structure, open to being represented by what I called earlier [. . .] the Other thing.

And that is the second characteristic of the Thing as veiled; it is by nature in the finding of the object, represented by something else.

You cannot fail to see that in the celebrated expression of Picasso, "I do not seek, I find," that it is the finding (*trouver*), the *trobar* of the Provençal troubadours and the *trouvères*, and of all the schools of rhetoric, that takes precedence over the seeking.

Obviously, what is found is sought, but sought in the paths of the signifier. Now this search is in a way an antipsychic search that by its place and function is beyond the pleasure principle. For according to the laws of the pleasure principle, the signifier projects into this beyond equalization, homeostasis, and the tendency to the uniform investment of the system of the self as such; it provokes its failure. The function of the pleasure principle is, in effect, to lead the subject from signifier to signifier, by generating as many signifiers as are required to maintain at as low a level as possible the tension that regulates the whole functioning of the psychic apparatus. (Lacan, *Séminaire* VII 143; *Seminar* VII 118–119)

The repetitive structure of most TV series offer a great example of what Lacan means by "searching" within the pleasure principle. They do not present the found object that breaks the frame of representation but seek to lead the viewer through an endless chain of substitutions, while assuring us that nothing has really changed. Mark Green will be the same sensitive but slightly troubled character from one episode to the next of *ER* so that even if he gets written out of the show after ten years, the structure is in place and continues on without him. There will be tensions and misadventures, but the basic reality, the foundation of our normative subjectivity, is never called into question. There is no answer of the Real: no ominously swinging traffic light; no mysterious corpse wrapped in plastic, as in *Twin Peaks*. The question therefore is not one of high versus popular culture or literature versus television and cinema, but one of the structure of signification.

To make my point more concrete, I will examine four sample texts, one each from Juvenal, Mallarmé, Leyner, and Sartre himself. I have deliberately chosen examples from different languages, genres, and periods. Thus, Juvenal represents satire from the Roman imperial period, Mallarmé highly wrought French symbolist poetry from the late nineteenth century,

Leyner contemporary American experimental prose, and Sartre the realist novel. What I am offering is not a theory of poetry or prose, a theory of modernity or classicism, or a theory of literary aesthetics or political engagement. It *is* an examination of the way in which certain practices of the letter "break apart the usual, univocal terms of language and reveal an irrepressible heterogeneity of multiple sounds and meanings" (Butler, *Gender Trouble* 81). It *is* an investigation into the literary as a linguistic practice that points beyond language and thus always stands as a critique of a given formation of the Symbolic. Furthermore, it is a meditation on the process of unveiling a radical new object that takes place between writer and reader in the literary moment.

My first example comes from Juvenal *Satire* 1, lines 147–49. In this poem, written at the beginning of the second century CE, Juvenal asks who today can avoid writing satire when poets drone on incessantly about mythological minutia and when senators' wives fight gladiators in the arena. It is the image of a world turned upside down. Such a view in itself, while well-anchored in the historical setting, would hardly represent a beyond of the Symbolic. It is rather its instantiation. Literary decadence, the inversion of gender roles, and the progressive degradation of traditional Roman morality are all standard tropes of Roman discourse from the time of Cato the Elder (second century BCE) to the coming into dominance of Christianity's messianic narrative. These are the classic bogeymen of Roman aristocratic and patriarchal ideology (Miller, *Subjecting Verses* 22–25), and Juvenal deploys them ably. The mere citation of them confirms their power rather than relativizes or points beyond it.

Juvenal, however, does far more than simply reproduce the founding assumptions of Roman ideology. He exposes the rhetorical mechanisms by which this ideology is produced. He reveals the sleights of hand and the rules of substitution and syntactical enchainment that permit it to function. In the process, he produces a rift in the fabric of the Symbolic, exposing the possibility of a world beyond—not so much a utopia as a world of unrelieved parapraxes from which all illusions of order have been swept away:

> *Nil erit ulterius quod nostris moribus addat*
> *posteritas, eadem facient cupientque minores,*
> *omne in praecipiti vitium stetit.*

> [Posterity can add nothing more to our customs
> Our descendants will do and desire the same,
> All vice stands at the edge of a precipice.]

What does it mean to say that time can add nothing more to our *mores*, our habits of life? History on this view appears to have stopped. Moreover, why is addition or increase bad? We seem to have reached a saturation point at which no additional form of behavior can be absorbed into the Roman system of morality without pushing it over the precipice (Ferguson 122). Thus, each new generation has brought an increasing variation in life (*addat*), and yet that increase can only be pictured as a decrease or falling-off within the existing Symbolic. "Our descendants will be less than ourselves," *minores*, a common Latin term that carries a moral charge, "because they will do and desire the exact same things," *eadem*. Thus increase, decrease, and stasis, movement in time and paralysis, all become aligned with one another in a fashion that is both completely consonant with the dominant ideology and reveals its logical absurdity. The ruling fantasy that gives consistency to our sense of social order has been unveiled. We can only go down from here, which will be indistinguishable from up.

Our second example is drawn from Mallarmé's "Sonnet en—yx," a poem whose complex intricacies of diction and etymological play go far beyond the scope of this paper.[6] I want to focus on one word, *ptyx*, a Greek term signifying a curve or fold (Cohn 141–42). It does not exist in normal French usage but appears in Homer in the first extant mention of writing in occidental poetry (Kromer 563–71). Before Mallarmé it appears only in Hugo's "Le satyre," where it is used as the name of a hill. The word signifies for Mallarmé the border between nonsense and meaning: the point at which existence folds back against itself in an act of reflection that conjures consciousness out of the nothingness enshrouding human existence. In the octave's rhyme scheme, *ptyx* is inserted between *Phénix* and *Styx*, corresponding to rebirth and nullity, respectively. It thus constitutes the fold of language, the "aboli bibelot d'inanité sonore."

> *Ses purs ongles très haut dédiant leur onyx,*
> *L'Angoisse, ce minuit, soutient, lampadophore,*
> *Maint rêve vespéral brûlé par le Phénix*
> *Que ne recueille pas de cinéraire amphore*
> *Sur les crédences, au salon vide: nul ptyx,*
> *Aboli bibelot d'inanité sonore,*
> *(Car le Maître est allé puiser des pleurs au Styx*
> *Avec ce seul objet dont le Néant s'honore).*

[Her pure nails very high dedicating their onyx,
Anguish, this midnight, sustains, lampadephore,

Many a vesperal dream burned by the Phoenix
That is not collected by any funerary amphora
On the credenzas, in the empty salon: no ptyx,
Abolished knickknack of empty sonority,
(For the master has gone to search for tears in the Styx
with this, the sole object with which Nothing is honored).]

The poem as a whole is a very complex meditation on nineteenth-century linguistic and historical theories, combined with a Hegelian reflection on the origin of consciousness in contradiction and conflict. Yet the whole is so tightly articulated and so overdetermined that the very act of synthesis it attempts reveals the impossibility of that gesture, thus pointing beyond the totalizing theories on which it rests.

The *ptyx* stands both as metonymy for the complex linguistic and historical theories out of which Mallarmé is fashioning this hermetic poem and as a metaphor for the impossible fold or curve that would arrest the dissemination of meaning to which these theories themselves endlessly attest. At the beginning of his quixotic mythology textbook, *Les dieux antiques*, Mallarmé describes how according to nineteenth-century historical linguistics and comparative mythology, the linguistic unity of the Indo-European people became fragmented, rendering a universal or perfect language impossible (1163–70). He argues that as a result of the migrations of the Indo-Europeans, sound and meaning became separated from one another, making direct expression unattainable. His solution to this perceived crisis of language was to imagine a work of self-conscious poetic, linguistic, and cultural recuperation that would "donner un sens plus pur aux mots de la tribu" ["give a purer meaning to the words of the tribe"] ("Tombeau d' Edgar Poe").[7]

The implications of this fall from an original state of linguistic grace and the subsequent need for a work of recuperation are central both to Mallarmé's conception of the "oeuvre pure" and the "Sonnet en—yx" (366). According to the myth, as he tells it, in the beginning there was linguistic and cultural unity. As a result of the fall into history, fragmentation and distortion occurred. It is the modern poet's task to recover this state of grace through a symbolic order that subsumes both the original unity and its subsequent fragmentation into a new, higher synthesis: "l'explication orphique de la terre" (Mallarmé 663; Langan 26–28). One means of creating this new symbolic order is through a thorough knowledge of the history of the language, its patterns of evolution, and their philosophical implications.

This interest in the poetic possibilities of historical philology is in many ways typical of the period (Balakian 85). In the latter half of the nineteenth century, the newly elaborated discourses of comparative mythology and Indo-European linguistics were providing revolutionary explanations for the historical origins of Western culture. The impact of these discursive practices on Mallarmé can be seen most clearly in *Les dieux antiques* and *Les mots anglais*. *Les dieux antiques*, a free translation of George Cox's *Manual of Mythology* supplemented with passages from *The Mythology of the Aryan Nation*, shows both a general knowledge of the field and of the work of Cox's mentor, Max Müller (Mallarmé 1159–63). By the same token, *Les mots anglais* displays a keen interest not only in the general theory of historical linguistics but also in the specific etymological roots of modern English and French (Mallarmé 901–02, 1050–51). Yet, where Cox and Müller supply what are comforting narratives of historical and racial continuity, providing the raw materials for what will be developed by other hands into a scientific racism that will reach its apogee in Nazism, Mallarme's poem presses these same concepts to the breaking point to reveal the radically incommensurate nature of the individual speaking subject to the historically constituted forms of signification out of which the possibility of meaning is formed:

> On the credenzas, in the empty salon: no ptyx,
> Abolished knickknack of empty sonority,
> (For the master has gone to search for tears in the Styx
> with this, the sole object with which Nothing is honored).

Mallarmé in the "Sonnet en—yx" uses the Latin and Greek etymologies of individual words,[8] as well as their mythological associations, to fashion a poem that enacts the roles of language and consciousness in the production and erosion of meaning in the pre-history of the West. In each case, the etymological roots and their mythic connotations refer either to the cosmic cycles of the stars and sun—which Mallarmé believed embodied for early man the primal struggle between being and nothingness—or to the corresponding cycles of life and consciousness found in individual human beings. Indeed it was Mallarmé's conviction, as well as Cox's, that all mythology and all religious and philosophical concepts stem from primitive humanity's attempt to name and understand the eternal cycling of the sun, its death and resurrection, or what Mallarmé termed "la tragédie de la Nature." Mythology itself was a product of the linguistic drift occasioned by the splitting up of the original Indo-European, linguistic plenum, which caused terms that were formerly concrete and descriptive to become detached from their original context (Mallarmé 1050–51, 1163–70, 1274; Cox 31–38; Cohn, *Towards*, 55, 140, 198).[9] The poet's impossible challenge, then, is not so much to deny history as to embody it within the compass of a single text. Hence, each of the etymologies examined in this sonnet refers to at least one of the following elements: light, dark, the curve as synecdoche for the cycle, or the convergence of opposites, as a synthetic movement embodying the previous three.

The first line is paradigmatic of the etymological patterning that runs throughout the poem. The relation of *ongles* and *onyx* is of particular interest. Set at opposite ends of the line, each is derived from a common Greek root, *onux*. *Onux* possesses a variety of meanings, but its primary sense is essentially that of *ongles*, the claws of an animal or the nails of a human. It is only by an extension of the initial set of qualities denoted by the word that it later came to mean a "veined gem," or more particularly "onyx" (Littré; Liddell and Scott). Thus, if we accept R. G. Cohn's interpretation of the *ongles* as "the distant cold stars which seem to be an organic part, a projection of the universal anguish" (i.e., the *Angoisse* at the beginning of the second line) (139–40), then we will observe a sort of overture being played on the harmonic relations that characterize the poem's imagery, the semantic content of its nouns, and their etymology. For, Mallarmé, by increasing the gap between sound and meaning that separates *ongle* from its "parenté originelle," *onux*, through a metaphorical transformation of nails into stars, has allowed the *ongles* to regain their original sound value [oniks], while permitting *onyx* to regain its original meaning ("nails").[10] Just as these two estranged moments of linguistic history converge at their point of derivation, *onux*, when they are projected to the apex of the night sky, so the line itself rolls up its ends to converge at the caesura between *haut* and *dédiant*. We thus find in this one line all the elements previously mentioned: light and dark; the cycle of the heavens; a convergence of opposites; and all achieved through an examination of the etymological root of the words at opposite ends of that same line. In the very first line, then, identity and difference are subsumed into a Hegelian unity of opposites.[11]

This sublimation of difference into unity, however, is but momentary. Its ideal self-identity is balanced by the powerful centrifugal forces inherent in the very history that produced it. The difference cannot be erased; *ongle* remains *ongle* and *onyx* *onyx*. They have not shifted positions on the page, nor been removed to a mythical vanishing point in Greek history, where the separate trajectories of their evolution would be annulled. The fold or *ptyx* that would allow them to be brought together exists neither within the poem, *nul ptyx*, nor in the French language. Even the imagery maintains this assertion of difference. For, while the white *ongles*, as the stars, are projected upon the dark night sky, the striped onyx remains a gem of the earth. The dualities effected by history are maintained, even in the moment of their denial. The white stars shine against the black background of night, while onyx consists in alternating bands of black and white. Unity and difference, light and dark, exist simultaneously, and are distributed equally throughout the line. Even the time of night *ce minuit*, reflects this dialectic, for midnight is by tradition the hour of greatest darkness, but also that in which the day begins its ascent. Yet, perhaps the most important indication of the mythic significance of this etymological and imagistic interaction resides in the observation that its effect is predicated on the initial projection by "Anguish" of the finite *ongles* onto the infinite heavens, thus ratifying their participation in the cyclic drama of the cosmos.

The "Sonnet en—yx" is a very different poem from Juvenal's. The moral and political eschatology of traditional Roman discourse has been replaced with the racialized metaphysical melancholy of *fin de siècle* France. In both cases, however, what distinguishes these passages as literary is a certain practice of the letter, a certain manipulation of the signifying substance that reveals the logical limits of the Symbolic structures that make signification possible. In neither case, however, are those manipulations extra-historical or extra-ideological. The literary is not only inconceivable outside of ideology; it, like any other speech-act, is constructed from the raw materials of social life. The question is not one of whether literature is contaminated by ideology but of what literature does with the ideological materials out of which it is rightly and necessarily made. Both Juvenal and Mallarmé reveal a beyond of the Symbolic but, in each case, a beyond that could only be constructed within a precisely located set of historically determined structures. In both cases, they reveal the ultimate impossibility of the Symbolic systems out of which they are constituted ever producing the stable, homogeneous sets of meanings and corresponding social unities of which their respective dominant ideologies dream. They do so less by adopting a position of conscious opposition to that ideology, which could only be articulated in the terms of the reigning Symbolic and thus subject to its immediate co-option, than through the invitation to the reader to collaborate in the unveiling of a fundamentally new object (or nonobject, more precisely) that reveals the limits of the Symbolic from within.

My penultimate example, from Mark Leyner's collection *I Smell Esther Williams*, is perhaps the best illustration of my thesis of the simultaneously local and transcendent nature of the literary. Leyner combines popular American culture with a camp writing style and absurdist sense of humor to produce a postmodern prose that pushes contemporary idiom to the breaking point.[12] His work is saturated with the most mundane elements of our immediate ideological universe, and yet he manages to reveal the depthless spaces that lie just below their signifying surface. The following is from his story "The Young American Poets":

> In lieu of kidnapping, more and more young people are having children of their own. Mayonnaise gone bad can be lethal and I wonder if being a stewardess is the vaunted career it once was. Ms. Eggnog left me a note: "Dear Mark, Go fuck yourself. I can't stand it anymore. They're lulling us into a false sense of security about radioactivity." I began to suspect some sleight of hand involving the bonds my grandparents held in escrow. I sent the little money I had left to Charo. (78)

In this passage, a series of deft maneuvers simultaneously reveals the vapidity of normal life, lacerates our reigning paranoia, and celebrates the weightless joy of pure semiosis. We move from the reversal of the expected tabloid headline on childless couples kidnapping babies from hospitals to the mock seriousness of "Hints from Heloise" warning us of the dangers of spoiled mayonnaise. The eggs in the mayonnaise, in turn—picture the jar of Helmans in your refrigerator—give rise to Ms. Eggnog, whose affair with the author has turned as sour as a carton of old milk ("Dear Mark, Go fuck yourself."). This association of mass-produced consumer products and sexuality turned bad (fucking eggnog!) in turn picks up on the earlier phrase lamenting the lost glories of the airline stewardess, that '60s and '70s icon of corporate-produced sexuality: "Coffee, tea, or me?" Yet it is not "Mark" or his "fucking" that Ms. Eggnog cannot stand but the radioactivity produced by the same dark corporate forces that have churned out the mayonnaise, holiday dairy products, and dimly remembered visions of sexy stewardae. That same constellation of late capitalist forces leads the narrator to fear the worst for his grandparents' bonds. Yet, these are the same forces he celebrates in that ultimate icon of the culture industry's vapidity: Charo—forever singing "goochie, goochie" as she dances for the doddering Xavier Cougat, who is old enough to be her grandfather. At least, she doesn't have to worry about her bonds.

The transitions in this passage are dizzying and the implications far from exhausted by this quick analysis. The amazing thing is not how disjointed it all seems but, just the opposite, how each disparate object seems deeply implicated in the next. The chain of association linking these found objects from the detritus of contemporary American life in Leyner's prose reveals the profound coherence and simultaneous inanity of our Symbolic ground. Postmodern American culture is revealed as an absurd, paranoid, and yet oddly joyous romp, a complex web of nothing. To follow the associative syntax and diction closely is ultimately to feel the foundations of contemporary existence shimmer lightly in the air.

The evacuation of the illusion of substance in an era whose clearest cultural icons are *Survivor* and Donald Trump may hardly seem counter-hegemonic. Contemporary consumer capitalism is itself a constant exchange of images with no real demand for foundational experiences and use values (Eagleton, *After Theory*, chapter 2). Yet, there is something sinister in Leyner's weightless world: the paranoia, the floating affect reveal a Symbolic system that has no legitimate claim upon us in any strong sense of the word and yet produces tangible effects and manipulations. The very sense of freedom this weightlessness celebrates, on one level, on another level is the sign of the sheer arbitrary nature and abjectness of our subjection. The revelation of that subjection, the unveiling of the *Ding* that lies behind and constitutes our freedom, remains a fundamentally demystifying gesture. Moreover, it is not at all clear that contemporary consumer capitalism, especially in the United States, views itself as the postmodern romp it has in many respects been seen to become. Reaganism, Thatcherism, and their ideological heir, Bushism, remain dependent on the belief that the solid bourgeois values of God, Country, Family, and Freedom underpin Western capital's continuing world hegemony: "This is what the terrorists hate." Such foundational beliefs may well be an illusion in the world of global consumer capitalism, but they have real consequences nonetheless. It would be very difficult to persuade thousands of American soldiers to kill and be killed in the sands of Iraq for Charo and Donald Trump. The illusion of solidity is more persistent than many people credit it.

My final example comes from Sartre himself. Although Sartre and Lacan differed on many things, most particularly their conceptions of language and the unconscious, their basic aesthetic positions, as outlined here, are not without certain important complementarities. This can no doubt be laid at the door as part of their respective well-known debts to Heidegger and Hegel, as well as their common Parisian intellectual milieu (Ragland-Sullivan 91; Roudinesco 98).

Nonetheless, this coincidence of interests would be nothing more than a mere cultural and intellectual curiosity if it did not have potentially powerful theoretical and political ramifications. Thus, for both Sartre and Lacan the subject remains central. This is what separates Lacan from many of his postmodern confreres (Žižek, *Sublime Object* 174–75). The Lacanian subject may be at its core a moment of sheer absence or the negation of all positive substance, but it is also absolutely central in that role. The talking cure depends on the existence of the tortured subject on the couch, perpetually discovering the facticity of its own constructions and defenses, its own constitutive relation to the Other (Lacan, *Séminaire* VII 347, 351; Freiberger 225–26, 237–38). Nor should it be forgotten that for Sartre himself in *L'être et le néant*, the authentic subject is on the side of *le néant*, not *l'être:* it is not a substance in itself, but a perpetual Hegelian negation. All the same, as noted above, Lacan accepts neither Sartre's position of the subject being a posited ontological given nor that of its ability through lucidity to come to an ideal self-presence of good faith. For Lacan, the subject is always constituted through language, and therefore always irremediably severed from itself (Dowling 91).

Nonetheless, once these allowances are made, the Lacan of the *Ethics* and the Sartre of *Qu'est-ce que la littérature* each have something to offer the other in terms of a theory of literature. Sartre brings three things to the table. The first is the urgency of the question: what is literature? What is this thing we think we read, produce, and study? The second is the formulation of literature not as a reified pre-existing object, a Platonic form, but as an invitation to a collaborative unveiling of a fundamentally new object that at once reflects and re-forms the world. The third is the consciousness of the necessarily political nature of any such collaborative unveiling of the literary object. Lacan offers three very different things. The first is his conception of the Imaginary, the Symbolic, and the Real as the three primary orders of existence. This triangular structure has the advantage of allowing us to theorize the relation of language to the subject in a very precise way without ever collapsing one term into the other. The second is his concept of *das Ding* as the pre-Symbolic kernel of our enjoyment. Last is his concept of the sublime object as that which is raised to the dignity of *das Ding*, i.e., as that which is created within the Symbolic in such a way as to always point beyond it and its pre-existing constructions.

Literature, then, is a practice of the letter that comes as an invitation to the reader to constitute or unveil a sublime object. That invitation comes in the form of a concentration of signifying effects that folds back a given Symbolic formation against itself and so points to its own beyond. Neither that beyond nor the Symbolic itself are static unchanging objects but situated moments whose precise contours are constituted in the instant of the issuing of the invitation: that is to say, when reader and text enter into the relation of co-constitution and unveiling.

Our final passage, then, is from the second volume of Sartre's *Les chemins de la liberté, Le Sursis*, and will show more precisely how this particular reading of Lacan and his heirs is able to offer a convincing answer to Sartre's question. *Le Sursis* is a vast multiperspectival novel set on the eve of the Second World War, in the days leading up to the French mobilization in September 1938. The novel is at once realistic and written in a kind of cinematic technique that involves rapid cuts between fictional characters and historical actors, leading to the possibility of a final synthesis in which all the individual points of view are taken up into a single larger historical and narrative vision. The passage in question is at once programmatic for the novel as a whole and an avowal of the fundamental impossibility, and simultaneous necessity, of its narrative project. This passage both acknowledges the necessity of the omniscient "God's eye" point of view that such a narrative style creates and denies the possibility of the existence of such a perspective *tout court*. As such, the single most programmatic statement in the novel, the one in which the author offers his most explicit metanarratological reflections, is also a deconstruction of the novel's own narrative technique. That technique, however, as is made clear, is not just a product of formal exigencies but also carries with it certain essential political, ethical, and epistemological demands:

> *Un corps énorme, une planète, dans un espace à cent millions de dimensions; les êtres à trois dimensions ne pouvaient même pas l'imaginer. Et pourtant chaque dimension était une conscience autonome. Si on essayait de regarder la planète en face, elle s'effondrait en miettes, il ne restait plus que des consciences. Cent millions de consciences libres dont chacune voyait des murs, un bout de cigare rougeoyant, des visages familiers, et construisait sa destine sous sa propre responsabilité. Et pourtant, si l'on était une de ces consciences on s'apercevait à d'imperceptibles effleurements, à d'insensibles changements, qu'on etait solidaire d'un gigantesque et invisible polypier. La guerre: chacun est libre et pourtant les jeux sont faits. Elle est là, elle est partout, c'est la totalité de toutes mes pensées, de toutes les paroles d'Hitler, de tous les actes de Gomez, mais personne n'est là pour faire le total. Elle n'existe que pour dieu. Mais Dieu n'existe pas. Et pourtant la guerre existe.*
> (Sartre, *Oeuvres Romanesques* 1024–25)

[A vast body, a planet, in a space of one hundred million dimensions; three-dimensional beings could not even imagine it. And yet each dimension was an autonomous consciousness. If one tried to look directly at the planet, it would fall to pieces, there would be only consciousnesses. One hundred million free consciousnesses, each one of which saw walls, the glowing end of a cigar, familiar faces, and constructed its destiny under its own responsibility. And yet, if one *were* one of these consciousnesses, one would become aware through the lightest of touches, through insensible changes, that one was part of a giant and invisible coral reef. The war: everyone is free and yet the bets are made. It's there; it's everywhere, it's the totality of all my thoughts, all Hitler's words, all Gomez's acts: but no one is there to add it up. It exists only for God. But God does not exist. And yet the war exists.]

As Jameson says, this is an "agonized and self-canceling passage" in which the simultaneous impossibility and necessity of totality is vividly evoked (57). The world must make sense because history has a direction. It is not random. In September 1938, the world of Western Europe was moving inexorably toward war. And yet, the illusion of the inexorable march toward war masks the countless independent actions of millions of responsible actors, no one of whose individual actions could be predicted with any certainty. In addition, such a vision of radical individual freedom was the very condition of the political solidarity that was necessary if war was to be stopped: for only an appeal to these individuals' ethical freedoms could justify a call to action that might stop the slide toward catastrophe. In a world where people are not responsible for their actions, the call for them to act differently is a non sequitur. And yet, the appeal to the individual actors' ethical freedom just as clearly masks the fact that they are indeed part of a vast process—an organism whose contours they cannot see or even posit, and yet it determines not only the context of their actions but their import as well.

These positions are contradictory. They cannot exist in the same logical universe, and yet they must if any sense is to be made either of the events of September 1938 or of those leading to the current war on terrorism. What Sartre's novel, in general, and this passage, in particular, achieve is the concretization and representation of this logical impossibility. "Totality is affirmed in the very moment whereby it is denied, and represented in the same language that denies it all possible representation" (Jameson 57). In doing so, Sartre marshals the categories and conventions of modernism's ethical pathos, the twentieth century's elegy for the bourgeois individual, to unveil an object that simultaneously transcends those categories and yet never falls into a facile deterministic materialism. It turns the very Symbolic resources of twentieth-century phenomenological philosophy and of Sartrean existentialism against themselves to create a sublime object that evokes the lost image of the reassuring totality—*das Ding* as the lost object—and mourns its loss as the condition of our acting as subjects in history.

If space allowed, similar demonstrations could be made of the practice of the letter in an even wider variety of texts. In fact, the range of examples is limited only by the knowledge of the reader. Literary analysis, as here described, moreover, in no way precludes examining these same texts as communicative acts. But literature itself is a practice of the letter that in its dialogic relation with the reading public simultaneously unveils and creates an object that not only reproduces the founding assumptions of the reigning Symbolic but pushes those assumptions to the point at which they reveal their own historical, structural, and, ultimately, ontological limitations, and hence their beyond. Through the literary an excess of meaning is produced that threatens the very ground of our experience, revealing a sublime object: *das Ding*, the point of flocculation, the ever-recurring yet historically specific navel of representation.

NOTES

1. Nabokov, *Lolita* 286. See also *Strong Opinions* 3, 121, 228–30; *Selected Letters* 242, 336.

2. All translations are my own unless otherwise noted.

3. As Eagleton himself recognizes in his most recent work (*After Theory* chap. 1).

4. Lacan thus collapses Kant's categories of the beautiful and the sublime, but, as Sussman (36) points out, beauty in Kant is a "way-station between pure reason and the sublime." It presents the antinomies of pure reason: demanding the particular be apprehended within the universal, while maintaining its particularity. See also Sussman (28–29).

5. Compare Bataille (158–59).

6. For an extended reading in these terms, see Miller ("Black and White Mythology"). Included there is a refutation of Riffaterre's argument that Mallarmé did not know the meaning of *ptyx*.

7. See Gilbert (110), "Mallarmé desired to return man and his world to their unique sources [. . .]. At these origins can be found the beginnings of all languages. During the course of history, adversity was established; expansion led to deterioration. Poetic language would return to this ideal source and be reborn as supreme."

8. See Chassé (39), "Pour arriver à la compréhension du poète, l'essentiel est d'abord de bien se persuader que le vers: 'Donner un sens plus pur aux mots de la tribu' était une formule de signification très précise. A son point de vue, cette phrase, en langage clair, se traduisait ainsi: 'employer les mots dans un sens strictement étymologique.'"

9. See also Chassé's claim that Mallarmé was trying to invent an ideal language as close to Sanskrit as possible (36).

10. It should be noted that the process that permits this metaphorical transformation is the same as that which originally allowed the Greek *onux* to refer to onyx as well as nails, an extension of meaning through an abstraction of the image.

11. See Hegel (§73), "Everything is grounded in the unity of identity and non-identity, of one and other, of sameness and distinction, of affirmation and negation. The Absolute is essentially dialectical. Dialectic is the essence of Being or Being as *essence*. Essence is the *sufficient ground* of all that seems to be non-absolute or finite. A is non-A: The Absolute maintains itself in that which seems to escape it."

12. I owe my discovery of Leyner to Moraru's insightful article.

WORKS CITED

Althusser, Louis. "Les mérites de l'économie classique." *Lire le Capital*. Paris: Maspero, 1968. 101–11.

———. "Letters to D." *Writings on Psychoanalysis: Freud and Lacan*. Eds. Olivier Corpet and François Matheron. Trans. Jeffrey Mehlman. New York: Columbia UP. 33–77.

Balakian, Anna. *The Symbolist Movement: A Critical Appraisal*. New York: New York UP, 1977.

Bataille, Georges. *L'érotisme*. Paris: Minuit, 1957.

Butler, Judith. *Gender Trouble: Feminism and the Subversion of Identity*. New York: Routledge, 1990.

———. *Subjects of Desire: Hegelian Reflections in Twentieth-Century France*. New York: Columbia UP, 1987.

Chassé, Charles. *Les clés de Mallarmé*. Paris: Aubier, 1954.

Clément, Cathérine. "La Coupable." *La jeune née*. Paris: Union Générale d'Edition, 1975. 8–113.

Cohn, R. G. *Towards the Poems of Mallarmé*. Berkeley: U of California P, 1965.

Contat, Michel and Geneviève Idt. "Préface" to Jean-Paul Sartre, *Oeuvres romanesques*. Ed. Michel Contat and Michel Rybalka, with the collaboration of Geneviève Idt and George H. Bauer. Paris: Gallimard, 1981. ix–xxxiii.

Cox, George W. *The Mythology of the Aryan Nations*. Vol. 1. London: Longmans, Green, and Co., 1870.

de Man, Paul. "The Dead-End of Formalist Criticism." *Blindness and Insight: Essays in the Rhetoric of Contemporary Criticism*. 2nd ed. Minneapolis: U of Minnesota P, 1983. 229–45.

Dowling, William C. *Jameson, Althusser, Marx: An Introduction to the Political Unconscious*. Ithaca: Cornell UP, 1984.

Eagleton, Terry. *After Theory*. New York: Basic Books, 2003.

————. *Literary Theory: An Introduction*. 2nd ed. Minneapolis: U of Minnesota, 1996.

Ferguson, John. *Juvenal: The Satires*. New York: St. Martin's, 1979.

Freiberger, Erich D. "'Heads I Win, Tails You Lose': Wittgenstein, Plato, and the Role of Construction and Deconstruction in Psychoanalysis and Ethics." *Lacan in America*. Ed. Jean Michel Rabaté. New York: The Other Press, 2000. 223–46.

Gilbert, Paula. *The Aesthetics of Stéphane Mallarmé in Relation to his Public*. Madison: Farleigh Dickinson UP, 1976.

Hanlon, Christopher. "Psychoanalysis and the Post-Political: An Interview with Slavoj Žižek." *New Literary History* 32 (2001): 1–22.

Hegel, G. W. F. *Encyclopedia of Philosophy*. Trans. Gustav Emil Mueller. New York: Philosophical Library, 1959.

Jameson, Fredric. *The Political Unconscious: Narrative as a Socially Symbolic Act*. Ithaca, NY: Cornell UP, 1981.

Julien, Philippe. *Pour lire Jacques Lacan*. 2nd ed. Paris: E.P.E.L., 1990.

Kristeva, Julia. *Black Sun: Depression and Melancholia*. Trans. Leon S. Roudiez. New York: Columbia UP, 1989.

————. "Le temps des femmes." *Cahiers de recherché de S. T. D. Paris VII* 5 (1979): 5–18.

Kromer, Gretchen. "The Redoubtable PTYX," *MLN* 86 (1971): 563–72.

Lacan, Jacques. *Le Séminaire. Livre VII: L'éthique de la psychanalyse*. Ed. Jacques-Alain Miller. Paris: Seuil 1986.

————. *Le Séminaire. Livre XI: Les quatre concepts fondementaux de la psychanalyse*. Ed. Jacques-Alain Miller. Paris: Seuil, 1973.

————. *Le Séminaire. Livre XX: Encore*. Ed. Jacques-Alain Miller. Paris: Seuil, 1975.

————. *The Seminar of Jacques Lacan. Book VII: The Ethics of Psychoanalysis, 1959–60*. Ed. Jacques-Alain Miller. Trans. Dennis Porter. New York: Norton, 1992.

Langan, Janine D. *Hegel and Mallarmé*. Lanham, MD: U Press of America, 1986.

Liddell, Henry George and Robert Scott. *A Greek English Lexicon*, 9th ed. Revised by Sir Henry Stuart Jones with the assistance of Roderick McKenzie. Oxford: Oxford UP, 1940.

Littré, E. *Dictionnaire de la langue française*. Paris: Hachette, 1876.

Mallarmé, Stéphane. *Oeuvres complètes de Mallarmé*. Eds. Henri Mondor and G. Jean-Aubry. Paris: Editions Gallimard, 1945.

Miller, Paul Allen. "Black and White Mythology: Etymology and Dialectics in Mallarmé's 'Sonnet en—yx.'" *Texas Studies in Literature and Language* 36 (1994): 184–211.

———. *Subjecting Verses: Latin Love Elegy and the Emergence of the Real.* Princeton, NJ: Princeton UP, 2004.

Mitchell, Juliet, and Jacqueline Rose, eds. of Jacques Lacan. "Seminar of 21 January 1975." *Feminine Sexuality.* Trans. Jacqueline Rose. New York: Pantheon, 1982. 162–71.

Moi, Toril. *Sexual/Textual Politics: Feminist Literary Theory.* New York: Routledge, 1985.

Moraru, Christian. "Intertextual Bodies: Three Steps on the Ladder of Posthumanity." *Intertexts* 5 (2001): 46–60.

Moxey, Keith P. F. "Semiotics and the Social History of Art." *New Literary History* 22 (1991): 985–99.

Nabokov, Vladimir. *Lolita.* 1955. New York: Berkley Publishing, 1977.

———. *Selected Letters 1940–1977.* Eds. Dmitri Nabokov and Matthew J. Bruccoli. San Diego: Harcourt, Brace, Jovanovich, 1989.

———. *Strong Opinions.* New York: McGraw Hill, 1973.

Ragland-Sullivan, Ellie. *Jacques Lacan and the Philosophy of Psychoanalysis.* Urbana: U of Illinois P, 1986.

Riffaterre, Michael. *Semiotics of Poetry.* Bloomington: Indiana UP, 1978.

Roudinesco, Elizabeth. *Jacques Lacan.* Trans. Barbara Bray. New York: Columbia UP, 1997.

Sartre, Jean-Paul. *L'être et le néant: essai d'ontologie phénoménologique.* Paris: Gallimard, 1943.

———. *Oeuvres romanesques.* Eds. Michel Contat and Michel Rybalka, with the collaboration of Geneviève Idt and George H. Bauer. Paris: Gallimard, 1981.

———. *Qu'est-ce que la littérature?* Paris: Gallimard, 1948.

Silverman, Kaja. *World Spectators.* Stanford: Stanford UP, 2000.

Sussman, Henry. *Psyche and Text: The Sublime and Grandiose in Literature, Psychopathology, and Culture.* Albany: State U of New York P, 1993.

Žižek, Slavoj. *Enjoy Your Symptom!: Jacques Lacan in Hollywood and Out.* New York: Routledge, 1992.

———. *Looking Awry: An Introduction to Jacques Lacan through Popular Culture.* Cambridge, MA: MIT Press, 1991.

———. *The Sublime Object of Ideology.* London: Verso, 1989.

2

Psychoanalysis, Religion, and Cultural Criticism at the Millennium

Henry Sussman

MILLENNIAL PSYCHOANALYSIS

The question the editors have put to us is a canny one. What is this love affair we maintain with psychoanalysis? Why do we continue it after all but the very few of us have abandoned the analytical *cabinet* with its verbal form of bulimia, spitting our privately nuanced signifiers, if not our guts out? Psychoanalysis continues as an academic pursuit, invoked, reconfigured, deployed in the environment of the classroom or the symposium. It is an academic obsession. Its relation to our clinical crunching, over and over again, the relevant data, memories, affects associated with those few Gordian knots, those few absolutely telling and prominent features on our psychic landscapes that make us, fatally and comically, who we are, is by no means clear. In managed health care systems, such as predominate primarily in the United States, pharmacological treatments have vastly outstripped the deployment of the "talking cure."

Psychoanalysis persists, regardless of how many of us, or how few, find our way to the therapeutic preserve of recapitulation, *revenant*,[1] reproach, resolve, revelation, apology, complaint, complicity, manipulation, transference, projection, regression, and fragmentary and always provisional healing. It persists not only as a longstanding and widely applied conceptual paradigm and "theoretical sub-specialization," but as a cultural venture and ethos experienced personally within a collective setting. In this connection, I wrote in *The Aesthetic Contract*:

> The psychotherapist is, whether she wants to be or not, implicitly a literary critic; the client is a philosopher. Teachers of literature and culture are in effect cultural psychoanalysts: they expose their students to the gender, race, ethnicity, class, and age-based

determinants of their lives. But the specificity of the analysis proceeds no further than the level of the group. The clinical psychoanalyst orchestrates a self-scrutiny or self-interpretation that takes
the above factors into account, but whose finitude goes all the way
to the client's personal experiences, associations, and memories.
A culturally astute educational system, then, should transform
every student into a cultural critic and a philosopher of her collectivity's experience. (196)

In my effort to elucidate certain of the cultural conditions to have prevailed
since the onset of Western modernity, that is since the emergence of capital
and urbanity as the driving forces in the societies predisposed to sustaining
them, and the programming of Protestantism as the revised onto-theology
rationalizing this sociocultural formation, I paralleled the linguistic negotiations performed by individuals and those by groups. I posited this analogy
because both individuated subjects and the collectivities they belong to,
whether defined by kinship, ethnicity, religion, or occupation and class, reside on a continuum, a middle—remember that in Deleuze and Guattari's
characterization of rhizomes there is nothing but middles (*Thousand Plateaus*
25)—extending from relatively stabilized public discourse and relatively
idiosyncratic private language. It is not difficult to visualize the exemplary
artist over the period chronicled, in different ways, already in Shakespearean
drama and Kleist's "Michael Kohlhaas" as a programmer constantly pushing the patois of acceptable public discourse into its hinterlands or margins.
The aesthetic contract of high modernism, whether practiced by Apolli-
naire, Mallarmé, Jarry, Joyce, Kafka, Stein, Proust, Picasso, futurism,
dadaism, or surrealism makes this foregrounding and delimitation of conventionality its driving force. Oddly, the initial clients of psychoanalysis,
whether Senatspräsident Schreber,[2] Anna von O,[3] the Wolf Man,[4] or the
Rat Man[5] find themselves in exactly the same position as the avatars of
modernism. They do not dismiss, deny, or repress a language of dreams,
symbols, emotions, and corporeal sensations that is horrifying and unprecedented to them. Under the tutelage of Freud in the psychoanalytic *cabinet*,
they above all negotiate and invent or reconstruct the interface between this
disturbing, highly idiosyncratic language and, on the one hand, the drives
and corporeality they have left behind, and on the other hand, the social
normativity that has excluded them. In relation to his patients, Freud occupies, among other roles, that of an artistic master, the major domus of an
aesthetic atelier. He is an exemplary master in an artform he has invented,
psychoanalytical therapy. Only in slightly different respects, his first patients
and disciples are novices in this artform, and until 1914 or so, he is only a

few steps ahead of them.[6] The psychoanalytical training institute has about it the air of a conservatory or atelier, a cloister arbitrary and idiosyncratic in a distinctive way, but at odds with the atmosphere of an academic department. Lacan provides the enormous contribution of restoring to psychoanalysis the linguistic thrust and acuity it manifested during the seminal Freudian moments, yet Lacan and indeed all the major post-Freudians, from Jung and Klein to Winnicott and Kohut, retain the aesthetic bearing of a modernist master reconciling *Burgertum* and conventionality to the impulses, expressions, and manifestations that simply will not capitulate.

We would not wish to begin to speculate on a common denominator linking the major variants of psychoanalytical practice, for it would not render justice to the true innovation and invention that has consistently transpired within the psychoanalytical sphere. Such an act of leveling and standardization could not account, for example, for a psychoanalytical performance, for the discourse of psychoanalysis as a medium of performance art, as it is routinely unpacked in the oral as well as written communications of Slavoj Žižek. Indeed, as I am arguing in other venues at the moment, those who take issue with Žižek's substantive calls on whatever—on the inevitability of governmental repression, the unconscious desire on the part of the oppressed for their worst nightmares, the appeal of Buddhism to U.S. New Agers—systematically err in seeking redress or correction to these Žižekian judgment calls.[7] For theory, in Žižek's work, is a secondary concern, at most. It is the stage or cultural venue for a discursive performance along the lines of psychoanalytical tropes, figures such as displacement, condensation, and regression. When it comes to critical or theoretical pronouncements, a rigorous philosopher or critical theorist will catch Žižek short every time. But conceptual rigor is largely beside the point in Žižek's performance, whose true work is meticulously and creatively marshaled in acts of *performing* displacement, condensation, and regression. Here I would insist, as a performance artist who allegorically, in every dimension of discourse, dramatically brings home the transpositions of language under the aura of psychoanalysis, Žižek succeeds brilliantly—and consistently.

But we can say, if we can resist the impulse to generalize, that psychoanalysis has, since its inception, served as a site and venue for undoing the disconnects that impede, in both public and subjective spheres, thoughtfulness, concentration, open-mindedness, and creativity, and for reconciling, if not integrating, otherwise antagonistic perspectives, points of view, voices, and experiences. Even when the fate of formal psychoanalysis and other variants of the "talking cure" is, through a variety of factors including managed healthcare and the prevalence of the deployment of psychopharmacological agents, up in the air, it is possible for universities and learned symposia to continue the work of psychoanalysis on the cultural plain—to creatively confront the inflections and torque upon the collective private language that has been programmed into the ethos and disposition of their communal members and participants.

Cultural psychoanalysis may be defined as the negotiation of the heavily nuanced and privatized language often inculcated by membership in various kinds of groups through an engagement, in a respectful but not repressively tolerant environment, with the discourses and artifacts of communities and interests that have been deemed, for whatever reasons, "inadmissible" to this point.[8] An engagement with Otherness and Others on their own terms out of the particular subcultures and local cultures into which we are first absorbed marks a pivotal educational hurdle, or raising of power, for all of us. It is a leap in conceptual ability as well as interpersonal outreach that is not accomplished by all. This embrace of the Other can be orchestrated only in part by the educational system, religious training, and their equivalents. Some of this opening to the Other transpires in institutional settings; some depends on experience in the street. To the extent that this engagement with Otherness can be orchestrated institutionally, this transformation is the moment at which the tired, tried, and true survey in Western Civilization opens into the impossibility, shock, and wonder of World Civilizations, an outrageous course to teach however long it lasts—and I teach it regularly—a course that begins to suggest the supplementarities available in Hinduism, Buddhism, indigenous cultures, and Chinese medicine, and parallel formations to the tendencies in the three "Abrahamic religions" and in classical Greek and Roman cultures that gave rise to "Western civilization." When deployed properly, the university or college curriculum can serve as the archive, the library lining the shelves of the office at 19 Berggasse, furnishing the materials for this crucial engagement. The instructional programmer who imagines education in this fashion becomes a cultural psychoanalyst, the occasion for students to work through the culturally induced blockages, biases, and blindnesses restricting an ethical engagement with Otherness, sabotaging an empathic bearing toward the experience of the communities imputed, at the moment, with Otherness, whether by religion, sexual preference, race, ethnicity, or age, preempting the dedication and drive to decipher at times the most exasperating and foreign tongues and tales they tell. And, as I argued in *The Aesthetic Contract*, the outreach and accommodation, integration if not homogenization, of inimical, alien, and possibly disturbing points of view that transpires in such a classroom demands an aesthetic acuity and resourcefulness very much akin to what Freud imbibed through osmosis from the memorable modernists and that shaped the program of modernism (40–50, 199–205).

One final general point indicative of my knee-jerk reaction to the challenging assignment the editors have sent my way: As is evident in Anthony Wilden's placement of what he has learned from Lacan in communication with cybernetics and information theory, if not from psychoanalysis's founding texts, psychoanalysis is, irreducibly, a systems theory; it extrapolates the widest parameters of what Freud terms the psychic and intrapsychic economies. In such works as "The Project," *Studies on Hysteria*, and *The Interpretation of Dreams*, Freudian theory sets into play—even if it leaves for the likes of Lacan, Wilden, and Žižek to fully elaborate their implications— the isomorphic structures, the loops of positive and negative feedback, and the morphogenetic evolution characteristic of systems' interactions with their environments, of the inputs and outputs, faculties, and agencies whose division of labor is a compelling topic from Spinoza and Leibnitz onward into the twentieth century.[9] We have eventuated at a moment in which a systems perspective is a minimal requirement of any cultural intervention with aspirations to an ethical purview.[10] We cannot begin to imagine the flows and interconnections facilitating globalization, for example, without projecting at the systematic level. Yet in a postmodern context, systematicity can maintain its relational features while abandoning its pretensions to functionality and scale. This is to say that a discourse or an inquiry can be systematic in the richness of the relations that it traces, associates, and combines without claiming a vast scale or relying on the classical mechanisms of systems, whether continuity between the parts and the whole, continuity of evolution, or parallelism between lower and higher levels of generality. Derrida can at every moment extrapolate the systematic pretensions— to presence, immediacy, purity, essentiality, Being, identity, endurance— around what he reads and articulates in a very local—Deleuze and Guattari would say *minor*—context. Any artifact that Derrida reads—it would be better to say any fragment of an artifact—is positioned such that it performs in specific respects the violation of the systematic terms and features that may be extrapolated from it. It is not without forethought that Derrida so often leaves unstated the encompassing systematic assembly of the concepts referenced in his exegeses. Simply the provision of the broader encompassing conceptual framework would dim the arbitrariness and richness of the tropes whose intransigent play constitutes the fullest extent of their meaning. Thus, the deconstruction of systems involves bracketing, to the degree possible, the traditional claims that have occasioned and rationalized them, and dedicating as much language as possible to what Wilden would call their "noise." Lacan's relentless pursuit of the intricate trajectory of the *petit objet a* and his ongoing measurement of the looming menace posed by the Big Other also belong to the deconstruction of systems as it transpires within the psychoanalytical field.

With regard to their approach to systems, Deleuze and Guattari are other, if not entirely antithetical, thinkers. Their approach to systems theory signals the distinction of their particular psychoanalytical intervention, one of particular interest to students attempting to address the worldly impacts and residues of symbolic processes while maintaining the linguistic focus and dedication to which Derrida exhorts us. Indeed, Deleuze and Guattari, particularly in their "Capitalism and Schizophrenia" diptych, maintain, even exaggerate the traditional aspirations and pretensions of Western conceptual systems, whose terms they ironically recast and paraphrase:

> Expression should be understood not simply as the face and language, or individual languages, but as a semiotic collective machine that preexists them and constitutes regimes of signs. A formation of power is much more than a tool; a regime of signs is much more than a language. Rather, they act as determining and selective agents. . . . *Is this not like an intermediate state between the two states of the abstract Machine?*—the state in which it remains enveloped in a corresponding stratum (ecumenon) and the state in which it develops in its own right on the destratified plane of consistency (planomenon). The abstract machine begins to unfold, to stand to full height, producing an illusion exceeding all strata, even though the machine itself still belongs to a determinate stratum. This is, obviously, the illusion constitutive of man (who does man think he is?). This illusion derives from the overcoding immanent to language itself. But what is not illusory are the new distributions between content and expression: technological content characterized by a hand-tool relation and, at a deeper level, tied to a social Machine and formations of power; symbolic expressions characterized by face-language relations and, at a deeper level, tied to a semiotic Machine and regimes of signs. (*Thousand Plateaus* 63)

The task here is not to mute or occult systemic claims but to subtract or deduct from them the pathos of subjectivity and the momentum of dialectical process. Indeed, Deleuze and Guattari leave us with the corpse or body of Western systematicity in the absence of the (logical and metaphysical) program that "animated" it. Rather than eliminate the systematic breadth of psychoanalytic thought, Deleuze and Guattari elect to refit it in a fashion more conducive to the indiscriminate flows and inarticulate connections, whether of thought, impulse, bodily fluid or word, that to them more accurately reflect the conditions of the postmodern world into which Western societies have eventuated. Deleuze and Guattari goad us into considering that the schizo state may have become a more normative form of psychological "organization" than integration; that the postmodern body is closer to a field for the shattering sensations of heroin than to serving as a homunculus of specialization and organization. Psychologically, Deleuze and Guattari's "subject" is not a neurotic system out of alignment, in need of correction, but an input oriented to subliminal hums, "noises," double messages. The schizo may not perform well according to the standard measures, but is exquisitely attuned to interfaces and interconnections that escape the rest of us. Indeed, it is the pursuit of uncanny resonances that can link the flows of money and goods, body fluids, symbols, ideologies, and events of history that defines the project that Deleuze and Guattari have, in the "Capitalism and Schizophrenia" diptych, set for themselves.

In at least impressionistic response to the editors' good questions, then, I can venture that at the millennium, psychoanalysis is something that happens more in a collective, cultural, and possibly educational context than in accordance with the protocols of a one-on-one intervention behind closed doors that initially defined it. It addresses the precipitating causes of blindnesses or disconnects on the part of groups rather than of individuals. It addresses, as ever, the gaps or discontinuities in knowledge and awareness preempting fully mindful or ethical reactions to people and conditions in the world. And, it gravitates to the systemic level in imagining or projecting the pathways, flow, and mechanisms of psychological information, thought, drive, and emotion.

THE NATURE OF AN INTERVENTION

I would like to address two tasks: to rephrase the terminology in which we would couch what constitutes an intervention within the parameters of this culturally psychoanalytical, systemically oriented milieu. I think that following the lead of Wilden and others who would translate therapeutic interactions into the terms of communications theory, with its inputs, outputs, loops of feedback and disconnection, it is most salutary to consider the cultural interventions available to us in terms that have been made possible by cybernetics. And I would like to posit a rationale for our need to return to religion as a major site for cultural and psychoanalytic work at the present and into the foreseeable future. As impossible as it has been for theoretically and philosophically astute scholars to reconcile the conditions of modernity and postmodernism with fundamentalist belief in any particular religious system, it is equally untenable for us to deny credence any longer to the power that religious thought and social systems exercise in the contemporary world. It can indeed be argued that recent current events, from the ongoing situation in the Middle East to 9/11 and the now-perpetual war between the West and the fundamentalist Islamist world, come to us courtesy of religious thought. There is no tenable psychoanalytical thought at the millennium, just as there is no viable deconstruction or Cultural Studies that does not address religious systems empathically, that is to say, not tendentiously or dismissively. Psychoanalysis and all viable current conceptual paradigms need to acknowledge that in the "advanced Western" societies, an informal, secular religion prevails. Even if obfuscated under the trappings of consumerism, entertainment, sports, and sexual ideology and fetishism, this informal religion is as prevalent and effective as the fundamentalisms of the Abrahamic world. Following the lead of deconstruction's "turn to religion," which arose tangentially out of the problematics of the trace and *archéécriture* a quarter of a century ago, and was pursued explicitly by Derrida himself for nigh on twenty of those years, cultural psychoanalysis needs, at a millennium whose primary import has been given in theological terms, to face the assertions, repressions, trade-offs, and inevitable conflicts within a religion of global dimensions and repercussions.

But first, for a few minutes, what of the intervention that psychoanalysis, or its cultural students and practitioners, can hope to make? We may have well eventuated at a moment when the medium of the critical essay no longer exhausts the possibilities for an informed cultural intervention on the part of a reader who may always be thought of in his or her own right as a potential cultural programmer and reprogrammer. The lessons we have learned from our own success in the fields of twentieth-century philosophy, psychoanalysis, semiotics, critical theory, and cultural studies may well now impel us more in the direction of informed *interventions* than that of well-documented scholarly contributions.[11] To calibrate interventions and impose them on a situation is a more slapdash and haphazard endeavor than contributing to an existing literature, itself corresponding to the standing parameters of the field of knowledge, whether these qualify as scholarship or criticism. The polymorphous notion we have gained of texts, the skepticism with which we would approach a priori divisions or genres of discourse strongly urge us toward the recognition that a screenplay, a lyrical poem, or even a musical composition or a Web site may constitute just as specific, nuanced, informed, and articulate a reading and processing of specific cultural artifacts and experiences as an explicit contribution to the critical literature. The same labor of reading, the same simultaneous act of agonized encoding and decoding, the same search for relevant contextual materials, surrounding such issues as an artifact's production, its times, extenuating factors in its emergence, the same combination of blindness and insight, of informed projection and almost willful obfuscation by which any coherent reading is extracted from an artifact, are demanded by an adaptation of an artifact from one medium to another and by the kind of overall cultural reprogramming that I am designating by the term intervention. We may well have eventuated at a moment where our own disciplines assure us that an intervention is every bit as legitimate a response to a cultural artifact as a learned essay.

There is a close and implicit rapport between the notion of intervention that I am developing here and the metaphors of cybernetics and programming. Imagine what happens when we replace the traditional scenario in which we are subjects better-read or worse-read, attached to larger or smaller backpacks of learning and erudition, marking us, in the eyes of literary departments, as superior or inferior specimens, with the notion that each cultural experience we have, each intense interaction we entertain with a cultural artifact, whatever its medium, joins the existing cultural programming, or inscription, we have assimilated. Each new interaction both deepens this programming, adds to the repertoire, but also reprograms prior interactions and reconfigures us as readers and therefore rewires or "re-primes" any subsequent interactions we are about to enter. The image of us as reading subjects slowly evolving from the time of our most basic competences and earliest cultural interchanges tends to emphasize the gradual accretion of our literacy and erudition, such that our latest acquisitions from the domain of culture are of limited impact. In such a view, we are really the subjective counterparts to a substantial library. Both what we have absorbed over the years and what we bring to an interpretative situation, in effect our "standing collections," far outweigh this year's or last year's acquisitions. The cybernetic model, in which reading and cultural interactions of different orders constitute a kind of programming, in which we are cultural programmers in an ongoing state of reprogramming, and in which our responses or interventions bear the capacity to reconfigure existing programs on the web of public response, gives the most recent interactions far more sway than they hold in the prior model of the reader or cultural subject as a human library. At any moment we may access the cultural artifact that may radically reconfigure our entire existing cultural program. Having been ourselves radically reprogrammed by cultural inscriptions constantly flooding the public sphere in a wide variety of media, we are at all times primed, through our own reconfiguration as cultural participants, to contribute significant responses that will participate in the generative reprogramming of our fellow participants in whichever intellectual webs we happen to join. The cybernetic model in which cultural artifacts exercise the capacity to reconfigure the cultural programming of the programmers that take them in, and in which the participants in culture are at all times susceptible to profound experiences resulting in significant changes, emphasizes the later moments in the interactions with the broader culture, which retain at all times the potential for radical transformation and for significant contribution to the public record. The view of us as subjects equipped with better or worse repositories of cultural literacy implicitly emphasizes the notion of inheritance and its sociopolitical pretext and dynamics. Some of us inherit a lot, whether in tangible or literate wealth, and some of us do not. Whereas there is something profoundly and radically democratic in the image of each of us as programmers in a manifestly international web of response to the cultural phenomena of the past as well as the present. The work in which we collectively join is rather a work of transformation and reprogramming rather than the competitive acquisition and hoarding of cultural sources and resources in a universe seen as closed and finite.

The state of our prior cultural programming at any given moment sets the parameters of any intervention we are prepared to issue in response to cultural artifacts we have extracted. Our interventions comprise works of cultural reprogramming issuing from a particular configuration—Benjamin would call it a constellation—of experience. Our interventions will be affected and modified by cultural interactions we entertain even during the time of the composition process, during the very act of programming. As cultural psychoanalysts, we are not only reprogramming the state of knowledge concerning specific events and artifacts, we are reprogramming the ground rules and other conditions of an interchange in which we all participate; in this broader sense, we are simultaneously, in whatever medium we couch the results of our reading, reprogramming each other. We are reprogramming each other at the same time that, through our daily cultural encounters and musings, we are constantly being reprogrammed, hopefully in a more constructive way than Hal is in Stanley Kubrick's *2001: A Space Odyssey*.

RELIGION REDUX

As students of cultural psychoanalysis, we need to return to the discipline of Religious Studies with vehemence. We need to retrace religion's understated role in a sequence of events seeming sometimes to unravel around us as if by chance. We need to appreciate religion's traditional role as an instrument of metaphysical ideology and an agent of multifaceted sublimation and in some cases repression in social configurations explicitly subscribing to its regime. In purportedly secular configurations in which religion's explicit authority has been shunted to the side, say, since the eighteenth century in Europe and the United States, we need to recognize its subliminal, displaced, occulted, and disguised transformations.

Psychoanalysis furnishes us with a breathtaking battery of tools and dynamics for conducting this collective work; through constructs such as displacement, repression, and regression, it enables us to discern religion's workings even in spheres from which it has presumably been separated. It helps us trace religion's involuted history even while participating in it. Religion may be regarded as a life-system extending into matters of health, sexual propriety, aesthetics, and even décor from its base in cosmology, eschatology, and day-to-day morals. Religion may be as prevalent and effective in its secularized substitutes as in its explicit dimensions of authority. It is intriguing to speculate on the informal secular religion coexisting, in the United States, Europe, and other regions of late capitalism; its elements surely number professionalism, entertainment, professional sports, shopping, and the stock market. Professionalism is not merely the name of the system in which we participate in the societal division of labor—in which we transform inherent and acquired skills, that is through education, the industry we have all joined in our own professionalization, into a specific job, more or less stable work conditions, and into, more broadly, a way of life.[12] Professionalism has, increasingly become, I believe, the matrix in which we collectively define our identities, determine the circle of our associations and the nature of our interactions within these loops, and synthesize our aspirations for ourselves, our families, our associations, communities, and even society at large. Where the metaphysics of religion, social class, and family or ethnicity has gone into remission, the arena of professionalism has come to the fore, but as yet, we have consecrated little work to its elucidation or deconstruction. In part, perhaps, because higher education constitutes itself not only as yet another profession but as one of the most esteemed and elite. There is much more work to be done on the psychoanalytical and sociological impacts of this increasingly transparent and hence pervasive phenomenon of professionalism. Yet we might well argue that as the consequence of a historical progression now almost five hundred years old, a person's profession is her ready-made religion, so why does he or she need to practice an explicit or traditional one? By the same token, an NFL or NBA game lasts about as long as a good religious service. Those of us graced with material wealth beyond

a hand-to-mouth existence—and this line is surely the Papal line of demar-
cation within the capitalist system—know that we will be collectively re-
warded both for buying a lot of SUVs, washing machines, designer clothes,
beauty products and for our speculative faith—Melville calls it confidence—
in Wall Street (*Confidence-Man* 68, 112, 119, 122, 148, 151, 178, 294–303).
Belief, faith, adherence in the system of finance and investment belongs to a
literal scheme of self-enrichment in our society.

It is not demeaning to any of us to admit that we have religious needs,
that certain questions, emotions, images, perspectives arise, particularly at
pivotal moments of transition, birth, catastrophic illness, death, puberty,
marriage, retirement, to which the organized religions, traditionally, offer
the most comprehensive and satisfying response. Derrida's religious interventions over the past twenty years, notably "Faith and Knowledge," "The
Eyes of Language," *On the Name, The Gift of Death*, and *Adieu to Emmanuel
Levinas*, lend the traditional religions at least this much credence. Yet at the
millennium we find ourselves sandwiched between (1) established Western
religious religions, which, to the degree that they are not fitted out to recent
social realities, phenomena including new media and technologies of communication, the multiculturalism resulting from long-established diasporas
and patterns of migration, and the explicitness of formerly nonconventional,
inadmissible sexual modalities, have to a significant degree become out-
moded or run their course, and (2) elements of the U.S.-Canadian-Euro-
pean-Pacific rim lifestyle and way of doing business that are deeply encoded
in a theological way but whose religiosity remains largely inexplicit, or, in
psychoanalytical terms, unconscious. We need the history, domain, and
tropology of psychoanalysis to assist us on both of these complementary
fronts, or rears. Our collective cultural context is immeasurably impover-
ished, at the moment, by the absence of commentators, cultural psychoanalysts that is capable of disclosing the rich theological coding and subtext to
such contemporary events as the War on Terrorism, the focus on Homeland Security, or the major vicissitudes of the stock market, which seem to
transpire with increasing frequency, always rendered explicable in terms of
faith or its loss. President Bush had already coded our response to the attacks on 9/11 as a Crusade by 9/12. Homeland Security is Eternal Vigilance
applied to the American Promised Land. The explosion of the oversized
bodhisattva statues at Bamiyan late in the domination of the Afghani Tal-
iban is indicative of a rigidly applied prohibition against representation in
Islam, but one that enters the theological regime by way of Genesis.

The world religions are interconnected. Their history is defined by
hostile takeovers at the exegetical margins of their canonical texts commit-

ted by competing creeds.[13] These usurpations transpire in a differential field of customs and laws, whether regarding dietary rules and fasting, Sabbaths and sabbaticals, or marriage and divorce. As one travels through certain geographical sectors of the world, the prohibition against eating pork morphs into one against beef, and into one against ingesting the flesh of living creatures altogether. The antagonistic positions that the world religions occupy in opposition to one another are the result of judgments and interpretations rendered of each other's canons far more than they are the aftermath of decisive victories and defeats delivered on the battlefield. Religions usurp one another—they steal each other's market share—through the propagation of hostile interpretations.

The major world religions, then, share a global climate at the same time that they diverge from one another systematically and on as many specific points as possible. They are linked, in other words, by a single Speidel watchband. When sectarian tensions tighten in one stretch of the religious community, religious opposition on a global level tightens all around. When the climate of religious opposition and undermining heats up in one region or neighborhood, the ecology of religious practice becomes aggravated all over the globe.

Unless the theological pretext of current affairs is rendered explicit, the public is disenfranchised from its rights to determine the degree of its implicit participation in the Abrahamic religions. I can well argue here that a healthy discourse of cultural criticism is essential to the preservation of the liberties bestowed upon us by French and American enlightenment thought, but I find no reference to literary criticism in the Constitution. There is the informal, unofficial religion that we unknowingly serve only too well in our shopping trips, catalog and Web orders, and our attendance at Broadway dramas, rock and roll concerts, and sporting events. Who knows? Maybe the campuses on which we spend so much of our time are also coded as "sleeper" religious institutions. Look at the physical plants of the Oxbridge colleges and the elite American universities modeled on them. And the faiths that assert themselves, perhaps as a calculated diversion, in place of this shadow religion, this unofficial American creed, have indeed in many respects, run their courses, exhausted themselves.[14] This is to say that our culture and society might well benefit, on what Freud termed the manifest level, from the collective devising of a New American Religion, with appertaining prayers, ceremonies, rituals, and customs, which does not assume, as a sociological matrix, the nuclear patriarchal family, the monoethnic nation-state, and a normativity of monogamous heterosexual reproduction.

Our dual accommodations of the official religion, whether we embrace or excoriate it, and our unavoidable participation in the unofficial but prevalent religion places us in an equally inevitable double bind, one bespeaking, in all likelihood, the schizo position, whether as characterized by Bateson (201–78) or Deleuze and Guattari (*Anti-Oedipus* 2–4, 15, 19, 33–35, 76–77, 86–87, 91, 112, 131–35, 244–46, 278–82). The shadow, or unofficial, religion draws on operating assumptions and core concepts of establishmentarian religions, which, even if putatively dismissed for generations, have become so pervasive as to be invisible. The succession between official and shadow religion is much like Benjamin's characterization of intergenerational links between technologies. At first, at least, painting dictates the compositional principles for photography and film alike. The case of religion in the United States is exacerbated by the fact that the society, in its grounding documents, believes itself to be areligious, to paraphrase the term by psychoanalyst Heinz Hartmann, a "nonreligious sphere."[15] The official religion of the United States is something like democracy, which is perhaps why we are so keen on extending it to areas like Afghanistan and the Middle East. Yet no sooner is it articulated than our democracy attains the universality and celebrates the direct relation of each American to this principle as "one nation under God." The official religion of the United States is a participatory democracy that structures and imparts a certain ethos to such closely related spheres as political process, ownership, and commercial transactions. One of the essential fundaments of this official American religion is never to resolve the ambiguity as to whether the nation is a strictly secular domain or whether it transpires under the aegis of God. The maintenance of this slippage enhances both sets of institutions and mores that the double-bond sets into play. (England, France, Spain, and Italy, on the other hand, as nations that remember only too well the condition of embracing, as an official religion, one of the standard Abrahamic faiths or an outgrowth of such a creed, were forced, oddly, as they evolved toward their present versions of liberal democracy, to draw a finer line between religion and the secular sphere than currently exists in the United States.)

The shadow, or unofficial, religion always obscures or occults the structures of the old establishmentarian religion persisting within its innovations. Rabid Oakland Raiders or New York Yankees fans revere these teams with a fervor deriving directly from the intertwined histories of religion and warfare, yet I would be dismissed as a cranky crackpot the moment I would posit this connection. French gastronomy and oenoculture embody a similar deterritorialization or sublimation of the sensuality coded in part through the Catholic Eucharist. The French consumer angles for his or her portion of fortune, that is, for her share in a world of elite, luxury commodities (e.g., champagne, perfume, fashion). It is a matter of secondary concern as to how much of these commodities the consumer attains or how often the reward becomes available. American consumption is more oriented to the Factory Outlet Mall, to the pervasive availability of inexpensive but desirable goods, toward a sort of democracy in acquisition, than toward the universal aura radiating from the traditional luxury items. Both national marketing models are saturated with values emanating from the long-standing "official religions," but the efficacy of marketing qua marketing depends on the erasure of the onto-theological subtext.

The official religion *enables* its disguised mutation, while the shadow religion offers its ideological foundation cultural continuity, a stay of execution in its march toward irrelevance and obscurity. The leeper religion acts out the seamy underside of the irreproachable official cant; it manages to reinforce the ideals of the prevailing official religion while seeming to violate them in every respect. This is not merely the exchange between hypocrisy and its debunking, or the more-or-less predictable dance between the conscious and the unconscious or the manifest and the latent. Rather, what we have here, in compliance with deeply rooted sociological laws, is the constitution of a schizo society requiring both the impeccable ideals and their unceremonious violation. This is, of course, the draw that the 2002 film *Far from Heaven* exerts on us. It is a tribute to the psychoanalytical theory of the past four decades, in part based upon Lacan's explicit openness to visual icons as a distinctive modality of thought and imagination, that film and other manifestations of popular culture are directly accessible to me when my parlance is in a psychoanalytical vein (or otherwise put: when I subscribe to the discursive and conceptual contracts pertaining to psychoanalysis). On the foundation of this work, I am empowered to segue directly, on reaching what is for me an excruciating tension and collusion between entire registers of ideals, pronouncements, and norms, to an example from current cinema, in the reassurance that the sociocultural imaginary of my auditors, constituted and cultivated above all visually, has been primed to respond to the example more vividly than to my extended formulations.

Far from Heaven dramatizes splendidly the interlacement between the unusually strident mores of the post–World War II U.S. society I grew up in and the subtext of strict racism and homophobia that contributed significantly to the shadow U.S. official religion of the moment. The film transforms Julianne Moore into a perfect visual icon of the double binds coming to a head and climax in her figure. The 1950s fashions that she wears are a kind of mode-sanctioned bondage gear. Any aggressiveness in her breasts bespeaks the rigidity of the harnesses they have been strapped into. She is no freer at the waist, from which her skirts flare dramatically outward. Her lips never lose their gloss, just as they never utter the conditions that have newly expressed themselves in her personal and familial existences: her husband is gay, and she has fallen in love, for good reasons, with a black man, a man incomparably more attuned and empathic toward her than her senior-executive spouse. Cathy Whittaker never looses her composure, whether she happens upon her husband in his only happy act of sexual self-expression, he strikes her, or he humiliates her at a party that she throws as a demonstration of the family's exemplariness. The immobility of her facial features, motivated as it is by unresolvable ideological and theological tensions, is the fullest expression of the supplementarity between counter-strands of onto-theology—"official" and shadow branches—that the film sets into play.

The unbearable tension between what Cathy Whittaker knows and will express or publicly acknowledge not only constitutes the visual artifacts of her unflappable facial expression, her indelible lip gloss, and the impenetrable veneer of her social manners; it characterizes in detail the rapport between the prevalent postwar U.S. creed of achieved freedom and democracy, industrial and technological dominance, happiness in wealth and technology, and clear-cut sociological and psychosexual mores and codes and the shadow-religion, not far from a shadow-economy, in which seemingly opposed values, apartheid racism and homosocial terror, operate toward the same ends. Indeed, her problematical husband Frank, who seeks psychiatric, not psychoanalytical treatment for his sexual-preference "problem," embodies the untenableness of this theological double bind as much as Kathleen does. His proclivity for queer encounters in the back of the local downtown cinema palace, when he's presumably working late, and for similarly married cabana boys on a forced vacation mandated by the company are at odds with the leadership potential he demonstrated during the war in the navy. The navy is both the source of his value to the company and of his initial gay experiences. Frank is a character at fundamental odds with the values of the secular religion he presumably exemplifies: he's not strictly aggressive in his bearing to the world, a family man, or even, in the terms on which the ideology and economy of the moment depend, a man.

The official and shadow religions do not, in dialectical fashion, overshadow or supplant one another. Rather, they uneasily coexist, in the configuration of an extended double bind. Frank's plan would be to continue as corporate fearless leader, exemplary family man, and closet gay person;

while Cathy's would be to facilitate this shadow-game or play of mirrors, so long as it were possible. But what might be possible on the part of characters crafted with psychological complexity and discretion is out of the question in terms of the social surround of 1950s Hartford, Connecticut, conjured up by the film. Frank's gayness is the intolerable antithesis of everything the company stands for and depends on, so it imagines, to succeed in the business climate of the time, and the neighbors will simply not brook Cathy's drive into the arms of the Afro-American landscaper's son and successor, as gracious, wise, responsible, and long-suffering as he may be. A crisis is set into play. Because of the mixing of the races, Cathy is demoted from social model to social pariah, and Raymond's eleven year-old daughter is stoned by some gung-ho youth acting out in the name of their community's honor. Frank takes the unspeakable leap, at the time, into a stable gay relationship, so his function at the company is adjusted. Raymond moves with his daughter to Baltimore. These are serious consequences, to be sure, but the show goes on. America barrels forward in its early steps to establish itself as undisputed democratic hegemon—leave the oxymoron to the literary critics—while the forces of radical racism and homophobia power this national campaign on. The official secular American religion prevailing in the heyday of this film is one of corporate, communal achievement and leadership in world democracy and tolerance; the shadow religion is one of homophobia and rigid separation along class as well as race lines.

It is in the sphere of religion where such disconnects and double binds in values, ethos, and aspiration emerge in fullest relief, and we who regard religion exclusively as a congenitally flawed venue of culture and hence unworthy of serious scrutiny talk ourselves out of what might constitute, as psychoanalytical thinkers, a good share of our greatest potential current social relevance. TV, film, and theatre, the entertainment industry, to be brief, serve as a stage for the religious imaginary, as the arts inevitably do, while religion, implicit or explicit, expressed or repressed, serves as an ideological repository and agent for attitudes serviceable to the prevalent sociopolitical configuration. Religion and the entertainment industry relate to one another as mutually encompassing frameworks: the entertainment industry can harbor the lineaments of a religion at the same time that informal religion can set the agenda for the entertainment industry. The secular-state religion can draw upon the entertainment industry for its imagery and self-mediation, its configuration of itself as various media; and at the same time, the media, often in the most indirect fashions imaginable, can synthesize the religious imaginary of the moment. As I am suggesting,

We should not be deterred, by dint of healthy academic skepticism, from an appreciation of the full persistent religious torque exerted upon both the fields of popular entertainment and national ideological self-definition.

Films such as *Far from Heaven* and *The Butcher Boy*, another example that leaps to mind,[16] are not only generous in their account of how contemporary, late-capitalistic societies nurture, call forth, and harvest their outcasts. They meticulously account for the symbolism and the process by which official, or what we term "organized," religion camouflages, occults, and extends itself into the venues that seem the most impervious to religious thought. This is an exercise that we need to continue in a postmodern historical and imaginary space in which the most archaic formations lurk just beneath the surface tension of public life, in which the religious motivations for the current events at center stage are capable of eluding vast segments of the population. This process may well be situated in the more collective arena of cultural psychoanalysis than in the clinical *cabinet* envisaged by Freud. But it is clear that psychoanalysis remains the model, tradition, and exigency for this indispensable scrutiny.

NOTES

1. This is a key term in Jacques Derrida's characterization of the spectral abyss implicitly installed within the Western "Abrahamic" religions and, by implication, throughout Western metaphysics. See, among other sites, Derrida 83–84, 208, 222–23, 252–53, 258–59, 278–79, 296, 372, 399.

2. The "subject," of course, of Freud's 1911 case study, "Psychoanalytic on an Autobiographical Account of a Case of Paranoia."

3. The write-up of her case history, along with those of the very first clients of psychoanalysis, among them Frau Emmy von M. and Fraülein Elizabeth von R., was included in the 1895 *Studies on Hysteria*, co-authored with Josef Breuer.

4. See Freud, "Infantile Neurosis."

5. See Freud, "Obsessional Neurosis."

6. In an essay entitled "The Subject of the Nerves: Philosophy and Freud," I trace the dynamic tension in Freud's thought and enterprise between the linguistic wonder evident in such early works as *Studies on Hysteria*, *The Interpretation of Dreams*, and *Jokes and Their Relation to the Unconscious* and the institutional aspirations and imperatives for psychoanalysis already evident in *Three Essays on the Theory of Sexuality*, and carried through to such major case histories as "The Wolf Man" and "The Rat Man" and such methodological cornerstones as "The Dynamic of the Transference" (1912). The year 1914 marks the beginning of the key "Metapsychological Essays," texts including "Instincts and their Vicissitudes" (1915), "Repression" (1915), and "The Unconscious" (1915), which encompass a

highly creative synthesis between the countermotivations in the overall Freudian enterprise. See *Hegelian Aftermath* 159–207.

7. For some of Žižek's characteristic pronouncements on these and related issues, see *Fragile Absolute* 1, 9, 46, 74–75, 108–09, and *Ticklish Subject* 94, 161, 186–87.

8. For elaborations on art as a cultural sector characterized by an ongoing negotiation between the prevailing state of public discourse, which approximates the Saussurian *langue*, and the innovations, variants, and individualistic linguistic appropriations contributed by the artist, see my *Aesthetic Contract* 165–69, 173–77, 181–91, 199–201. This scenario, if viable, receives a pedagogical and educational extension in the notion that one major purpose of "higher education" is the cultural psychoanalysis, in a collective and public ambiance, of the segmentations that result in the idioms pertaining to specific social communities, whether determined by geography, demography, nationality, ethnicity, class, race, religion, or other factors. See, again, *Aesthetic Contract* 191–99.

9. See esp. Wilden 164–78, 202–12, 356–67. I am most grateful to Todd Balazic, a student in my Fall 2002 seminar on systems-theory at Buffalo, for making this work known to me and for explaining it with enormous lucidity.

10. A speculative fiction writer such as Jorge Luis Borges stands out in his engagement of issues of systematicity and lends a vivid figurative rendition of the features of systems into which certain specific hypothetical characteristics have been embedded. It is in the context of Borges's *Ficciones* that I hazard a few of my own general formulations regarding systems. See my "Writing of the System."

11. The critical intervention, as I understand it from my work in recent years, is a response nuanced by the arbitrariness of an existing state of affairs, one largely imposed on it. Such interventions are improvisational at the core, and take less solace from the ongoing battery of explicitly conceptual and logical tools and figures than discourse addressed to the philosophical academy. In a provisional, but nonetheless persistent way, I work through this discursive division of labor in my *The Task of the Critic: Poetics, Philosophy, Religion.*

12. Professional life numbers among the many factors of individuation under the broader modernity that Max Weber traces out in his classic study *The Protestant Ethic and the Spirit of Capitalism.* See 29, 54–55, 160–63, 166–70.

13. As the teacher of a general education "World Civilizations" course over the past decade and a half, I have drawn considerable inspiration, while observing global historical developments at a "large grain," from the scenario of periphery-center shifts staged by the historian William H. McNeill. As a critical theorist, I could not help but notice the strong affinity between Derrida's investigations of marginality as an infrastructural fulcrum, or "handle," on the repressive tendencies of metaphysical systems and the tendency, observed "clinically" or "empirically" by McNeill, for civilizations to be considerably enriched and upgraded when they are taken over, even under hostile conditions, by the "barbarians." See McNeill 50–59, 200, 213–19, 253, 257–83.

14. Against the backdrop of current events (e.g. the War against Terrorism), heavily nuanced by the history of the Abrahamic faiths, the present essay closes on a leitmotif of the often bewildering tension between explicit, traditional religion and its occulted simulacrum, what I term a "shadow religion," in contemporary public life. I am reminded by Kaja Silverman that this is, in all substantial respects, the extension of a distinction that Louis Althusser, in his essay "Ideology and Ideological State Apparatuses," drew between the State proper and the Ideological State Apparatus (ISA). The latter term already incorporated organized religion when the essay was written in 1967. Althusser would have no difficulty in acknowledging the roles of contemporary sports, fashion, and entertainment in today's American (and indeed global) ISA. See Althusser 134, 143, 148–55, 157, 167, 171, 177–81.

15. This is, of course, a play on Heinz Hartmann's notion of the therapeutic environment as a "nonconflictual sphere" (144–48).

16. This 1998 Irish film by Neil Jordan, based on Patrick McCabe's 1992 novel of the same title, does a splendid job in tracing the incursion of imagery from American popular culture and current events (e.g., *The Lone Ranger*, *The Fugitive*, *The Brady Bunch*, the Bay of Pigs Invasion, the Tate–La Bianca murders) within the sensibility of its benighted child-hero who grows up deprived and overburdened on a cultural as well as geographical margin of Irish society. Both the novel and its cinematographic adaptation carefully explore the role of Irish Catholicism in the evolution of the teenaged protagonist from an endearing if mischievous boy into a sociopathic murderer. See my "On the Butcher Block" for a detailed analysis of this film.

WORKS CITED

Althusser, Louis. "Ideology and Ideological State Apparatuses." *Lenin and Philosophy*. Trans. Ben Brewster. New York: Monthly Review Press, 1971.

Bateson, Gregory. *Steps to an Ecology of Mind*. New York: Ballantine, 1972.

Deleuze, Giles, and Félix Guattari. *A Thousand Plateaus*. Trans. Brian Massumi. Minneapolis: U of Minnesota P, 1987.

———. *The Anti-Oedipus*. Trans. Robert Hurley, Mark Seem, and Helen R. Lane. Minneapolis: U of Minnesota P, 1983.

Derrida, Jacques. *Acts of Religion*. Ed. Gil Anidjar. New York: Routledge, 2002.

Freud, Sigmund, and Joseph Breuer. *Studies on Hysteria. The Standard Edition of the Complete Psychological Works of Sigmund Freud*. Trans. James Strachey. Vol. 2. London: Hogarth, 1955. 1–305.

Freud, Sigmund. "From the History of an Infantile Neurosis." *The Standard Edition*. Vol. 17. London: Hogarth, 1955. 7–122.

———. "Notes Upon a Case of Obsessional Neurosis." *The Standard Edition*. Vol. 10. London: Hogarth, 1955. 155–318.

————. "Psychoanalytic Notes on an Autobiographical Account of a Case of Paranoia (Dementia Paranoides)." *The Standard Edition*. Vol. 12. London: Hogarth, 1958. 9–82.

Hartmann, Heinz. *Essays on Ego Psychology*. New York: International Universities Press, 1981.

McNeill, William H. *A History of the Human Continuity*. 5th ed. Upper Saddle River: Prentice Hall, 1997.

Melville, Herman. *The Confidence-Man*. Ed. H. Bruce Franklin. Indianapolis: Bobbs-Merrill, 1967.

Sussman, Henry. *The Aesthetic Contract: Statutes of Art and Intellectual Work in Modernity*. Stanford: Stanford UP, 1997.

————. *The Hegelian Aftermath: Essays on Hegel, Kierkegaard, Freud, Proust, and James*. Baltimore, MD: Johns Hopkins UP, 1982.

————. "On the Butcher Block: A Panorama of Social Marking." *The New Centennial Review* 4 (2004): 143–68.

————. *The Task of the Critic: Poetics, Philosophy, Religion*. New York: Fordham UP, 2005.

————. "The Writing of the System: Borges's Library and Calvino's Traffic." *Literary Philosophers*. Eds. Jorge Garcia, Karolyn Korsmeyer, and Rodolphe Gasché. New York: Routledge, 2002.

Weber, Max. *The Protestant Ethic and the Spirit of Capitalism*. Trans. Talcott Parsons. London: Harper Collins, 1991.

Wilden, Anthony. *System and Structure*. London: Tavistock, 1972.

Žižek, Slavoj. *The Fragile Absolute*. London: Verso, 2000.

————. *The Ticklish Subject*. London: Verso, 1999.

Part Two
Psychoanalysis and Collectivity

3

Lacan's Four Discourses

A Political Reading

SLAVOJ ŽIŽEK

What Lacan calls the "desire of the analyst" appeared already before psy-choanalysis proper—Lacan discerns it in different historical figures, from Socrates to Hegel. It answers a key question, and it best encapsulates the anti-Buddhist spirit of psychoanalysis: Is desire only an illusion? Is it pos-sible to sustain desire even after one gains full insight into the vanity of the human desire? Or is, at that radical point, the only choice the one between serene Wisdom and melancholic resignation? The Buddhist stance is ulti-mately that of Indifference, of quenching all passions which strive to estab-lish differences, while psychoanalysis asserts a violent passion to introduce a Difference, a gap in the order of being.

I

The further dilemma to which this one is linked is that of the collective: when Lacan introduces the term "desire of the analyst," it is in order to un-dermine the notion that the climax of the analytic treatment is a momentous insight into the abyss of the Real, the "traversing of the fantasy," from which, the morning after, we have to return to sober social reality, resuming our usual social roles—is psychoanalysis an insight which can only be shared in the precious initiatic moments? Lacan's aim is to establish the possibility of a *collective* of the analysts, of discerning the contours of a possible *social link* of analysts (which is why, in his scheme of four discourses, he talks about the *discourse* of the analyst as the "obverse" of the Master's discourse). The dis-course of the analyst is a link sustained not by a Master-signifier but by the excess of the Real embodied in the *objet petit a*, or the cause of desire. The stakes here were high: Is every community based on the figure of a Master

(Freud's version in *Totem and Taboo*), or its derivative, the figure of Knowledge (modern capitalist version)? Or, is there a chance of a different link? Of course, the outcome of this struggle was a dismal failure in the entire history of psychoanalysis, from Freud to the late Lacan and his École: psychoanalytic communities regularly ended up as proto-totalitarian initiatic groups. But the fight is worth pursuing: the cause of the failure was not that the attempts were too radical, but that they were not radical enough. This is the properly *Leninist* moment of Lacan—recall how, in his late writings, he is endlessly struggling with the organizational questions of the School. The psychoanalytic collective is, of course, a collective of and in an emergency state. When Saint Paul defines the Messianic state of emergency as a state in which the end of time is near, in which we only have the time which remains, and are thus obliged to suspend our full commitment to worldly links ("possess things as if you do not possess them," etc.), does the same not go also for the patient, who, while in analysis, also has to suspend his social links?

The link between the analyst and the patient is not only speech, words, but also money: one *has* to pay a price that hurts. The link is thus not only symbolic, at the level of the signifier, but also real, at the level of the object—this point is crucial, especially today. Is the analyst the contemporary miser? Yes and no. The link between psychoanalysis and capitalism is perhaps best exemplified by one of the great literary figures of the nineteenth-century novel, the Jewish money lender, a shadowy figure to whom all the big figures of society come to borrow money, pleading with him and telling him all their dirty secrets and passions (recall Gobseck from Balzac's *La comedie humaine*)—this figure is a disillusioned wise man, well aware of the vanity of all human endeavors, hidden from the public gaze, with no visible power, but nonetheless the secret master who pulls the strings of the entire social life. This figure, cruelly indifferent, deprived of any compassion and empathy, is much closer to the analyst than the church confessor or the old wise trustee. Against Foucault's *History of Sexuality*, the thesis of which is "the birth of psychoanalysis out of the spirit of [the Christian] confession," one should rather assert "the birth of psychoanalysis out of the spirit of thrift."

The line separating the analyst from the miser is thin. For Lacan, it is the miser, rather than the heroic transgressor, who goes to the end, violating all moral constraints, who is the exemplary figure of desire: if we want to discern the mystery of desire, we should not focus on the lover or murderer in the throws of passion, ready to put at stake anything and everything for it, but on the miser's attitude towards his chest, the secret place where he keeps and gathers his possessions. The mystery, of course, is that, in the figure of the miser, excess coincides with lack, power with impotence, avaricious hoarding with the elevation of the object into the prohibited/untouchable Thing one can only observe, never fully enjoy.

It is against this background that one should approach Lacan's *L'envers de la psychanalyse*, the Seminar XVII (1969–1970) on the four discourses, his response to the events of 1968. Its premise is best captured as his reversal of the well-known antistructuralist graffiti from the Paris walls of 1968: "Structures do not walk on the streets!"—if anything, this Seminar endeavors to demonstrate how structures *do* walk on the streets (i.e., how structural shifts *can* account for social outbursts like that of 1968). Instead of the one symbolic Order with its set of a priori rules that guarantee social cohesion, we get the matrix of the passages from one to another discourse: Lacan's interest is focused on the passage from the discourse of the Master to the discourse of the University as the hegemonic discourse in contemporary society. No wonder that the revolt was located at the universities: as such, it merely signaled the shift to the new forms of domination in which the scientific discourse serves to legitimize the relations of domination. Lacan's underlying premise is skeptic-conservative—Lacan's diagnosis is best captured by his famous retort to the student revolutionaries: "As hysterics, you demand a new master. You will get it!" This passage can also be conceived in more general terms, as the passage from the prerevolutionary *Ancien Régime* to the postrevolutionary new Master who does not want to admit that he is one, but proposes himself as a mere "servant" of the People—in Nietzsche's terms, it is simply the passage from Master's ethics to slave morality, and this fact, perhaps, enables us a new approach to Nietzsche: when Nietzsche scornfully dismisses "slave morality," he is not attacking lower classes as such, but, rather, the new masters who are no longer ready to assume the title of the Master—"slave" is Nietzsche's term for a fake master.

II

What Lacan calls "discourse" is not simply a specific form of speech but the underlying structure of the social link that situates the speaker and the addressee—for example, "Master's discourse" is not only what a Master figure says, but the entire social link constituted in this way. The starting point of the matrix of the four discourses is Lacan's well-known "definition" of the signifier: a signifier is that which "represents the subject for another signifier"—how are we to read this obviously circular definition? The old-style hospital bed has at its feet, out of the patient's sight, a small display board on which different charts and documents are stuck specifying the patient's temperature, blood pressure, medications, etc. This display represents the patient, but for whom? Not simply and directly for other subjects (say, for the nurses and doctors who regularly check this chart), but primarily for other signifiers, for the symbolic network of medical knowledge in which the data on the panel have to be inserted in order to obtain their meaning. One can easily imagine a computerized system where the reading of the data on the panel proceeds automatically, so that what the doctor obtains and reads are not these data directly but the conclusions which, according to the system of medical knowledge, follow from these and other data. The conclusion to be drawn from this definition of the signifier is that, in what I say, in my symbolic representation, there is always a kind of surplus with regard to the concrete, flesh-and-blood addressee(s) of my speech, which is why even a letter that fails to reach its concrete addressee in a way does arrive at its true destination, which is the big Other, the symbolic system of "other signifiers." One of the direct materializations of this excess is the symptom: a ciphered message whose addressee is not another human being (when I inscribe into my body a symptom that divulges the innermost secret of my desire, no human being is intended to directly read it), and which nonetheless has accomplished its function the moment it was produced, since it did reach the big Other, its true addressee.

Lacan's scheme of the four discourses articulates the four subjective positions within a discursive social link that logically follow from the formula of the signifier (which is why psychosis is excluded: it designates the very breakdown of the symbolic social link). Its four elements—the subject, the Master-Signifier, the chain of signifiers which stands for Knowledge, and the "indivisible remainder" of this operation, the object-cause of desire—consecutively occupy four structural places: that of the agent of a discourse, of its other (addressee), of the truth (the true position from which the agent speaks), and of the product-remainder of the speech act. The whole construction is based on the fact of symbolic *reduplication*, the redoubling of an entity into itself and the place it occupies in the structure, as in Mallarme's *rien n'aura eu lieu que le lieu*, or Malevitch's black square on white surface, both displaying an effort to formulate place as such or, rather, the minimal difference between the place as an element that precedes the difference between elements. *Reduplication* means that an element never "fits" its place: I am never fully what my symbolic mandate tells me that I am. For that reason, the discourse of the Master is the necessary starting point, insofar as in it, an entity and its place *do* coincide: the Master-Signifier effectively occupies the place of the "agent" which is that of the master; the *objet petit a* occupies the place of "production," which is that of the inassimilable excess, etc. Also it is the redoubling, the gap between the element and the place, which then sets the process in motion: a master hystericizes himself by starting to question what effectively makes him a Master, etc. So, on the basis of the discourse of the Master, one can then proceed to generate the three other discourses by way of successively putting the other three elements at the place of the Master: in the university discourse, it is Knowledge that occupies the agent's (Master's) place, turning the subject ($) into that which is "produced," into its inassimilable excess-remainder; in hysteria, the true "master," the agent who effectively terrorizes the Master himself, is the hysterical subject with her incessant questioning of the Master's position, etc. So, first,

$$\frac{S_1}{\$} \qquad \frac{S_2}{a}$$

The discourse of the Master provides the basic matrix: a subject is represented by the signifier for another signifier (for the chain or the field of "ordinary" signifiers); the remainder—the "bone in the throat"—that resists this symbolic representation— emerges (is "produced") as *objet petit a*, and the subject endeavors to "normalize" his relationship toward this excess via fantasmatic formations (which is why the lower level of the formula of the Master's discourse renders the matheme of fantasy $\$ - a$). In an apparent contradiction to this determination, Lacan often claims that the discourse of the Master is the only discourse that excludes the dimension of fantasy. How are we to understand this? The illusion of the gesture of the Master is the complete coincidence between the level of the enunciation (the subjective position from which I am speaking) and the level of the enunciated content (i.e., what characterizes the Master is a speech act that wholly absorbs me in which "I am what I say"; in short, a fully realized, self-contained, performative). Such an ideal coincidence, of course, precludes the dimension of fantasy, since fantasy emerges precisely in order to fill in the gap between the enunciated content and its underlying position of enunciation: fantasy is an answer to the question "You are telling me all this, but why? What do you really want by telling me this?" The fact that the dimension of fantasy nonetheless persists thus simply signals the ultimate unavoidable failure of the Master's discourse. Suffice it to recall the proverbial high manager who, from time to time, feels compelled to visit prostitutes in order to be engaged in masochist rituals where he is "treated as a mere object": the semblance of his active public existence in which he gives orders to his subordinates and runs their lives (the upper level of the Master's discourse: $S_1 - S_2$) is sustained by the fantasies of being turned into a passive object of other's enjoyment (the lower level: $ - a$). In Kant's philosophy, the faculty of desire is "pathological," dependent on contingent objects, so there can be no "pure faculty of desiring," no "critique of pure desire," while for Lacan, psychoanalysis precisely *is* a kind of "critique of *pure* desire." In other words, desire *does* have a nonpathological (a priori) object-cause: the *objet petit a*, the object that overlaps with its own lack.

One can see, now, in what precise sense one is to conceive of Lacan's thesis according to which what is "primordially repressed" is the binary signifier: the symmetrical companion to the One, to the Master-Signifier, the signifier the presence of which would guarantee the inherent balance and harmony of the Symbolic order. What the Symbolic order precludes is the full harmonious presence of the couple of Master-signifiers, $S_1 - S_2$ as *yin-yang* or any other two symmetrical "fundamental principles." The fact that "there is no sexual relationship" means precisely that the secondary signifier (that of the Woman) is "primordially repressed," and what we get in the place of this repression, what fills in its gap, is the multitude of the "returns of the repressed," the series of the "ordinary" signifiers. In Woody Allen's Tolstoy parody *War and Love*, the first association that automatically pops up, of course, is: "If Tolstoy, where then is Dostoyevsky?" In the film, Dostoyevsky (the "binary signifier" to Tolstoy) remains "repressed"; however, the price paid for it is that a conversation in the middle of the film as it were accidentally includes the titles of all of Dostoyevsky's major novels: "Is that man still in the underground?" "You mean one of the Karamazov brothers?" "Yes, that idiot!" "Well, he did commit his crime and was punished for it!" "I know, he was a gambler who always risked too much!" Here we encounter the "return of the repressed," that is, the series of signifiers that fills in the gap of the repressed binary signifier "Dostoyevsky." This is why the standard deconstructionist criticism, according to which Lacan's theory of sexual difference falls into the trap of "binary logic," totally misses the point: Lacan's *la femme n'existe pas* aims precisely at undermining the "binary" polar couple of Masculine and Feminine—the original split is not between the One and the Other but is strictly inherent to the One it is the split between the One and its empty place of inscription. This is how one should read Kafka's famous statement that the Messiah will come one day after his arrival. This is also how one should conceive of the link between the split inherent to the One and the explosion of the multiple: the multiple is not the primordial ontological fact; the "transcendental" genesis of the multiple resides in the lack of the binary signifier (i.e., the multiple emerges as the series of attempts to fill in the gap of the missing binary signifier).

Thus, there is no reason to be dismissive of the discourse of the Master, to identify it too hastily with "authoritarian repression": the Master's gesture is the founding gesture of every social link. Let us imagine a confused situation of social disintegration, in which the cohesive power of ideology loses its efficiency: in such a situation, the Master is the one who invents a new signifier, the famous "quilting point," which again stabilizes the situation and makes it readable; the university discourse that then elaborates the network of Knowledge that also sustains this readability by definition presupposes and relies on the initial gesture of the Master. The Master adds no new positive content; he merely adds a signifier that all of a sudden turns disorder into order—into "new harmony," as Rimbaud would have put it. Think about anti-Semitism in Germany of the 1920s: people experienced themselves as disoriented, thrown into undeserved military defeat, economic crisis melted away their life-savings, political inefficiency, moral degeneration, and the Nazis provided a single agent which accounted for it all: the Jew, the Jewish plot. Therein resides the magic of a Master: although there is nothing new at the level of positive content, "nothing is quite the same" after he pronounces his Word. . . .

The difference between S_1 and S_2 is thus not the difference between two opposed poles within the same field, but, rather, the cut within this field—the cut of the level at which the process occurs—inherent to the one term. Topologically, we get the same term at two surfaces. In other terms, the original couple is not that of two signifiers, but that of the signifier and its *reduplication*, i.e., the minimal difference between a signifier and the place of its inscription, between one and zero. How, then, do S_1 and S_2 relate? Did we not oscillate between two opposed versions: in the first version, the binary signifier, the symmetric counterpart of S_1, is "primordially repressed," and it is in order to supplement the void of this repression that the chain of S_2 emerges, i.e., the original fact is the couple of S_1 and the Void at the place of its counterpart, and the chain of S_2 is secondary; in the second version, in the account of the emergence of S_1 as the "enigmatic term," the empty signifier, the primordial fact is, on the contrary, S_2, the signifying chain in its incompleteness, and it is in order to fill in the void of this incompleteness that S_1 intervenes. How are the two versions to be coordinated? Is the ultimate fact the vicious circle of their mutual implication?

$$\frac{S_2}{S_1} \qquad \frac{a}{\$}$$

The university discourse is enunciated from the position of "neutral" Knowledge; it addresses the remainder of the Real (say, in the case of pedagogical knowledge, the "raw, uncultivated child"), turning it into the subject ($). The "truth" of the university discourse, hidden beneath the bar, of course, is power, i.e., the Master-Signifier: the constitutive lie of the university discourse is that it disavows its performative dimension, presenting what effectively amounts to a political decision based on power as a simple insight into the factual state of things. What one should avoid here is the Foucauldian misreading: the produced subject is not simply the subjectivity that arises as the result of the disciplinary application of knowledge-power but its remainder, that which eludes the grasp of knowledge-power. "Production" (the fourth term in the matrix of discourses) does not stand simply for the result of the discursive operation, but rather for its "indivisible remainder," for the excess that resists being included in the discursive network, i.e., for what the discourse itself produces as the foreign body in its very heart.

Perhaps the exemplary case of the Master's position that underlies the university discourse is the way in which medical discourse functions in our everyday lives: at the surface level, we are dealing with pure objective knowledge that desubjectivizes the subject-patient, reducing him to an object of research, of diagnosis and treatment; however, beneath it, one can easily discern a worried hystericized subject, obsessed with anxiety, addressing the doctor as his Master and asking for reassurance from him. (One is tempted to claim that the resistance of doctors to be treated just like other scientists resides in their awareness that their position is still that of the Master,[1] which is why we do not expect the doctor to tell us just the bare (objective) truth: he is expected to tell us the bad news only insofar as our knowledge of our bad condition will somehow help us to cope with it— if it would only make things worse, he is expected to withhold it from the patient.) At a more common level, suffice it to recall the market expert who advocates strong budgetary measures (cutting welfare expenses, etc.) as a necessity imposed by his neutral expertise devoid of any ideological biases: what he conceals is the series of power relations (from the active role of state apparatuses to ideological beliefs), which sustain the "neutral" functioning of the market mechanism.

$$\frac{\$}{a} \qquad \frac{S_1}{S_2}$$

In the hysterical link, the $ over a stands for the subject who is divided, traumatized, by what for an object she is for the Other, what role she plays in the Other's desire: "Why am I what you're saying that I am?," or, to quote Shakespeare's Juliet, "Why am I that name?" This, for Lacan, is the primordial situation of a small child, thrown into a cobweb of libidinal investments: he or she is somehow aware of being the focus of others' libidinal investments, but cannot grasp *what* others see in him—what she expects from the Other-Master is knowledge about what she is as object (the lower level of the formula). Racine's Phèdre is hysterical insofar as she resists the role of the object of exchange between men by way of incestuously violating the proper order of generations (falling in love with her stepson). Her passion for Hyppolite does not aim at its direct realization-satisfaction, but rather at the very act of its confession to Hyppolite, who is thus forced to play the double role of Phèdre's object of desire and of her symbolic Other (the addressee to whom she confesses her desire). When Hyppolite learns from Phèdre that he is the cause of her consuming passion, he is shocked— this knowledge possesses a clear "castrating" dimension, it hystericizes him: "Why me? What for an object am I so that I have this effect on her? What does she see in me?" What produces the unbearable castrating effect is not the fact of being deprived of "it," but, on the contrary, the fact of clearly "possessing it": the hysteric is horrified at being "reduced to an object," that is to say, at being invested with the *agalma* that makes him or her the object of others' desire.

$$\frac{a}{S_2} \qquad \frac{\$}{S_1}$$

In contrast to hysteria, the pervert knows perfectly what he is for the Other: a knowledge supports his position as the object of the Other's (divided subject's) *jouissance*. For that reason, the formula of the discourse of perversion is same as that of the analyst's discourse: Lacan defines perversion as the inverted fantasy—i.e., his formula of perversion is $a - \$$, which is precisely the upper level of the analyst's discourse. The difference between the social link of perversion and that of analysis is grounded in the radical ambiguity of *objet petit a* in Lacan, which stands simultaneously for the fantasmatic lure/screen and for that which this lure is obfuscating, for the void behind the lure.

So, when we pass from perversion to the analytic social link, the agent (analyst) reduces himself to the void that provokes the subject into confronting the truth of his desire. Knowledge in the position of "truth," below the bar under the "agent," of course, refers to the supposed knowledge of the analyst, and, simultaneously, signals that the knowledge gained here will not be the neutral "objective" knowledge of scientific adequacy but knowledge that concerns the subject (analysand) in the truth of his subjective position. Recall, again, Lacan's outrageous statements that, even if what a jealous husband claims about his wife (e.g., that she sleeps around with other men) is true, his jealousy is still pathological. Along the same lines, one could say that, even if most of the Nazi claims about the Jews were true (they exploit Germans and seduce German girls), their anti-Semitism would still be (and was) pathological—because it represses the true reason *why* the Nazis *needed* anti-Semitism in order to sustain their ideological position. So, in the case of anti-Semitism, knowledge about what the Jews "really are" is fake—irrelevant—while the only knowledge at the place of truth is the knowledge about why a Nazi *needs* the figure of the Jew to sustain his ideological edifice. In this precise sense, what the discourse of the analyst "produces" is the Master-Signifier, the "swerve" of the patient's knowledge, the surplus-element that situates the patient's knowledge at the level of truth: after the Master-Signifier is produced, even if nothing changes at the level of knowledge, the "same" knowledge as before starts to function in a different mode. The Master-Signifier is the unconscious *sinthome*, the cipher of enjoyment, to which the subject was unknowingly subjected. The crucial point not to be missed here is how this late Lacanian identification of the subjective position of the analyst as that of *objet petit a* presents an act of radical self-criticism: earlier, in the 1950s, Lacan conceived the analyst not as the small other (a), but, on the contrary, as a kind of stand-in for the big Other (A, the anonymous symbolic order). At this level, the function of the analyst was to frustrate the subject's imaginary misrecognitions and to make them accept their proper symbolic place within the circuit of symbolic exchange, the place which effectively (and unbeknownst to them) determines their symbolic identity. Later, however, the analyst stands precisely for the ultimate inconsistency and failure of the big Other, i.e., for the Symbolic order's inability to guarantee the subject's symbolic identity.

III

So, if a political Leader says, "I am your Master, let my will be done!," this direct assertion of authority is hystericized when the subject starts to doubt his qualification to act as a Leader ("Am I really their Master? What is in me that legitimizes me to act like that?"); it can be masked in the guise of the university discourse ("In asking you to do this, I merely follow the insight into objective historical necessity, so I am not your Leader, but merely your servant who enables you to act for your own good."); or, the subject can act as a blank, suspending his symbolic efficiency and thus compelling his Other to become aware of how he was experiencing another subject as a Leader only because he was treating him as one. It should be clear, from this brief description, how the position of the "agent" in each of the four discourses involves a specific mode of subjectivity: the Master is the subject who is fully engaged in his (speech) act, who, in a way, "is his word," whose word displays an immediate performative efficiency; the agent of the university discourse is, on the contrary, fundamentally disengaged: he posits himself as the self-erasing observer (and executor) of "objective laws" accessible to neutral knowledge (in clinical terms, his position is closest to that of the pervert). The hysterical subject is the subject whose very existence involves radical doubt and questioning, his entire being is sustained by the uncertainty as to what he is for the Other; insofar as the subject exists only as an answer to the enigma of the Other's desire, the hysterical subject is the subject par excellence. Again, in clear contrast to it, the analyst stands for the paradox of the desubjectivized subject, of the subject who fully assumed what Lacan calls "subjective destitution," i.e., who breaks out of the vicious cycle of intersubjective dialectics of desire and turns into an acephallous being of pure drive.

As to the political reading of this matrix, it is thus that each of the discourses clearly designates a political link: the Master's discourse represents the elementary mode of political authority sustained by fantasy; the University discourse is the discourse of postpolitical "expert" rule; hysterical discourse obeys the logic of protest and "resistance," of demands which, according to Lacan's formula, really want to be rejected because "*ce n'est pas ça*" (because, if fully met, the literal satisfaction of the demand robs it of its metaphoric universal dimension—the demand for X "really was not about X"); the analyst's discourse designates the radical revolutionary-emancipatory politics in which the agent is *a*, the symptomal point, the "part of no part," of the situation, with knowledge at the place of truth (i.e., articulating the agent's position of enunciation and thus regaining the explosive effect of truth); and $ represents the addressee of the agent, the ex-master who is now hystericized, since the agent questions his position by way of "producing," deploying openly, explicating as such, the Master-Signifier and thus rendering it inoperable (like in the paradox of the "states which are essentially by-products": once it is questioned, authority loses its self-evidence). How, then, within this frame, are we to read more closely the university discourse?

In the University discourse, is not the upper level ($ − *a*) that of *biopolitics* (in the sense deployed from Foucault to Agamben)? Of the expert knowledge dealing with an object that is a—not subjects but individuals reduced to bare life? And does the lower level of the formula not designate what Eric Santner called the "crisis of investiture," i.e., the impossibility of the subject to relate to S_1, to identify with a Master-Signifier, to assume the imposed symbolic mandate? The usual notion of the relationship between excess-enjoyment and symbolic identification is that symbolic identity is what we get in exchange for being deprived of enjoyment; what happens in today's society, with its decline of the Master-Signifier and the rise of consumption, is the exact obverse: the basic fact is the loss of symbolic identity, the "crisis of investiture," and what we get in exchange for this loss is that we are all around bombarded with forms and gadgets of enjoyment.

The key point here is that the expert rule of "biopolitics" is grounded in and conditioned by the crisis of investiture; this crisis generated the "post-metaphysical" survivalist stance of the Last Men, which ends up in an anemic spectacle of life dragging on as its own shadow. Another aspect of the same shift is the rise of the term "ideology" in the very epoch of the dissolution of the hegemonic role of the Master discourse. In its classic Althusserian formulation, ideology is characterized in the terms of the interpellation by the Master-signifier, i.e., as the version of the discourse of the Master; however, one started to speak about "ideology" in the late Napoleonic period, i.e., in the very historical moment when the Master's discourse started to loose its hold—one should thus say that one starts to speak about "ideology" at the very point when ideology started to lose its immediate "natural" character and to be experienced as something artificial, no longer substantial but, precisely, a "mere ideology." It is the same as with the Oedipus complex, whose very theorization by Freud was conditioned by the crisis and decline of Oedipus in social reality.

However, the "object" of the discourse of the University has two aspects that cannot but appear as belonging to two opposite ideological spaces: that of the reduction of humans to bare life, to *homo sacer* as the *disponible* object of the expert caretaking knowledge, and that of the respect for the vulnerable Other brought to the extreme, of the attitude of narcissistic subjectivity that experiences itself as vulnerable, constantly exposed to a multitude of potential "harassments." Is there a stronger contrast than the one between the respect for the Other's vulnerability and the reduction of the Other to "mere life" regulated by administrative knowledge? But what if these two stances nonetheless rely on the same root; what if they are the two aspects of the same underlying attitude; what if they coincide in what one is tempted to designate as the contemporary case of the Hegelian "infinite judgment," which asserts the identity of opposites? What the two poles share is precisely the underlying refusal of any higher Causes, the notion that the ultimate goal of our lives is life itself. Nowhere is the complicity of these two levels more clear than in the case of the opposition to the death penalty—no wonder, since (violently putting another human being to) death is, quite logically, the ultimate traumatic point of biopolitics, the politics of the administration of life. To put it in Foucauldian terms, is the abolition of the death penalty not part of a certain "biopolitics" that considers crime the result of social, psychological, and ideological circumstances, such that individuals are not responsible for the crimes they commit, so they should not be punished? The notion of the morally/legally responsible subject is an ideological fiction whose function is to cover up the network of power relations. Is, however, the obverse of this thesis not that those who control the circumstances control the people? No wonder the two strongest industrial complexes are today the military and the medical, that of destroying and that of prolonging life.

The ultimate example of this ambiguity is arguably the *chocolate laxative* available in the United States, with the paradoxical injunction "Do you have constipation? Eat more of this chocolate!"—the very thing that causes constipation. Do we not find here a weird version of Wagner's famous "Only the spear which caused the wound can heal it" from *Parsifal*? And is not a negative proof of the hegemony of this stance the fact that true unconstrained consumption (in all its main forms: drugs, free sex, smoking, etc.) is emerging as the main danger? The fight against these dangers is one of the main investments of today's biopolitics. Solutions here are desperately sought, which would reproduce the paradox of the chocolate laxative. The main contender is "safe sex"—a term that makes one appreciative of the truth of the old saying "Is having sex with a condom not like taking a shower with a raincoat on?" The ultimate goal would be here, along the lines of decaf coffee, to invent "opium without opium": no wonder marijuana is so popular among liberals who want to legalize it—it already *is* a kind of "opium without opium."

The structure of the "chocolate laxative," of a product containing the agent of its own containment, can be discerned throughout today's ideological landscape. There are two topics that determine today's liberal tolerant attitude toward Others: the respect of Otherness, openness toward it, *and* the obsessive fear of harassment—in short, the Other is okay insofar as its presence is not intrusive, insofar as the Other is not really Other. . . . In the strict homology with the paradoxical structure of chocolate laxative, tolerance coincides with its opposite: my duty to be tolerant toward the other effectively means that I should not get too close to him, not intrude into his or her space, in other words, that I should respect his or her *intolerance* toward my overproximity. This is what is more and more emerging as the central "human right" in late-capitalist society: *the right not to be "harassed,"* i.e., to be kept at a safe distance from the others. A similar structure is clearly present in how we relate to capitalist profiteering: it is okay *if* it is counteracted with charitable activities: first you amass billions, then you return (part of) them to the needy. The same goes for war, for the emergent logic of humanitarian or pacifist militarism: war is okay insofar as it really serves to bring about peace, democracy, or to create conditions for distributing humanitarian help. And does the same not hold more and more even for democracy and human rights: human rights are okay if they are "rethought" to include torture and a permanent emergency state; democracy is okay if it is cleansed of its populist "excesses" and limited to those "mature" enough to practice it. . . .

IV

This same structure of the chocolate laxative is also what makes a figure like George Soros so ethically repulsive: does he not stand for the most ruthless financial speculative exploitation combined with its counteragent, the humanitarian worry about the catastrophic social consequences of the unbridled market economy? Soros's very daily routine is a lie embodied: half of his working time is devoted to financial speculations, and the other half to "humanitarian" activities (providing finances for cultural and democratic activities in post-Communist countries, writing essays and books), which ultimately fight the effects of his own speculations. . . . Figures like Soros are ideologically much more dangerous than direct and raw market profiteers— it is here that one should be a Leninist, i.e., react like Lenin when he heard a fellow Bolshevik praising a good priest sincerely sympathizing with the plight of the poor. Lenin exploded back that what Bolsheviks need are priests who get drunk, rob the peasants of the last bits of their meager resources, and rape their wives—they make the peasants clearly aware of what priests objectively are, while the "good" priests confuse their insight.

A conference entitled "Fighting Terrorism for Humanity: A Conference on the Roots of Evil" took place in New York on 22 September 2003, the result of an initiative taken by Kjell Magne Bondevik, then prime minister of Norway, and Elie Wiesel, the Nobel Peace Prize laureate and professor. The conference was organized by the International Peace Academy and the Norwegian Mission to the United Nations, and it was held at the Inter-Continental, The Barclay Hotel in New York. The purpose of the conference was stated to be "to help distinguish the real roots and origins of terrorism from factors that have a weaker link with terror and to discuss new policy measures in the global campaign against terrorism. Focusing on the true causes will enable us to fight terrorism more effectively. We need to identify the breeding grounds and the origins of hate in order to eliminate them, and we need to formulate medium and long-term policies in addition to the immediate action we have adopted to protect citizens and prevent these crimes." What looked especially promising was Session 3 of this conference, the "Round Table of World Leaders" who were invited to comment on the findings of the Oslo conference and other sources of knowledge about the causes of terrorist acts; as the official program specified, after this session "[t]here will be a closed lunch for participants at the Round Table of World Leaders. Aides, experts and other participants will be invited to a buffet lunch." They ate, bringing us to throw it up—how should one not recall here Brecht's acerbic fable about the origins of the Frankfurt School: in his old age, a rich capitalist, haunted by pangs of bad conscience, dedicated a large sum of money to a group of wise men and charged them to find the origin of misery and suffering in the world—forgetting the fact that he himself was this origin, i.e., the sources of Evil discussing the roots of Evil. . . .

However, when one talks about biopolitics, one should be careful to note that the category of "pure (or mere) life" has nothing whatsoever to do with any biological or experiential immediacy; it is thoroughly determined by its symbolic context. Two different examples may clarify this point. A pack of cereals is a (symbolic) envelope containing the reality of cereals; an envelope which contains the expiration date that determines the way we perceive the reality of cereals. Recall the horror that arises when we perceive that we are already past that date: all of a sudden, we perceive *the same* cereal that a minute ago appeared to promise healthy pleasure as a suspicious, potentially harmful trash. The Real (the "*objet petit a*") here is the invisible X in the object whose presence or absence decides that what I see is a delicious meal or rotten trash, even if the thing in reality looks exactly the same. In a different field, when King Hussein of Jordan was already "clinically dead" in February 1999 (his internal organs ceased to function, and he was kept alive only through machines that regulated his heart beating), his death (disconnection from the machine that kept his heart beating) was postponed until proper preparations were made for the regular transfer of power—do we not have here a nice case of the distinction between the two deaths?

This brings us to the link between S_2 and the agency of the superego: superego is not directly S_2; it is rather the S_1 of the S_2 itself, the dimension of an unconditional injunction that is inherent to knowledge itself. Recall the information about health we are bombarded with daily: "Smoking is dangerous!" "To much fat may cause a heart attack!" "Regular exercise leads to a longer life!" etc., etc. It is impossible not to hear beneath it all the unconditional injunction, "You should enjoy a long and healthy life!" Hegel successfully resisted this danger: his theory of monarchy is the ultimate proof that he occupied the unique position in between the discourses of the Master and the University: while rejecting the abolition of the Master, aware of the necessity of the Master's exceptional position as the safeguard against the terror of Knowledge, he no longer succumbed to its charisma but reduced it to the stupidity of an empty signifying function.

The modern Master justifies himself through his expert knowledge: one does not become a Master through birth or mere symbolic investiture; one should rather earn it through education and qualification—in this simple and literal sense, modern power is knowledge, grounded in knowledge. The passage from Master to University discourse means that the State itself emerges as the new Master, the State run by qualified expertise of bureaucracy. And Hegel, from his position in between this shift, was able to perceive what remains hidden before and after, as is clear from his deduction of the necessity of the monarch in a rational state—a monarch reduced to a pure signifying function, deprived of any actual power. Hegel was thus aware of the necessity to maintain the gap between S_1 and S_2: if this gap gets obliterated, we get the "totalitarian" bureaucracy as S_2.

The University discourse as the hegemonic discourse of modernity has two forms of existence in which its inner tension ("contradiction") is externalized: capitalism, its logic of the integrated excess, of the system reproducing itself through constant self-revolutionizing, and the bureaucratic "totalitarianism" that is conceptualized in different guises as the rule of technology, of instrumental reason, of biopolitics, as the "administered world." How, precisely, do these two aspects relate to each other? That is to say, one should not succumb to the temptation of reducing capitalism to a mere form of appearance of the more fundamental ontological attitude of technological domination; one should rather insist, in the Marxian mode, that the capitalist logic of integrating the surplus into the functioning of the system is the fundamental fact. The Stalinist "totalitarianism" was the capitalist logic of self-propelling productivity liberated from its capitalist form, which is why it failed: Stalinism was the symptom of capitalism. Stalinism involved the matrix of *general intellect*, of the planned transparency of social life, of total productive mobilization—and its violent purges and paranoia were a kind of "return of the repressed," the "irrationality" inherent to the project of a totally organized "administered society."

What this means is that the two levels, precisely insofar as they are two sides of the same coin, are ultimately incompatible: there is no meta-language enabling us to translate the logic of domination back into the capitalist reproduction-through-excess, or vice versa. Which, then, is the way out of this predicament? How do we break the circle of this mutual implication? Perhaps, one should begin with an elementary insight. A lot of today's claims that the twentieth century was the most catastrophic in all of human history, the lowest point of nihilism, the situation of extreme danger, etc., forgets the elementary lesson of dialectics: the twentieth century appears as such because the criteria themselves changed. Today, we simply have much higher standards of what constitutes the violation of human rights, etc. The fact that the situation appears catastrophic is thus in itself a positive sign, a sign of (some kind of) progress: we are today also much more sensitive to the things that were going on in previous epochs. Recall feminism: only in the last two hundred years was the situation of women progressively perceived as unjust, although it was "objectively" getting better. Or recall the treatment of disabled individuals: even a couple of decades ago, the special entrances to restaurants, theatres, etc., which enable them to have access, would have been unthinkable.

NOTE

1. See Clavreuil on this point.

WORKS CITED

Clavreuil, Jean. *L'ordre médical*. Paris: Seuil, 1975.

Foucault, Michel. *The History of Sexuality*. Trans. Robert Hurley. New York: Pantheon, 1978.

Freud, Sigmund. *Totem and Taboo: Some Points of Agreement Between the Mental Lives of Savages and Neurotics. The Standard Edition of the Complete Psychological Works of Sigmund Freud*. Vol. 13. Trans. James Strachey. London: Hogarth, 1955. 1–161.

Lacan, Jacques. *Le Séminaire. Livre XVII: L'envers de la psychanalyse*. Paris: Seuil, 1991.

Racine, Jean. *Phèdre*. Paris: Seuil, 1946.

Santner, Eric. *My Own Private Germany*. Princeton, NJ: Princeton UP, 1996.

4

Signs of Desire

Nationalism, War, and Rape in *Titus Andronicus,*
Savior, and *Calling the Ghosts*

Deneen Senasi

The history of nations is a history of desire: a desire for identity, for dominion, and perhaps above all, for signification, a desire for signs of the nation itself repeating infinitely in the names and bodies of individual human beings. As a study of such histories, this essay, too, is marked by its own desires. Foremost among these is the desire to confront an array of issues surrounding this nexus of collective drives as they are brought to bear upon individual subjects, and the corollary question of what this collection (itself a kind of textual "collective") thematizes as a "desire for psychoanalysis." Taken together, what do these instances of collectivized and collectivizing psychic forces embedded in the phenomenon of "nationalism" suggest about the role of psychoanalysis in the new millennium? What, if anything, can a desire for psychoanalysis do with or for our understanding of the desires of nations? How are such desires localized, made manifest or legible? Of course, the collective of the nation has no "body"; it is an abstract concept, a nominalist term in which signifier and signified can never converge in anything like a fixed and stable form. The signifier through which the deferred presence of the nation is inscribed, by definition, cannot be localized in a single body, not even that of a king or a queen. In day-to-day life, in conflict and in war, individual bodies perish, and territories are won or lost, while nations persist. However infinitely the sign of the nation may be repeated, the bodies to which it seems to point—bodies of flesh and of earth—are invariably variable. Susceptible to admixture and alteration in almost every conceivable fashion, the relative stability of the sign itself is undercut and threatened by the mutability of the bodies to which it struggles to refer.

However much the signifier gestures toward the signified, it cannot encompass or absorb it. In this way, the figure, or form, that constitutes the material ground of that signified remains disconcertingly elusive, even "immaterial," in that the sign and its one "true" body can never meet. This quality of material estrangement renders the relationship between the sign of national identity and those bodies that come to bear it extremely unstable, tenuous, and at times, dangerous for the individual subjects caught in this web of signification and desire. Such separation threatens those desires by raising the questions of whether the nation is to be found in its sign or in its "bodies" and of what may happen when the two fail to correspond. If a body bearing the sign of the nation, in other words, is somehow read as heterogeneous, how can the "integrity" and stability of the sign itself be maintained? Such a threat has, throughout the history of nations, led to acts of violence that attempt to force bodies and signs, signifiers and signifieds, to converge, stabilize, and homogenize, whatever the cost. In this way, the psychic origins of nationalistic violence are linked to the symbolic order of signs and bodies through which the desires of nations materialize.

This scenario is exemplified in the nationalistic violence of rape, in which the violation of the woman's body is inextricable from the violation of the sign of national identity she bears. My central concern in this paper is with those women forced to bear the unbearable and with those who attempt to read and respond to this nexus of bodies, signs, and desires. Specifically, the essay will explore three representations of women and their experience of nationalistic violence: William Shakespeare's ambivalent tragedy of empire and nation, *Titus Andronicus*, and two films: *Savior*, a feature film focusing on the Bosnian war, and *Calling the Ghosts*, a documentary featuring survivors of that conflict. There are, of course, important differences between a sixteenth-century play and two twentieth-century films, as well as generic distinctions between the films themselves. There is also the apparent difficulty of widely disparate historical periods and cultural locales separating Shakespeare's early modern imagining of Rome, as a nation, empire, and state, from the Balkans of the twentieth-century, issues I will return to in more detail later.

As is all too clear, however, rape in war is, tragically, a transhistorical, transcultural phenomenon; understanding the dynamics of one in relation to the other calls for analysis that complicates and ultimately transcends those boundaries. At this point, I wish to emphasize that what these representations share is the exploration of a series of scenarios in which, for the women concerned, gender, ethnicity, and "nation" converge, coalesce, and expand, effectively overshadowing all other aspects of identity. As Anne McClintock has argued, "all nationalisms are gendered; all are invented, and all are dangerous" (89). She suggests further that nations and the nationalisms associated with them represent "historical practices through which social difference is both invented and performed" (89). In particular, I will be focusing on ways in which such "invention and performance" is carried out through acts of violence, localized in women's bodies, which are bound up with speech acts and with signs. In this context, the negotiation of silence and speech becomes a history of another kind of desire—this time one that is inscribed in the women's passage from *bearing the sign* of nationalistic hatred and anxiety to *bearing witness* to their own experience.

If the history of nations is a history of desire, the history of nationalism as a field of inquiry is a history of dichotomies. Scholars of nationalism are usually categorized as either "primordialist" or "modernist," while recent studies often turn on attempts to describe the phenomenon in terms of "eastern" or "western" nationalisms, reason versus emotion, or the untheoretical versus the theoretical, just to name a few. For the purposes of the present analysis, perhaps the most significant of these is the distinction between the "primordialist" and the "modernist" approach. Nationalism has most often been described as a manifestation of modernity, a phenomenon that emerges in the eighteenth and nineteenth centuries. Therefore Umut Özkirimli begins his overview of the field in *Theories of Nationalism* with "a discussion of the eighteenth and nineteenth centuries, when the doctrine of nationalism was first framed" (14). Özkirimli justifies this point of departure by referencing what he describes as "the great classics of the modernist approach" (55): Ernest Gellner's *Nations and Nationalism*, Benedict Anderson's *Imagined Communities*, and Eric Hobsbawm and Terence Ranger's *The Invention of Tradition*, each of which designates this period as the origin of the phenomenon. While this perspective has dominated studies of nationalism since the early 1980s, it has recently been challenged by scholars Özkirimli describes as "primordialists," those who see nations and nationalisms as "perennial entities" (60) existing well before the eighteenth century.

Adrian Hastings, in his book-length study *The Construction of Nationhood: Ethnicity, Religion, and Nationalism*, calls into question the influential work of Hobsbawm, a fellow historian, Gellner, and Anderson, as well as John Breuilly's *Nationalism and the State*, as representatives of "the principal current orthodoxy in nationalist studies, but one increasingly challenged by medievalists and others" (2). Hastings argues that the treatment of nationalism as an exclusively "modernist" phenomenon constitutes a problem to such a degree that he finds himself "speaking across the frontline of an historiographical schism" (2). From his position across that divide, he argues instead that "if nationalism became theoretically central to western political thinking in the nineteenth century, it existed as a powerful reality in some places long before that" (4). Here Hastings expands the field of study pertinent to the topic of nationalism to encompass examples that precede conventional historical parameters. He describes it as arising "chiefly where and when a particular ethnicity or nation feels itself threatened in regard to its own proper character, extent or importance, either by external attack or by the state system of which it has hitherto formed a part; but nationalism can also be stoked to fuel the expansionist imperialism of a powerful nation-state" (4).

Hastings argues that "Hobsbawm wrote a history of nineteenth- and twentieth-century nationalism, but not a history of nationalism" (11). He disavows the "primordialist" label such an argument would seem to invite, suggesting instead that "What has to be asserted counter to modernism is not any kind of primordialism—a claim that every nation today, and just those nations, all existed in embryo a thousand or fifteen hundred years ago—but, rather, a finely constructed analysis of why some ethnicities become nations while others do not" (11–12). In challenging the history of nationalism as written by Hobsbawm and others, Hastings describes the emergence of a nation as primarily a linguistic phenomenon. While he focuses on the importance of an emerging vernacular literature as one of the hallmarks of a nation, my own analysis focuses on the semiotic sign-systems of nation and ethnicity as they are "written" over and into the identity of individual women. This distinction aside, however, in what follows I will examine instances of the "powerful reality" of nationalism in representations of both "pre-modern" and "modern" cultures, since I too believe, as Hastings so aptly puts it, that "understanding nations and nationalism will only be advanced when any inseparable bonding of them to the modernization of society is abandoned" (9).

The resonance between a sixteenth-century play by Shakespeare and representations of women in the Balkan conflicts in the twentieth century is especially significant in the context of studies of nationalism. In "Theoretical Difficulties in the Study of Nationalism," Yael Tamir suggests that the greatest obstacle to constructing a viable theory of nationalism is the assumption that the incidents themselves are "so diverse and contextualized that they defy all attempts to generalize them" (68). Nevertheless, certain patterns are discernible between such experiences of trauma, even in widely disparate times and places; indeed, as Tamir argues, "if the plurality of particular experiences hampers the possibility of developing a theory of nationalism, it must be an impediment to the formation of political theories in general" (67–68). I would argue further that such kinships foreground ways in which these are problems not just for history, political philosophy, or social science, but for psychoanalysis as well, presenting issues of desire, power, appropriation, collective identity, and interpretation that we must work to articulate and theorize in this new millennium. Tamir suggests that another reason why nationalism has so often been represented as a "phenomenon that cannot, and need not, be theorized" (67) is that "nationalistic claims often lend themselves to unfavorable interpretations according to which they are no more than erratic outbursts of emotion from which no set of principles can be deduced" (68). The relationship between nationalism and emotion Tamir points to further underscores the importance of psychoanalytic readings. In spite of the challenges involved and the conventional wisdom to the contrary, Tamir writes, "I argue that theories of nationalism can be constructed and urge more scholars to join the effort to improve them" (68). This essay is, in part, my own response to Tamir's call for such theorization.

In *Bloodlines: From Ethnic Pride to Ethnic Terrorism*, Vamik Volkan asserts the need for psychoanalytic readings of nationalistic phenomena. Volkan suggests that "despite the resurgence of ethnic and related large-group conflict, and evidence of complex and intertwined psychological issues in many cases, the tools and practices of foreign policy and intergroup relations have responded slowly to the changing international environment" (17). Therefore, he writes, "*Bloodlines* seeks to fill this gap in the literature of diplomacy by using the principles of psychoanalysis to search for the meaning of cultural identity, ethnic attachment, and the passions related to such relationships" (18). While Volkan persuasively sets out the reasoning behind such work, grounding his analysis in Freud's *Group Psychology and the Analysis of the Ego*, his reading of the Balkan conflicts focuses almost exclusively on one "large-group identity," that of the Serbs. In doing so, perhaps inevitably, he oversimplifies the problem by examining only one set of psychological issues, rather than the entire matrix of motivations and desires that constitute the basis for nationalistic conflict *between* ethnic groups.

By contrast, I would argue that we must work to locate such group identities within a more complex series of semiotic relationships, as a means of elucidating one of the major vehicles, the signs of ethnic or national identity, through which nationalistic desires materialize. Volkan does gesture toward such a reading, arguing that "Serb propagandists began accusing Muslims of preparing a jihad against them" and that "the more such projections occurred, the more Bosnian Muslims were perceived, consciously and unconsciously, as Ottoman Turks, the enemy in the Serbs' chosen trauma" (73). In this way, the sign of identity of one group, the Bosnian Muslims, is culturally overwritten with the sign of another, the Ottoman Turk. While Volkan points out that it is important to consider "the role of the Bosnian Muslim leadership in establishing Bosnia as an attractive target for these projections" (73), he stops short of exploring other projections within the conflict groups that may lead to additional semiotic transpositions.

This point returns us to the central concern of this paper, and that is the women whose bodies become the locus for acts of nationalistic violence bound up with speech acts and signs. As they negotiate the passage from bearing such signs to bearing witness to the violence perpetrated upon them, they move from being read *as a sign* by others to *deploying signs* in their own right, as the speech acts of their testimony serve to foreground their status as speaking subjects. Here I wish to emphasize the value and significance of such speech acts for the speaker, placing other effects on the listener, the community, and the nation in a secondary position. Such an emphasis runs counter to analysis found in the influential work of Shoshana Felman and Dori Laub in their book *Testimony: Crises of Witnessing in Literature, Psychoanalysis, and History*. For Felman and Laub, the dynamics of witnessing are situated most notably in the figure of the listener, whom they describe in the following terms:

> The professionally trained receivers of the testimonies which bear witness to the war atrocities—the listeners and interviewers whose own listening in fact *enables* the unfolding of the testimonial accounts of Holocaust survivors—cannot fulfill their task without, in turn, passing through the crisis of experiencing their boundaries, their separateness, their functionality, and indeed their sanity at risk. (xvii)

Here the listener is not secondary, but primary, both in terms of Felman and Laub's emphasis on the effect of such accounts but also, and more tellingly, in their assertion that the listener "*enables*" (a word they emphasize with italics) the entire process. Implicitly this suggests that without the listener there can be no witnessing, an assertion that limits the ways in which witnessing can take place; textual accounts, for example, require no "listener" *per se*. More importantly, the dynamics of witnessing posited in the passage above effectively reenact the semiotic violence carried out against the trauma survivor, making of him or her a sign to be read by others who then become the primary repositories of value and significance in the testimony that emerges.

This point is made even more explicit in the second chapter of *Testimony*, written by Laub and titled "Bearing Witness or the Vicissitudes of Listening." Laub's play on words in that title—the vicissitudes of *bearing* witness are located explicitly here in the listener—effectively conflates the reception of testimony with the act of bearing witness in the sense of a first-person account of trauma. Laub asserts that "massive trauma precludes its registration: the observing and recording mechanisms of the human mind are temporarily knocked out" (57). Therefore, she suggests "the victim's narrative—the very process of bearing witness to massive trauma—does indeed begin with someone who testifies to an absence, to an event that has not yet come into existence, in spite of the overwhelming and compelling nature of the reality of its occurrence" (57). In this way, the reality of trauma is imagined as a kind of phantasmatic "absence" that can only be rendered as "present" through the registering consciousness of the listener. Laub is quite explicit on this point, arguing that "the trauma—as a known event and not simply an overwhelming shock—has not truly been witnessed yet" and that the listener "is a party to the creation of knowledge *de novo*. The testimony to the trauma thus includes its hearer, who is, so to speak, the blank screen on which the event comes to be inscribed for the first time" (57). At this point, Laub positions the listener and the trauma survivor in a kind of semiotic dialectic through which the phenomenon of testimony is constituted as such.

That dialectic is ultimately disavowed, however, as Laub radically reduces the significance of the survivor in the construction of testimony, arguing that "the trauma survivor who is bearing witness has no prior knowledge, no comprehension, and no memory of what happened" (58). Here Laub contradicts her earlier assertion that the listener is a "blank screen," suggesting instead that it is the survivor who is empty and "blank," devoid of anything akin to knowledge or memory of her or his own experience and who is, therefore, wholly dependent upon the listener for the inscription of such "cognizance" (58). While I recognize that the listener does indeed play a crucial role in the reception of testimony, Laub's dismissal of the significance of the speaking subject strikes me as overly reductive, problematic, and dangerous, in particular in the context of nationalistic violence carried out against women. To suggest that the trauma survivor has no "prior knowledge, no comprehension" of the event implicitly reduces her to a passive repository of apparently meaningless signs without the intercession of the listener, whose agency and understanding are assumed at the outset to supersede her own.

By contrast, I will offer an alternative reading of the dynamic processes of bearing witness, one in which the survivor does in fact retain memory and knowledge of her own experience. As the following examples illustrate, Laub's sense of the listener is sometimes dangerously idealized, as the survivor must often struggle against those who position themselves as her "enablers" and their self-interested attempts to appropriate meaning through readings of the sign that, to them, she has become. The question I wish to consider is whether the primary value of the psycholinguistic act of witnessing should be situated in those who speak or in those who listen; whose desires are addressed in such acts and, ultimately, whose are being heard?

In Shakespeare's *Titus Andronicus*, the title character is a Roman general, renowned for his service and devotion to the state. Upon his return to Rome from the battlefield, Titus and his surviving sons offer Alarbus, the eldest son of Tamora, the Queen of the Goths, as a sacrifice. When Tamora pleads for her son, Titus remains unmoved, thereby setting in motion a chain of events driven by the desires of nationalistic identity, dominion, and revenge. While Titus's victory over the Goths is in keeping with Hastings's suggestion that nationalism can "fuel the expansionist imperialism of a powerful nation-state" (4), the play goes a step further, effectively continuing the nationalistic conflict after the final battle in the heart of Rome itself. While she acknowledges the defeat that made her a prisoner of war, Tamora's appeal on behalf of her son resorts to universal, rather than nationalistic logic:

> Sufficeth not that we are brought to Rome
> To beautify thy triumphs, and return
> Captive to thee and to thy Roman yoke;
> But must my sons be slaughtered in the streets
> For valiant doings in their country's cause?
> O, if to fight for king and commonweal
> Were piety in thine, it is in these. (1.1.109–15)

Titus refuses to recognize such logic, insisting instead on the rights of Roman culture. In typical nationalistic fashion, Titus privileges the practices of his own culture as inherently superior, while simultaneously dehumanizing his "enemy," Tamora, dismissing her love for her children and the very life of Alarbus as immaterial. As Tamir points out, "The implication of resorting to general justifications is that all nations have the same rights; hence, one's nation is only one among others, obliged by the law of nations. It is no coincidence that nationalists are reluctant to acknowledge this message, as it implies that they ought to see other nations' rights as a source of self-restraint" (73). Titus clearly does not see the rights of the Goths or of Tamora as a fellow parent as "a source of self-restraint." Seen in this light, the subsequent hewing and hacking of Alarbus's limbs, described by Lucius as "Our Roman rites" (1.1.146) prefigures the mutilation of Lavinia as, at least in part, an act of nationalistic revenge carried out by Alarbus's younger brothers, Demetrius and Chiron.

Tamora's presence in the moments immediately preceding that assault underscores this connection: when Lavinia begs her for mercy, Tamora replies, "Remember, boys, I poured forth tears in vain to save your brother from the sacrifice, but fierce Andronicus would not relent" (2.2.163–65). Here Tamora reads Lavinia not as an individual subject but as a sign of her father and the "Roman rites" that govern his identity. To violate Lavinia is therefore to violate Titus and Rome. The brothers tear out her tongue, in a recitation of the Ovidian story of Philomela, and then take that source one step further, by cutting off her hands. They taunt Lavinia with her inability to speak or to employ the instruments of writing. Demetrius tells her, "So, now go tell, and if thy tongue can speak, Who 'twas that cut thy tongue and ravished thee" (2.3.1–2), and Chiron says, "Write down thy mind, bewray thy meaning so, And if thy stumps will let thee, play the scribe" (2.3.3–4), underscoring the ways in which Lavinia's mutilation is designed to prevent her from deploying "signs and tokens" as a speaking subject. As a result, they assume she is immured within her own body and its enforced silence. To use Felman and Laub's terms, the brothers' rape and mutilation of Lavinia is presumed, by them, to be "an event without a witness—an event eliminating its own witnesses" (xvii).

The moment of Lavinia's discovery by her uncle, Marcus, a Roman tribune, seems to confirm this perspective; though he begs her to speak, she cannot. This is the moment Demetrius and Chiron have provided against, the moment of witnessing. Significantly, Lavinia's relationship with language has been problematized even before her assault, making the possibility of her bearing witness all the more tenuous. While she is on stage for much of the first act, she remains almost entirely silent; except for a speech of filial piety, emphasizing her "tributary" (1.1.159) relations to her father and the name of the Andronici, she speaks only briefly and usually only when spoken to. This preponderance of silence has led prominent Shakespeare critic Coppèlia Kahn to describe Lavinia as a "signifier," one who has "no access to agency" (60–61). For both Kahn and the brothers who rape her, Lavinia's "access to agency" is seen as inextricable from her access to language. Because she speaks little before her rape and mutilation and not at all after, she is assumed to exist as a kind of evacuated sign, one who can only be given meaning through the registering consciousness of others.

Demetrius and Chiron assume that she cannot "tell" because she cannot deploy signs and therefore, to use Laub's terms, the event of her trauma will always remain "absent," since it cannot be "heard" and given meaning by a listener. For Kahn, Lavinia's silence is equivalent with her status as a sign. Because the audience or reader cannot "hear" her either before or after her assault, Kahn assumes that Titus's daughter never really exists as an independent dramatic subject. Seen in this light, access to language is assumed as a precondition for both witnessing and subjectivity itself, but as in Laub's analysis, that access is assumed to take on meaning only once it is registered and received by an outside listener. Nevertheless, while Marcus initially associates Lavinia's wounds with those of Philomela, Shakespeare suspends the realization that she has been raped, not allowing it to emerge clearly until *much* later in the play. This delay is significant because instead of being read as a sign by Marcus and her father, it remains for Lavinia to assert the truth later in the play.

The deferred moment of witnessing is followed by a period of appropriation, as Titus assumes the role of Lavinia's interpreter, placing himself in a position analogous to that of an analyst and his daughter to that of an analysand. He tells Marcus, "I understand her signs: Had she a tongue to speak, now she would say that to her brother which I said to thee" (3.1.144–46). Here Titus conflates Lavinia's signs with his own speech, assuming an untroubled correspondence between them. In contrast to Felman and Laub's sense of the listener as an "enabler," such an attitude is congruent with Julia Kristeva's assertion that "interpretation necessarily represents appropriation, and thus an act of desire and murder" ("Within the Microcosm of 'The Talking Cure'" 33). Lavinia's silence here is congruent with the "tributary" silence of the dutiful daughter in the play's first act; in Kristeva's terms, Titus's murder of his daughter begins at this point, in the appropriation of her "signs" in the service of his own desires. Titus has already murdered one of his children because Mutius refused to subsume his speech to that of his father. In the case of Lavinia, he expects to encounter no such willful interference, and insistently asserts his authority as her interpreter:

> I can interpret all her martyred signs.
> She says she drinks no other drink but tears,
> Brewed with sorrow, mashed upon her cheeks.
> Speechless complainer, I will learn thy thought.
> In thy dumb action will I be as perfect

As begging hermits in their holy prayers.
Thou shalt not sigh, nor hold thy stumps to heaven,
Nor wink, nor nod, nor kneel, nor make a sign,
But I of these will wrest an alphabet
And by still practice learn to know thy meaning. (3.2.36–45)

While Titus suggests that he already "understands" these signs fully, these lines present a more ambiguous picture, in which Titus, the analyst, must through "practice" learn to interpret the meaning of Lavinia's signs. But what Titus reads are not the signs she *makes*, but the sign that, to him, she increasingly *becomes*—an embodied sign of his enemies and his dissipating power. His need to "wrest an alphabet" from Lavinia's signs, with its implicit suggestion of violence, also returns us to Kristeva's point about the threat of appropriation implicit in the desire for interpretation.

In fact, Titus comes to understand the full import of her assault only when Lavinia bears witness to it in her own right. She gestures violently to the story of Philomela in the *Metamorphosis* and then guides Titus's staff with her feet and mouth to write in the sand, identifying the names of her assailants and the nature of the assault. Lavinia's return to legible signification, independent of her avowed "listener" and analyst, represents a turning point in her fate. Titus now sets in motion his plan for revenge, one that encompasses the death of Lavinia by his own hand, fulfilling the second half of Kristeva's formulation. Instead of "enabling" and "inscribing" her testimony of trauma, Titus continues it, acting in a manner that corresponds to the assumptions of her original attackers. While Lavinia's memory and cognizance of what she suffered are not dependent on his reception of her testimony, her life is. The disparity between his interpretation of her "matry'rd signs" and the truth of her experience lead Titus to exact revenge not only on her assailants but also on Lavinia herself. In Lavinia's story we, therefore, find a tragic trajectory, as she moves from bearing the sign of Rome and its rites to the enemy Goths, to bearing the sign of the Goths and their revenge within her father's Roman imaginary.

Yet as a subject and not a sign, her act of witnessing complicates the trajectories of desire projected onto her; that moment reveals Titus's analysis for what it is—not transparent meaning but imposed desire. For Lavinia, the act of witnessing is therefore counterpoised against Titus's desire for Rome in its "pure" form. Signification independent of her self-declared interpreter comes with a price because of the threat to the Symbolic order implicit in that definitive speech act. The sign of one nation's identity converging with another in a single woman's body threatens both with disappearance, revealing the tenuous relations between the sign of the nation and the bodies that bear it. Lavinia is sacrificed to this vulnerability of nations at the level of the sign. Her body and the sign of Rome, in Titus's imaginary, can no longer coexist—his desire for Rome is therefore equivalent with his destruction of his daughter.

This disturbing equivalency between nationalistic desire and the destruction of women is also apparent in two films depicting more recent conflicts, *Savior* and *Calling the Ghosts*. In fact, each of these films demonstrate that what we see in *Titus* is not simply a function of Shakespeare's early modern imagination but is, in fact, very much a part of the psychic structures of violence and nationalism in our own time. Both focus on the Balkan conflicts in contemporary Bosnia Herzegovina and on the stories of women who suffer, survive, and bear witness to trauma. As Hastings notes:

> The near invisibility of Bosnia as a specific identity of more than a geographical kind is one of the most remarkable characteristics of almost all pre-1992 literature relating to Yugoslavia. The absence of even a category of "Bosniaks" among the "nations" in the Yugoslav constitution is itself extraordinary. Every other "state" had its corresponding "nation." Bosnia did not. (139)

The semiotic ambiguity surrounding Bosnia both before and after the collapse of the Yugoslav federation that Hastings outlines has significant resonance for both films. *Savior*, a feature film directed by Peter Antonijevic, depicts a Serbian woman who is raped by Muslims, rejected by Serbs, and murdered by Croats. *Calling the Ghosts* is a documentary featuring two Bosnian women—one Muslim, one Croat—who were raped and tortured by Serbs at the infamous Omarska concentration camp outside the town of Prijedor.

In *Savior*, we first see Vera in a scene depicting an exchange of prisoners between Muslims and Serbs. The camera pans over the crowd without pausing on the dark-haired young woman, obviously pregnant, among them. It then returns to focus on her, as she approaches the two men waiting to take her home—one Serbian and one American, a mercenary played by Dennis Quaid. Quaid's character Joshua becomes involved in the conflict as a result of the death of his wife and child in a terrorist bombing; his presence, therefore, carries with it the violence enacted in the name of nationalistic desire and the consequences of such conflict at the level of individual lives. In the moments immediately following the death of his family, Joshua walks to the nearest mosque and, in an act of ethnic hatred and revenge, murders the men praying there. He flees, joining an international mercenary group engaged as support in the Bosnian war. When Vera arrives, the Serbian soldier, Goran, immediately begins to insult and harangue her for submitting to those who raped her in the Muslim camp. She says only "I don't want to talk to you" and then remains silent as the three set off for their village. Her silence infuriates Goran, intensifying his verbal assault until he stops the jeep in a tunnel and drags her, heavily pregnant, out onto the pavement. Calling her "Muslim whore," he beats and kicks her. When his attack brings on her labor, she says only "Evo ga" ("he's coming") as Goran aims his rifle between her legs. Quaid's character then shoots Goran, killing him. With his assistance, she delivers her child— a girl—on the pavement where Goran had thrown her.

After the child is born, Vera refuses to hold her. Once they arrive at her parents' home, responsibility for the baby appears to pass to her mother, but this is only temporary. When Vera's father and brother learn what's happened, she and her child are immediately thrown out of the house. Through it all, Vera has remained almost completely silent and with the exception of Goran and Joshua, each of whom tries to get her to speak for his own reasons, those she encounters seem neither to expect her to speak nor to desire it. Her silence is, in this way, congruent with the presence of the child, which all concerned interpret as a kind of embodied narrative account of what has happened. As with Goran, to her father she has become a sign of the enemy, just as to that enemy she was an embodied sign of the Serbs. In commentary on the film, Antonijevic explains that during the Bosnian war, both sides engaged in such practices, capturing women and raping them, holding them prisoner until they became visibly pregnant, then sending them home. The violation of the woman's body, as we have seen, is inextricable from the violation of the sign of national identity she bears. And once again, the role of the "listener" is complicated by the silence of the survivor, a silence that does not prevent others from interpreting her "marty'rd signs" but nevertheless defers her own interpretation. In this case those signs are, to return to the work of Kristeva, demonstrably polymorphic. Though no account is given in the linguistic sense, one is clearly legible at the level of semiotics, what Kristeva describes as a "'multilayered' model of psychic *significance*, one that incorporates heterogeneous *marks and signs*" (*New Maladies of the Soul* 33). Reading her silence and her body in tandem with that of the child, Vera's father responds to that heterogeneity of national origins, signs, and desires and expels it, in an echo of Titus's rejection of his daughter. Like Lavinia, Vera's presence (and, in this case, that of her child) constitutes a threat to the Symbolic order, while her silence holds in suspension her own response to the trauma she endures.

That response, at first, appears to correspond with her father's rejection. At one point, she seems to consider throwing the child from the moving jeep, but changes her mind in the last moment. When Joshua stops at a farm to try to get some milk for the baby, Vera remains alone with her, and when she cries, begins to breast-feed her. At this point, her father and brother catch up with them, ready to kill them both as restitution to the community for the death of Goran and the violation of the ethnic sign of identity. Significantly, the community demands the death of Vera and the child once they discover Goran's body. When one of the villagers asks Vera's father whether or not he will carry out this act of internal "ethnic cleansing," he replies in the affirmative, once again placing his desire for the community over that of his desires for the life of his daughter. What follows is a pivotal scene in which Vera refuses her father's gun as a means to take her own life, refusing also to participate any longer in his interpretation of her rape and its threat to the Symbolic order of the community. Here, she speaks at length for the first time, initially to her father in Serbo-Croatian and then to Joshua in English. Her silence, unlike Lavinia's, was self-imposed, but once she accepts the baby and rejects the cultural order whose re-inscription her silence had previously enabled, she no longer appears to desire it.

Vera's rejection of silence and the semiotics of national hatred is made fully explicit in her final moments in the film, when she is captured by a group of Croatian soldiers rounding up Muslims and Serbs along the road. The people are forced into the water at the river's edge, while the soldiers stand on the shore with guns. One soldier comes forward with an enormous hammer and begins to single out victims to bludgeon to death. Vera knows that she will die; she also knows that Joshua and her baby are just a few yards away, hidden in an abandoned houseboat. While the soldier kills, she begins to sing a Serbian lullaby: "Zaspi mi, zaspi mi, djetence, zaspi mi čedo mamino"—which means "Sleep for me, little child, sleep for me mother's dear." The word "čedo" is of special significance here— it refers not just to any "dear" one but to one's own baby, one who is an inextricable part of oneself. The song draws the soldier's attention to Vera; as she continues to sing, he draws back her hair and forces her to kneel in the shallow water. She falls silent only when the hammer strikes. This is Vera's moment of witnessing, the performance of a speech act that defines her refusal of the Symbolic order and claims the child as her own.

As in *Titus*, the trajectory is tragic but with a difference—Lavinia's death is carried out in order to protect Titus's Roman imaginary; stage directions give no indication of whether she participates in her own death or resists. By contrast, Vera openly refutes the Symbolic order, then embraces what she once rejected, bearing witness to her own passage from bearing the sign of national hatred to bearing a child of mixed ethnic origins for whom she can feel love. Of course, the Symbolic order still frames Vera's story; her death at the hands of the Croatian soldiers is carried out because, for them, she still bears the sign of the enemy, as a Serb. Returning to Felman and Laub's model, it is important to note that in this moment of witnessing there is an unusual specificity in the addressee. Vera's infant daughter and the child's protector are the "listeners" here, and they are not "blank screens" (Laub 57). Neither are they her "enablers"; what Vera does in the moments preceding her death constitutes a clear choice, made in light of her own prior "knowledge" and "comprehension" (Laub 58) of the circumstances, on behalf of the child and Joshua, who might otherwise have tried to save her.

Instead, Vera's moment of witnessing "enables" them, the man and the child, ensuring their survival, and ultimately Joshua's redemption. Further, the meaning of Vera's testimony clearly emanates from the speaking subject herself, as her knowledge of past trauma converges with her present understanding. To return to the question raised earlier, the primary value of the psycholinguistic act of witnessing, in this case, appears to reside in both the speaker and the listener, in the kind of dialectic Laub first posits, then discards. It should be noted, however, that the desires of the speaker, in this case, are clearly the ones being addressed and heard. Vera's moment of witnessing is a function not only of knowledge and comprehension but agency, a decision to speak in a moment when she might indeed have "preferred silence" (Laub 58) but makes an altogether different choice.

After Vera's death, the focus of the film shifts to concentrate on the fate of her child, and in doing so, offers implicit commentary on the effects of both bearing witness and listening to it. When the Croatian soldiers move on, Joshua takes the baby and finds his way by bus to a Red Cross center in Split. He leaves the child in a van bearing the aid agency's emblem, telling her "Your mother loved you very much," as he tucks a piece of paper with the name "Vera" written on it into her blankets. He then walks away, exhausted and still wounded. After tearing up his military identification and dropping it along with his gun into the sea, he collapses nearby on a bench. As he sits beside the Adriatic weeping, a woman who traveled with them on the bus appears carrying the child. She asks, "Is this your baby?" Without hesitating, Joshua replies, "Yes, she is mine." The woman then offers to take Joshua and his baby to a hospital. In this way, Antonijevic's film comes full circle in its dramatization of the effects of nationalistic violence on individual lives.

The baby, now bearing her mother's name (which in Serbo-Croatian means "hope"), is born out of such violence, born out of the reading of her mother's body as a sign of ethnic origin, just as her mother is killed in a subsequent reading of her life in those same terms. Joshua, who enters the Bosnian conflict as a result of such violence in his own life, at this moment acknowledges the child as his own, and so she is, for her existence is congruent with the violence of his response to the loss of his family. This then is the effect for Joshua of listening to Vera's moment of bearing witness, not the loss of the listener's sanity, as Laub cautions, but the recuperation of it. In the film's final scene that moment of witnessing is reenacted, as the woman who returns the baby to Joshua begins to sing the same lullaby. As she sings "Zaspi mi, zaspi mi, djetence, zaspi mi čedo mamino," the credits begin to roll and the song is taken up by many voices, underscoring yet again the ways in which the child's existence is inextricable from the violence through which she was born, even as the hopeful quality of her name calls for her to be acknowledged and embraced, not just by Joshua, but by all who are enmeshed in such conflicts.

I conclude by turning to one final example in the negotiation of silence and speech for women forced to bear the unbearable. *Calling the Ghosts*, a documentary written and directed by Mandy Jacobson and Karmen Jelinčić, recounts the experiences of women subjected to rape in the former Yugoslavian republic and their response in the aftermath of the conflict. Jadranka Cigeli and Nusreta Sivac were imprisoned, raped, and subjected to psychological torture in the infamous Omarska concentration camp near the town of Prijedor in northwest Bosnia in 1992. In *Calling the Ghosts*, we first see Ms. Cigeli, whose first name "Jadranka" is derived from the Serbo-Croatian word for the sea, alone beside the water, long after her ordeal has taken place. The problem she articulates there is whether to speak or remain silent. She says:

> In the beginning I had only the reruns of my own film. There was a period of self-questioning before me. To stay silent or to speak. If I stay silent, how moral would that be? When I remember the night when I was first taken out my own broken bones start to hurt. If I speak how good is that for me? I would actually have to expose myself.

Jadranka's statement emphasizes the resilience of her memories of trauma, which recur at both psychological and physical levels. She offers an articulate rendering of what is at stake in negotiating silence and speech for the trauma survivor. The implicit answer she finds to that dilemma lies in both the testimony of the film itself and the work of bearing witness that she and her childhood friend, Nusreta, initiate on behalf of themselves and other women.

Unlike Lavinia and Vera, Jadranka's body bears no visible sign that might communicate her experience to others. The signs of that trauma, therefore, materialize most fully in her and Nusreta as signs of an alternative form of desire, a desire for bearing witness that overcomes the desire for the relative safety and seclusion of silence. That desire is expressed in direct opposition to Laub's assertion that "the speakers about trauma on some level prefer silence so as to protect themselves from the fear of being listened to—and of listening to themselves" (58). While Jadranka considers remaining silent, she ultimately makes another choice, precisely because she feels an obligation to herself and others to speak. Moreover, as it is depicted in the documentary, Jadranka's decision to make the passage from silence to speech is entirely her own; it is not mediated by a listener but instead appears to come directly from her own memories and cognizance of the trauma she has survived. In this way, the film implicitly emphasizes the agency of the survivor and her sense of self-possession in both the decision to speak and the account she narrates.

The memories of both women are recounted with detail and precision. Jadranka states that "on the thirtieth of May at 4:20 a.m., that is when the real suffering began." The film goes even further back, contextualizing these events in memories of happier times associated with Prijedor, times when both grew up as friends in the same school and later colleagues in the same profession. Significantly, before the war both Jadranka and Nusreta were involved in the active articulation of principles of justice: one as a lawyer, the other as a judge. When both were taken to Omarska, it was a part of the roundup in the Prijedor region of Muslim, and in some cases, Croat, leaders and intellectuals. In Jadranka's description of her first experience of rape at the camp, we see similarities to Antonijevic's film: the assault begins with a verbal attack, calling her "whore," and then beating. She is raped not once but several times, by several different men in a single room over the course of a single night, a pattern that is subsequently repeated on numerous occasions. On the mornings that follow, the head of the camp regularly announces that any woman who has been raped or assaulted should notify him immediately, and then laughs when they remain silent, a scenario that recalls the mockery of Demetrius and Chiron in Shakespeare's play.

When journalists began to investigate the Omarksa camp, officials strenuously denied that there were any women being held there. After their release, when charges were brought before the international tribunal at the Hague, one of the primary perpetrators of rape and torture at Omarska, Dusko Tadic, continued the strategy of mockery and denial. In a statement he suggests that the charges of rape filed against him by Jadranka were baseless because, he said, she was too old and unattractive for him to be interested in sexually. In addition to the obvious insult to Jadranka as a woman, Tadic's statement clearly elides the crucial point: that the rapes carried out at Omarska are not only violations of individual women but also of the signs of national or ethnic identity they bear. As we have seen, such violation carries with it a residual effect in which the survivor's own ethnic group, even her closest filial ties, may be challenged or eradicated altogether. Nusreta describes the reunion with her husband and his complete acceptance of all that had happened to her at Omarska. He does not read her then as a sign of the "enemy," as a result of the trauma she suffered. Not all women who suffered the same trauma at Omarska experienced the same response, however, and Nusreta goes on to recount the story of a woman whose husband divorced her after her release. Nusreta says quietly of the man, "He just couldn't take it."

Neither the mockery of Dusko Tadic nor the response of others in their own communities dissuaded Jadranka and Nusreta from their intention to serve as official witnesses at the International Tribunal. But they also did something more—as women educated in the law, they decided to work toward a wider scope of witnessing, collecting testimony from an array of women who endured similar experiences, not only at Omarska, but throughout the country. In the film they articulate in lucid terms what is at stake in the act of witnessing. When Jadranka says that in order to obtain the story you must "violate the witness," forcing her to "live through it again," she returns us to those opening moments by the sea, where she confronts the possibility of "exposing herself" in the act of witnessing. She expresses that concern in moral terms, but there is another related dimension we should attend to here, and that is how the speech act of witnessing is defined, as a psychic structure, by the locus of significance attributed to it. In terms of a moral responsibility to history and cultural memory, that locus is traditionally assumed to lie outside the witness herself—in the perpetrators of the crime, who must try to prevent it, in her family or national community who may try to revenge it, and, according to Felman and Laub, in the analyst, who must listen and try to interpret it.

Yet, what these women achieve in their gathering of testimony draws our attention back to the speaking subject herself, as a subject and not a sign, because in this collectivity of witnesses, we find the psychic structures of desire, in particular the desire for interpretation, being radically redefined. Here the witness is at one and the same time speaker, interlocutor, *and* listener. If retracing such memories is a violation, both are violated, both are vulnerable. This "multilayered psychic significance," to use Kristeva's terms, seems to hold out the promise of what she describes as a necessary "equilibrium" in psychoanalytic discourse between "truth and jouissance, authority and transgression" (*New Maladies of the Soul* 35). In this way the survivors of Omarska provide us with a dramatically different model from the ones represented in both the distillation of appropriation and murder Kristeva delineates and the eradication of the speaking subject implicit in the work of Felman and Laub. Through their desire to bear witness, in all its senses and syntactical positions, these women demonstrate that interpretation without appropriation in the conventional sense is conceivable *and* that the trauma survivor is not dependent on the listening and interpretation of others for her memory and comprehension of her own experience. That memory and comprehension lies within them, and it is through their agency and desire, and theirs alone, that it culminates in anything like meaning. Jouissance, authority, and truth converge in speaker and listener alike in this scenario, mediating without ignoring the transgressive "violence of analytic interpretation" (Kristeva 34). In this way, the desire for witnessing may gesture toward a reimagining of what it means to "desire psychoanalysis" for a speaking subject who cannot be reduced to an empirical (and therefore normative) case study, from which others, whether nationalists or analysts, "wrest an alphabet," while the subject herself remains immured in silence.

Like Jadranka and Nusreta, I, therefore, find myself ending where I began, with the question of desire. If there is a difference between the history of nations as a history of desire and the history of psychoanalysis as much the same thing, that distinction lies in the significance of the moment of witnessing for the speaker herself. In theorizing the dynamics of bearing witness, it is of crucial importance to distinguish between speaker and listener and the effects of the experience upon each within their respective positions. To conflate the two is to implicitly subject the survivor to yet another form of semiotic violence, laying claim to her voice and the words she speaks as our own without really hearing them *as hers*, and as a result threatening her with a form of subjective erasure. Even if the listener were, as Laub describes it, "a participant and a co-owner of the traumatic event"

(57) he or she could never "participate" or "own" that event in the same way or in the same terms as the survivor. If there is a dialectic at work in this scenario, it is not one that emerges from this sense of "twinned" experience, but instead must, at the most logical level, proceed from the differences and desires that continue to obtain between those who speak and those who listen.

At the end of *Calling the Ghosts*, Jadranka and Nusreta are at the Hague, where they have come to offer testimony. While there, they decide to send postcards to their former colleagues in Prijedor, once they leave the courtroom. Having been read as embodied signs of ethnic hatred, they respond by deploying signs as speaking subjects instead, both in the courtroom and more informally on the street outside. That psycholinguistic transition is enormously instructive in any attempt to theorize in more concrete terms the dehumanizing effects of nationalism. Such effects are in part carried out through the process outlined here, in which the individual is reduced to an embodied sign of ethnicity, empire, or nation, devoid of feelings, rights, or individual subjectivity. To paraphrase McClintock, Jadranka and Nusreta "invent" and "perform" their response to the violent effects of nationalism through their own testimony and through collecting that of others, thereby re-inscribing their sense of themselves as women and as Bosnians over and above the signs of hatred they had previously been forced to bear. On the street outside the Hague, they direct their postcards bearing the signs of that resilient subjectivity to those who participated in or benefited from their persecution back home. They laugh together at the response their gesture might elicit, then drop the cards into the post and continue on their way. I find this moment intriguing because even before judgment has been rendered at the international tribunal, before anything like a guarantee of justice, and without, therefore, the interpretative "validation" provided by the listening of others, they already seem to be in a different place, not just geographically, but psychologically. That place is one they found, in my view, in the desire that motivates their passage from bearing the sign of nationalistic hatred to bearing witness against it.

WORKS CITED

Calling the Ghosts. Dir. Mandy Jacobson and Karmen Jelinčić. Women Make Movies, 1996.

Felman, Shoshana, and Dori Laub. "Foreword." *Testimony: Crises of Witnessing in Literature, Psychoanalysis, and History*. New York: Routledge, 1992. xiii–xx.

Hastings, Adrian. "The Nation and Nationalism." *The Construction of Nationhood: Ethnicity, Religion, and Nationalism.* Cambridge: Cambridge UP, 1997. 1–34.

———. "The Southern Slavs." *The Construction of Nationhood: Ethnicity, Religion, and Nationalism.* Cambridge: Cambridge UP, 1997. 124–47.

Kahn, Coppèlia. "The Daughter's Seduction in *Titus Andronicus*, Or Writing Is The Best Revenge." *Roman Shakespeare: Warriors, Wounds, and Women.* London: Routledge, 1997. 46–76.

Kristeva, Julia. "In Times Like These, Who Needs Psychoanalysts?" *New Maladies of the Soul.* Trans. Ross Guberman. New York: Columbia UP, 1995. 27–44.

———. "Within the Microcosm of the 'Talking Cure.'" *Interpreting Lacan.* Ed. Joseph H. Smith and William Kerringan. New Haven: Yale UP, 1983. 33–57.

Laub, Dori. "Bearing Witness or the Vicissitudes of Listening." *Testimony: Crises of Witnessing in Literature, Psychoanalysis, and History.* New York: Routledge, 1992. 57–74.

McClintock, Anne. "'No Longer in a Future Heaven': Gender, Race, and Nationalism." *Dangerous Liasons: Gender, Nation, and Postcolonial Perspectives.* Minneapolis: U of Minnesota P, 1997. 89–112.

Özkirimli, Umut. "Discourses and Debates on Nationalism." *Theories of Nationalism: A Critical Introduction.* New York: St. Martin's, 2000. 12–63.

Savior. Dir. Peter Antonijevic. Perf. Dennis Quaid, Natasa Ninkovic. Columbia, 1997.

Shakespeare, William. *The Most Lamentable Tragedy of Titus Andronicus. William Shakespeare: The Complete Works.* Ed. Stanley Wells and Gary Taylor. Oxford: Clarendon UP, 1986. 125–52.

Tamir, Yael. "Theoretical Difficulties in the Study of Nationalism." *Theorizing Nationalism.* Ed. Ronald Beiner. Albany: SUNY Press, 1999. 67–89.

Volkan, Vamik. "Deadly Distinctions: The Rise of Ethnic Violence." *Bloodlines: From Ethnic Pride to Ethnic Terrorism.* New York: Farrar, Straus and Giroux, 1997. 3–18.

———. "Ancient Fuel for A Modern Inferno: Time Collapse in Bosnia-Herzegovina." *Bloodlines: From Ethnic Pride to Ethnic Terrorism.* New York: Farrar, Straus and Giroux, 1997. 50–80.

Part Three

Psychoanalysis and the Author

5

Moving beyond the Politics of Blame

Let Us Now Praise Famous Men

KAJA SILVERMAN

> Lay your sleeping head, my love,
> Human on my faithless arm;
> Time and fevers burn away
> Individual beauty from
> Thoughtful children, and the grave
> Proves the child ephemeral:
> But in my arms till break of day
> Let the living creature lie,
> Mortal, guilty, but to me
> The entirely beautiful.
>   —W. H. Auden, "Lay Your Sleeping Head, My Love"

If I had been asked to explain the original meaning of the phrase "the personal is political" a few weeks ago, I would have defined it as the rallying cry of a group of feminists in the 1960s who fought to make room within leftist politics for a host of issues related to the private domain. I was stunned to learn, after tracking down the essay out of which this phrase emerged, that its real purpose was to defend feminists who attended group therapy sessions from the accusation that they were apolitical (Hanisch, "Personal" 3). I was also amazed to discover that the primary function of these sessions themselves was to protect those who attended them against "the bad things that [were] said about [them] as women," and to help them "stop blaming [themselves] for [their] sad situations" and their "failures" (4). By declaring the "personal" to be "political," Carol Hanisch—the author of the eponymous essay—sought to exonerate herself and her colleagues for their attempt to escape another kind of condemnation.

Few of us would be likely to turn to group therapy for this purpose today. Regardless of its political rationale, the goal of collective "consciousness-raising" is generally to increase one's sense of culpability, not diminish it—to make the participants "shoulder" their "responsibilities" and be "answerable" for their deeds. This is not because we inhabit a more permissive society than our predecessors, one that sometimes fails to equip its members with a conscience; our culture is every bit as punitive as that against which the Women's Movement rebelled. It is, rather, because the claim that the personal is political has been—as Hanisch herself puts it— "revised or ripped off or even stood on [its] head and used against [its] original, radical intent" (Hanisch, "Introduction" 1). Instead of protecting us from judgment, the concept of the "private" now provides new opportunities for super-egoic invigilation.

This is as true of oppositional groups as it is of mainstream America; indeed, those of us on the Left often find ourselves more harshly judged by our allies than we are by our enemies. It is no longer enough to behave in a politically correct way; our desires and our identifications must also conform to this standard, and signs of psychic dissonance are construed as "racism," "sexism," or "classism." To judge someone for unconscious impulses is absurd, since these impulses would not be repressed if they were not as abhorrent to that person's consciousness as they are to our own. Far from demonstrating that we don't harbor the same desires, moreover, our moral indignation is almost proof positive that we do. And contradictions of this sort are not an accidental feature of subjectivity. We are divided in relation to our pleasure and ambivalent in our relationships with others because human desire originates in and is sustained through prohibition (see Freud, *Civilization* 114).

Freud imputes this kind of "infighting" to the "narcissism of minor differences," but I believe that it has another cause: moral sadism. Moral sadism is my name for the erotically charged pleasure we derive when we are able to treat someone else in the way that our super-ego usually treats us. The super-ego is created through the introjection of the paternal law—the voice that says "thou shall not commit murder," and backs up this prohibition with the threat of punishment. But no sooner is it created than it begins to measure us against the standard of the ego-ideal and to berate us for our failure to approximate it. Because the super-ego reaches deep into the unconscious, it is also able to ferret out desires that are so deeply repressed that we do not even know that we have them. Cruelly, it refuses to distinguish between them and the desires that we act upon; as far as it is concerned, the unconscious wish to commit murder *is* murder. And since the super-ego's life-blood is aggression, the more we resist the temptation to direct ours outwards, the more violently it treats us.[1] No one can tolerate this pressure forever. Sooner or later, we all succumb to the temptation to rid ourselves of it by re-exteriorizing our aggression. Now, however, we no longer recognize it as aggression, because it has been "sanitized" by its detour through the super-ego. We are not injuring others; we are—rather—protecting the oppressed, and punishing their oppressors.

We are more in need of psychoanalysis today than we ever have been before, not just as a therapeutic practice and a powerful hermeneutic, but also as a corrective to the dangerous fantasy that if human beings try hard enough, they can achieve absolute "goodness." We also need to make room in our politics for the messiness of human desire, both because blame is an atomizing force, and because, in spite of all of its ambivalence, it is within Eros that our transformative potential resides. Our best guide in this domain is not, I suggest, Freud or Lacan, but rather James Agee, a leftist writer who looks at the problem of Southern poverty from the dual vantage point of psychoanalysis and his own mortal and guilty subjectivity. The resulting book—his and Walker Evans's *Let Us Now Praise Famous Men*—not only takes the blame out of leftist politics, it also replaces it with something that isn't "supposed" to be there: libido.

I

In the summer of 1936, James Agee traveled to rural Alabama, where he stayed for approximately two months. He had been commissioned by *Fortune* magazine to write an article on cotton tenantry, and he went to Alabama in the hope of meeting some typical white farmers.[2] The editors of *Fortune* wanted Margaret Bourke-White, who was then a media star in her own right, to produce the photographs for this essay. Not only did Agee refuse to work with her, he included in the Appendix to the text he eventually wrote a series of ostensibly adulatory but in fact extremely incriminating quotations about her from society magazines. He chose the much more retiring and aesthetically scrupulous Walker Evans as his collaborator instead, and the latter accompanied him on his journey to the South. The two men ended up staying for approximately one month with the Gudgers,[3] a white tenant farming family of six, in order to see how they lived and worked. Agee and Evans also remained throughout this period in close contact with two other white tenant farming families, the Ricketts and the Woods.

Evans produced the photographs that were to accompany Agee's text during the period of their visit. Agee, however, needed more than three years to complete his part of their joint project, and when it was done it bore little relation to the text he had been assigned to write. Instead of a magazine article, it had become a lengthy book, which would eventually be published under the surprising name *Let Us Now Praise Famous Men*.[4] And rather than a semi-journalistic account of poverty in the South, it offered a stunning example of high modernist prose.

Agee describes the relationship between Evans and himself as a "collaboration." This is upon first reading a baffling claim. Although included in the same volume as Agee's text, Evans's portraits of white tenant farmers and their places of abode do not seem organic to it; they are consigned to the front of *Let Us Now Praise Famous Men*, without verbal commentary of any kind.[5] They also seem to privilege the signified over the signifier, and to blur the distinction between signified and referent. As William Stott puts it, theirs is a "beauty of the literal, of the world as it is" (273). Finally, it is not easy to locate Evans within his photographs; they seem almost authorless. Agee's part of the book, on the other hand, is intensely "rhetorical." Not only is his text made up of words, and his prose flamboyantly self-referential, but he is everywhere in *Let Us Now Praise Famous Men*, both as author and as man.[6] Agee's account of his and Evans's project constantly circles back either to himself or to the two of them. "I spoke of this piece of work we were doing as 'curious,'" he writes in the opening sentence of the book (8). In the concluding sentence he writes, "[My and Evans's] talk drained rather quickly off into silence and we lay thinking, analyzing, remembering, in the human and artist's sense praying, chiefly over matters of the present and of the immediate past . . . until at length we too fell asleep" (471). Agee's part of *Let Us Now Praise Famous Men* is also studded with his own memories and sexual fantasies, as well as his personal feelings about the three tenant farming families. Upon closer inspection, however, Evans and Agee's project can indeed be seen to be a joint one.

When Agee and Evans first arrived at their destination in rural Alabama, Evans avoided staging his photographs, and attempted to surprise the tenant farmer families into doing the same. Late in *Let Us Now Praise Famous Men*, Agee describes in detail Evans's first photographic encounter with the three families. We learn that he shot a series of images of Fred Ricketts, George Gudger, and Fred Woods on the sly, while talking with them. He then photographed other members of these three families as they returned from work, before they found time to wash or change their clothes. Evans apparently thought that the less time the tenant farming families had to put on a public face, the truer his account of them would be. These families themselves, however, experienced these "candid" photographic sessions as a violation. Agee writes that they viewed the camera as a weapon, an evil eye, and a stealer of images and souls—as a witchcraft "colder than keenest ice, and incalculably cruel" (364). He adds that he attempted to reassure the three families with his eyes that "however it must seem it [was] all right, truly and all the way all right"—that he and Evans were their friends (365). However, at the end of this section of *Let Us Now Praise Famous Men*, Agee talks about the "mutual wounding" that this initial encounter with the tenant farming families inflicted (370). He also notes in passing that love alone would be able to heal these wounds (370). "Love"—as I will explain later—is for Agee an ambiguous word; while signifying "care," in an almost Heideggerian sense, it is not entirely separable from sexuality.

Rather quickly, it seems, Evans began to make room in his photographs for his subjects' self-presentations. He waited to shoot the tenant farmers and their children until they had arranged themselves as they wished to be shot and no longer felt uncomfortable in front of the camera. He showed a similar deference in the face of their houses and belongings.[7] As Lincoln Kirstein puts it, "even the inanimate things" in Evans's photographs—"bureau drawers, pots, tires, bricks, signs"—seem "waiting in their own patient dignity, posing for their picture" (197). John Hersey writes in his Introduction to the 1988 edition of *Let Us Now Praise Famous Men* that Evans solicited the involvement of the tenant farming families because he wanted them to feel "at home in their setting, and in command of themselves" (xxviii). The continuing transparency of his photographs was presumably determined in part by a similar principle. By excluding from these images all reference either to themselves or their author, he attempted to "make room" for what they show—to provide the members of the Gudger, Ricketts and Woods family with a representational abode.[8]

As Agee makes clear in the sections of *Let Us Now Praise Famous Men* devoted to money (115–21), "at home in their setting, and in command of themselves" was precisely what the tenant farming families were not in their actual lives. Their houses and in many cases their farming implements and mules were loaned to them by their landlord, to whom they were, for all intents and purposes, permanently indentured. George Gudger, for instance, who was the head of the household in which Evans and Agee lived during their stay in Alabama, was obliged to reimburse his landlord not only with his labor and the labor of his family but also with half of his corn, cotton, and cottonseed. He was also required to pay back the rations money annually advanced to him by his landlord, with interest, as well as the cost of the fertilizer, again with interest (115–16). Since this arrangement held no matter how good a year he had, there was always the possibility that he would not earn anything from his crops.

Evans's photographs thus became a form of restitution. They made good at the level of representation the injuries that the tenant farming families suffered in reality. They did so, moreover, not merely by depicting a reality that was at odds with the tenant farmers' world, but also by installing this reality—by means of the tenant farmers' self-presentation— within that very same world. As should be clear by now, under the cover of abandoning representation for reality, Evans redefined both terms. He showed that representation can inhabit reality, and reality representation.

II

In the "Colon" section of *Let Us Now Praise Famous Men*, Agee suggests that it was also *his* desire to provide something like a representational abode for those who were without a home of their own. The metaphors that he uses to describe his project, however, are "to set" and "to give" in "regard." "[I want to] set in regard as I can the sorry and brutal infuriate yet beautiful structures of the living which is upon the [tenant farmers] daily, and this in the cleanest terms I can learn to specify" (99), he writes at one point in his text. "I will be trying . . . *to give*" things as in my "*regard they are*" (242), Agee observes at another.

We usually speak not of "setting" or "giving" but rather of "holding" something "in regard." To hold something in regard is, of course, to respect and esteem it. As I will indicate in a few pages, this last action is not extraneous to Agee's concerns; it is, on the contrary, at the center of his text. By using the verb "to give" instead of the verb "to hold" in the second of the passages I have just quoted, Agee expresses his desire to do something for the tenant farming families *in addition* to, not *instead* of, holding them in regard. He conveys his hope, that is, that he will be able to transmit or communicate the respect and esteem that he entertains for them to someone else. Unlike the action of holding something in regard, which requires only one participant, that of giving something in regard requires at least two; it originates within one psyche and completes itself within another.

As the first of the epigraphs with which Agee begins Book 2 of *Let Us Now Praise Famous Men* helps us to understand, the someone else to whom he hopes to communicate his feelings for the tenant farmers is the reader. In this epigraph, which is taken from Shakespeare's *King Lear*, the second-person pronoun figures prominently. Its referent is ostensibly "pomp," but this abstract concept finds its locus within us:

Poor naked wretches, whereso'er you are,
That bide the pelting of this pitiless storm,
How shall your houseless heads and unfed sides,
Your loop'd and window'd raggedness, defend you
From seasons such as these? O! I have ta'en
Too little care of this! Take physick, pomp;
Expose thyself to feel what wretches feel,
That thou may'st shake the superflux to them
And show the heavens more just.

Agee explicitly designates the reader as the person to whom he hopes to convey his regard for the Gudgers, the Ricketts, and the Woods in his Preface to *Let Us Now Praise Famous Men*. He also makes the completion of his project dependent upon his success in doing so. "This is only a *book* by necessity," he writes. "More seriously, it is an effort in human actuality, in which the reader is no less centrally involved than the authors and those of whom they tell" (xlviii).

The verb "to set" has a more stubbornly material significance than the verbs "to hold" or "to give." We use it to describe the congealing of concrete into a particular form; the placement of a chair in front of a desk; and the arrangement of plates and utensils on a table in preparation of a meal. It might seem a very odd word to associate with affect, which is immaterial and unlocatable. With the verb "to set," however, Agee attempts to thematize not his feelings themselves but rather the exteriorization and contextualization to which he must subject them if he is to transmit them to the reader. He speaks to the necessity, that is, of embedding his regard for the tenant farming families in what Heidegger calls a "thingly" form if he is to communicate it to the reader—of housing it in a structure that others can visit and enter.[9]

For the author of "The Origin of the Work of Art," it apparently does not matter whether this form is architectural, musical, linguistic, literary, sculptural or painterly. For Agee, however, form constitutes an enormously vexed issue. Sometimes, like Evans, he seems to believe that he will only succeed in the task that he has given himself if he manages to enclose the farmers themselves within his text. At such moments, he is radically discontent with the medium in which he works. As Alan Spiegel has recently argued, this Agee is a poststructuralist *avant la lettre*; he knows that there is no reconciling words and things (58–59). In order to incorporate the Gudgers, Ricketts, and Woods into his book, he would have had somehow to undo it as a book. "If I could do it, I'd do no writing here," he confides early in *Let Us Now Praise Famous Men*. At other times, Agee's enemy is illusionism, rather than the dissonance of language and reality. Then he rails against all forms of art-making, as well as imagination in some larger sense, and the responses for which it seems to call (11–12, 239–40).

Whether lamenting the lack of covenant between word and thing or the inevitable illusionism of art, Agee almost always expresses his preference for photography over literature. The camera is in his view "incapable of recording anything but absolute, dry truth" (234). It may even be *part* of the reality it depicts—a thing rather than a representation. Early in *Let Us Now Praise Famous Men*, he groups photographs together with "fragments of cloth, bits of cotton, lumps of earth, records of speech, pieces of wood and iron, phials of odors, plates of food and of excrement," as if all these things belonged to the same ontological order (13).

One often has the sense when reading Agee's text that the camera is an ideal to which he himself aspires.[10] If he could see in the way the camera sees, he would be able to value the tenant farming families even more, and if he could work with photography instead of with words, he would succeed in communicating this affect to the reader. At such moments, "respect" and "esteem" seem to be extensions of that objectivity for which the photographic apparatus has so often been celebrated.

In Agee's view, everything is equally visible to the camera, and equally important (245). Its lens seemingly possesses the capacity to level the cultural distinctions by means of which we privilege certain elements of a visual field over others. In addition, from the perspective of the camera no two objects are identical; everything in the world is singular. It would thus seem capable of circumventing the systems of classification through which we subsume a four-legged domestic animal to the species "dog," or a vaporous fluff of whiteness to the category "clouds." Finally, the camera as described by Agee renders evident the way in which one significant and unique thing relates to other equally significant and unique things; it shows them in their "ramified kinship and probable hidden identification with everything else" (245).

However, not a single one of Evans's photographs can be said to perform all of these functions—at least not in isolation from the spectator's gaze. Agee's own text, on the other hand, abounds in passages instantiating the kind of looking he associates with the camera. A good example is the passage in which he describes his and Evans's encounter with a little white Alabama church. When they discover it for the first time, Evans sets up his camera in front of the church, and Agee then attempts to look at that structure in the way that he imagines the photographic apparatus to be doing.

In the passage in which Agee recounts what he sees, he gives equal attention to the boards out of which the church is constructed; a "small white porcelain knob"; and a button lying in the sun. He also emphasizes the irreducible particularity of each of the church's elements. He does so, paradoxically, by emphasizing the resemblances between it and things that seem to be completely different.[11] Agee speaks, for instance, about the "wrung stance of thick steeple, the hewn wood stoblike spike at sky, the old hasp and new padlock, the randomshuttered windpowglass whose panes [are] like the surfaces of springs, the fat gold fly who [sings] and [botches] against a bright pane within" and "the little stove with long swan aluminum in the hard sober shade" (39).

Agee succeeds in looking in this way, moreover, only by accessing his own private history. He establishes the ramifying kinships that both individuate and extend what he sees through metaphors and similes, and he finds these metaphors and similes within his own memory reserve. As he puts it near the beginning of this passage, " I . . . search[ed] out and register[ed] in myself all [of the church's] lines, planes, [and] stresses of relationship" (39). In a later section of Agee's narrative, he makes even more explicit the role of memory in his writing. "I will be trying to write here of nothing whatever which did not in physical actuality or in the mind happen or appear," he vows; "and my most serious effort will be, not to use these 'materials' for art, far less for journalism, but *to give them as they were and as in my memory and regard they are* . . . the truest way to treat a piece of the past is as such: as if it were no longer the present" (242).

Agee's account of memory anticipates to an extraordinary degree what Lacan would later call a "language of desire" (see esp. Lacan 19–127). He represents it not as a temporal continuum but rather as a spatial grid, across which associations can be mapped. Like Lacan, moreover, Agee seems to understand that these relations are always libidinally established—that they come into play when the energic charge of one memory is displaced onto another, and that they work to illuminate. Finally, like Lacan, Agee links these associations to truth; he says, indeed, that they are "the 'truest' thing" about experience:

> The "truest" thing about . . . experience is . . . neither that it was from hour to hour thus and so; nor is it my fairly accurate "memory" of how it was from hour to hour in chronological progression; but is rather as it turns up in recall, in no such order, casting its lights and associations forward and backward upon the past and then the future, across that expanse of experience. (244)

By putting quotes around the word "truest," the author of *Let Us Now Praise Famous Men* might seem to call that notion itself into question, much as contemporary theorists tend to do. He might seem to suggest, that is, that there is finally no truth but the truth that there is no truth. However, this particular Agee would have had no patience with the poststructuralist axiom that since there is no accessing the real, the most genuine account of the past is the one that most fully acknowledges its fantasmatic bases. For him, representation does not spell the death of reality; rather, representation constitutes the site within which the real might be said to "realize" itself.[12]

III

In the passage where Agee describes the story about the white church, he first writes: "I helped get the camera ready and we stood away and I watched what would be trapped, possessed, fertilized, in the leisures and shyness which are a phase of all love for any object" (39). The slippage between Evans's camera and Agee's look is at its most extreme here. We cannot say whether the final phrase—"in the leisures and shyness which are a phase of all love for any object"—qualifies the former or the latter. This ambiguity is heightened by the fact that we are asked to look at the church not from the vantage-point of the camera, but rather from Agee's own fantasmatic approximation of that apparatus. His look thus explicitly emerges as the prototype for what it purports to imitate. I will take the liberty of reformulating Agee's sentence in recognition of this fact: "the human look possesses and fertilizes what it sees in the leisures and shyness which are a phase of all love for the object." Love, we recall, is the agency through which the wounds inflicted by Evans's early photographs were to be healed. It is a synonym for "to care" or to "hold in regard." What does it mean to characterize love in this way?

In one of those uncanny coincidences that point to a more profound connection, the first of the metaphors through which Agee characterizes the look is also used by John Hersey to characterize the relationship between the countless inhabitants of Hiroshima killed by the atomic bomb and the flowers that sprung up in the devastated landscape afterward (*Hiroshima* chap. 4). Those flowers, Hersey tells us in his account of post-atomic Japan, were nourished by the ashes of the dead. As a result, they grew to an unprecedented size. Marguerite Duras and Alain Resnais also evoke this metaphor in *Hiroshima, mon amour*. They suggest that the love of the French woman for the German soldier fertilizes her relation to the Japanese architect. As a result, that relationship becomes "special" and "wonderful."[13] Love functions in a similar way in *Let Us Now Praise Famous Men*; it, too, nourishes by creating relationships between the present and the past. As a result of being linked to Agee's memories, the Gudgers, the Ricketts, and the Woods undergo an enlargement; they become "famous," or what I would like to call "more-than-real."

But fertilization is not the only action that Agee associates with love. The latter also entraps and possesses what it looks at. In the section of *Let Us Now Praise Famous Men* entitled "Near a Church," Agee characterizes the second of these verbs in unequivocally negative terms. Fascinated by the exterior of the white church, and desirous of seeing the interior, he and Evans consider forcing a window open. At the moment that they do so, a black man and woman pass by. They do not speak, but their simple presence is a reproach; as Agee puts it, "they made us . . . ashamed and insecure in our wish to break into and possess their church" (39–40).

In the context of the later passage, however, the action of possessing seems to have a radically different meaning. Like the verb "to trap," which conventionally enjoys an even more negative meaning, it is linked to "leisures" and "shyness," and characterized as "a phase of all love for any object." I think that Agee is linking the words "trap" and "possess" to love because he knows this affect to be more complicated than it is generally assumed to be. To love someone, he tells us over and over again in *Let Us Now Praise Famous Men*, means to release that person into her essence. It means to let her be herself. We perform this liberating action, however, not by withholding the word that would make her our own but rather by extending it to her; not by renouncing our claim upon her but rather by imposing it. At least in this context, appropriation is the only path to freedom.[14]

We "own" another person by incorporating her into our language of desire—by making her a signifier for all that we have previously loved. Because to claim her in this way means to see her from a place from which she cannot see herself, and to confer upon her a meaning that is alien to the one she imputes to herself, it might seem the apogee of egoism. To interpret appropriation in this way, however, would be to misunderstand it radically; it would be to confuse the "I" with the "me"—to conflate the subject of desire with the ego. We speak our language of desire not by consolidating the ego but rather by withdrawing libido from it and investing it in another. And since—as Freud tells us—the ego shrinks or expands depending upon its libidinal reserve (*Group Psychology* 111–16), to "own" someone in the way I am describing here is actually to diminish it.

The meaning that another person assumes when she becomes the signifier of our passion is also not an external imposition; rather, it is always somehow solicited by that person herself. That the latter is not always aware of addressing us in this way does not discredit my claim; the appeal that travels from her to us is in the first instance formal, not psychic. It may not only remain completely unconscious but be in conflict with what she consciously demands of us. The solicitation about which I am speaking is synonymous with a person's physical being—with her color, pattern, and shape.

In my lexicon, "desire" signifies the state of ineradicable lack into which each of us is inducted at the moment that we accede to language: the lack of presence or the "here" and "now." To speak one's language of desire is thus not merely to establish signifying relations between one memory and another; it is also to symbolize this lack—to give feature and name to what we have sacrificed to meaning. When we engage in this activity, we emerge as the subjects of our own desire. More often, however, we opt to be objects—to bind our libido to those ideal images through which the ego is constituted and sustained.[15]

It is primarily at the level of our look that we speak our language of desire. We do so either by allowing our perceptual past to coalesce with our perceptual present, or—as in the case of dreams—by condensing two or more memories into a composite formation. Such signifying events do not always take the same form. Sometimes, our look functions as the agency whereby the present is subsumed to the past, and so derealized. At other times, we allow a recent memory or the perceptual present to re-embody what has been before. It is when we look in this second way that we induct what we see into a heightened reality.[16]

IV

Desire also enjoys the status I have just imputed to it in *Let Us Now Praise Famous Men*. Agee, however, adds several things to the account I have offered. He helps us to understand, first of all, that although looking is our most important way of speaking our language of desire, that faculty is frequently inflected by the other senses. The signifier of Agee's passion almost always has a tactile and an olfactory dimension. His account of the oil lamp by which he reads one night in Alabama is representative in this respect. After a detailed presentation of the lamp's visual qualities, Agee describes the oil by means of which it burns. The latter is "not at all oleaginous," he writes, "but thin, brittle, rusty feeling, and sharp; taken and rubbed between fore-finger and thumb, it so cleanses their grain that it sharpens their mutual touch to a new coin edge. . . . I run my thumb upon it and smell of my thumb, and smooth away its streaked print on the glass" (50). Hearing is also a privileged activity in Agee's text;[17] the book begins and ends with a meditation upon that sense, and it abounds with references to music. Agee tells us that it was even "written with reading aloud in mind" ("Preface" xlvii).

Agee also teaches us that the subject has more ruses than an identification with ideality for evading her *manque-à-être*.[18] At various moments in his text, he excoriates himself for his shortcomings as a writer or man and expresses his desire for humiliation or punishment.[19] These are moments of what I will henceforth call "false care"—moments at which Agee disguises an intensely narcissistic masochism as concern for another or a group of others. Although ostensibly self-sacrificing, these passages are always indicative of the kind of heroic fantasy that Freud associates with childish daydreaming ("Creative Writers").

Let Us Now Praise Famous Men provides two particularly egregious examples of false care. The first occurs at the moment in that text when, after terrifying a black man and woman who pass by the Alabama church by running after them, Agee fantasizes throwing himself flat on his face, and "embrac[ing] and kiss[ing] their feet" (42). The second transpires when he imagines saving Emma Woods from her grim fate by dying for her. The narcissistic nature of this last fantasy is indicated through the sheer number of times in which the first-person pronoun appears in the surrounding passage. "I would have done anything in the world for her," Agee writes about Emma, ". . . and all I could do . . . the very most I could do was not to show all I cared for her and what she was saying, and not to even try to do, or to indicate the good I wished I might do her and was so helpless to do" (64–65).

Finally, *Let Us Now Praise Famous Men* permits us to see that there is an ambivalence inherent in desire itself that can militate against its assumption. In Agee's writing, there is always a fine line between desire in the broadly existential sense, and sexual desire. The former is always on the verge of metamorphosing into the latter. At the moment that this metamorphosis occurs, *manque-à-être* becomes subject to a destructive logic that is antithetical to appropriation. The negative meaning that resurfaces at the site of the verbs "to trap" and "to possess," no matter how robust the attempt to banish it, marks the difficulty of separating care from Eros in *Let Us Now Praise Famous Men*.

Agee manifests an unusually acute self-consciousness about the facility with which he moves from the first of these states to the second. In a remarkable passage late in the book, he broods darkly upon what is for him the perhaps unavoidable devolution of that phase of love in which we "feed, enrich and honor" another into those "desperate battlings of the body . . .

which soon blunt and blind the delicate munificence" of the exchange (468). Many other passages in *Let Us Now Praise Famous Men* prove the truth of this observation. Agee's meticulous account of tenant farming repeatedly metamorphoses into erotic reveries, reveries that are on at least four occasions associated with violence.

The first time that care devolves into Eros in Agee's text is when he imputes to Emma Woods the desire to sleep not only with George Gudger, her sister's husband, but also with Evans and himself, as an anticipatory compensation for being consigned for the rest of her life to a solitary existence with a husband she does not love (62).[20] Since there is little in the text to corroborate Agee's notion that this is her fantasy, it cannot help but emerge as his own. He himself underscores its implicit violence. "There is tenderness and sweetness and mutual pleasure in such a 'flirtation' which one would not for the world restrain or cancel," he observes, "yet there is also an essential cruelty, about which nothing can be done . . ." (61–62).

Agee engages in another erotic reverie in the "Shelter" section of *Let Us Now Praise Famous Men*, where he again thematizes sexuality as a violation. Here, however, it is manifestly his own sexuality that is at issue. Alone in the Gudger's house, while the others work the fields, he examines the objects that they have left behind. His solitude and the heat of the house trigger a memory from early puberty—the memory of being alone in his grandfather's house, "hot" with lust. After wandering through all the rooms, rifling through the drawers, looking at books of nudes, and reading old love letters, he masturbated on every bed (136–37).

The next important passage in which Agee's sexual desire erupts into the pages of his text is perhaps the most troubling, since it involves a young girl, and since it turns upon her psychic violation. Sitting in the Gudger house for the first time, during a heavy rainstorm, he stares intensely at Louise, one of the Gudger children, until chills run through him, "a sort of beating and ticklish vacuum of the solar plexus" (400). After a short pause, he gazes at her again until he feels a warmth, and the need to protect her from himself. The new look that he now gives her in effect asks her to forgive him for subjecting her to his lust: "If I have started within you any harmful change," he attempts to communicate to her with his eyes, "if I have so much as reached out to touch you in any way you should not be touched, forgive me if you can . . ." (401). Between these lines, which occur late in the book, and the final pages of *Let Us Now Praise Famous Men*, are sprinkled a whole series of related passages.

There is nothing particularly surprising about the fact that Agee can be at one moment psychically affirming the "loveliness, strength, and defenseless mortality, plain, common, salt and muscled toughness of human existence of a girl" (469), and at the next moment be afflicted by that expense of spirit so brilliantly described by Shakespeare.[21] Care and Eros are two different dispositions of the same energy, perhaps even different "vicissitudes" of the same drive. What is perhaps more surprising is that Agee would not have edited his sexual fantasies and memories out of his account of tenant farming. What do these fantasies and memories have to do with the Gudgers, the Ricketts, and the Woods?

I believe that Agee returns again and again to the topic of sexuality not out of a pornographic imperative but rather because he can only speak his language of desire, and thereby claim the tenant farming families, by accessing the moment immediately before it finds expression. For Agee, this moment represents the most divine form that human desire can take. It is also a powerful solvent for the ego; whenever Agee succeeds in sculpting his void in the image of one of the tenant farmers, without at the same time falling over the precipice into Eros, he loses his egoic coordinates.

In an extraordinary passage near the end of Agee's narrative, he and Evans are alone on the porch of the Gudger house, listening to the call and antiphon of two distant animals. A typical chain of associations (Mozart, a line from Shakespeare, walking down streets or driving in the country, looking at African Americans) leads him to the recollection of "that delicate stage of love" when a girl "first begins, not in pleasure alone, but in a kind of fear and deep gentleness, to use her light, slow, frank hands upon your head and body." Moments like this, he tells us, at which we are poised upon the threshold of the sexual, are "unassailably beyond any meaning of tenderness and of trust, so like the opening of the first living upon the shining of the young earth in its first morning, that an overwhelming knowledge of God and of his non-existence fight in [us]." We feel it impossible, Agee adds, to look in the other's eyes for one more moment and not be so "distended by incredulous joy that [we] are of one size and ignorance and fleshlessness with space itself" (468).

Through the notion of an internal struggle between the knowledge of God and the knowledge of his nonexistence, Agee thematizes the paradoxical nature of the moment before sexual expression. On the one hand, it is spiritual in nature; in this privileged instant, the psyche altogether escapes its fleshly prison. On the other hand, it is irreducibly sensuous in nature. When we experience the expanded state of consciousness celebrated by Agee, which he consistently associates with joy, it is not to soar heavenward; rather, it is to take up residence within another body.

In the passage from which I have just quoted, Agee holds out to us the possibility of becoming one with space itself, but the entity with which he most often describes forming a corporeal identification is Beethoven's

Seventh Symphony, or Schubert's C-Major Symphony (15–16). In the first of these passages, Agee describes this ecstasy in the form of an exhortation to the reader; we, too, he tells us, should lose ourselves in the music of one of these composers. "Get a radio or phonograph capable of the most extreme loudness," Agee writes in the Preamble to *Let Us Now Praise Famous Men*,

> and sit down to listen to a performance of Beethoven's Seventh Symphony or of Schubert's C-Major Symphony. . . . Turn it on as loud as you can get. Then get down on the floor and jam your ear as close into the loudspeaker as you can get it and stay there. . . . Concentrate everything . . . into your hearing and into your body. You won't hear it nicely. If it hurts you, be glad of it. As near as you will ever get, you are inside the music; not only inside it, you are it; your body is no longer your shape and substance, it is the shape and substance of the music. (15–16)

Listening to music remains the primary paradigm for conceptualizing this recorporealization throughout the whole of *Let Us Now Praise Famous Men*. Virtually every subsequent time that Agee speaks about it, he invokes Beethoven, Bach, or Mozart. However, the passage in which the moment before sexuality emerges as the occasion for appropriation turns not upon music but rather upon the Gudger family.

Early in Agee's narrative, in the section entitled "A Country Letter,"[22] he sits writing late at night in the Gudgers's house by the light of an oil lamp. Everyone else in the house is asleep. After a meticulous description of his surroundings, Agee begins a meditation upon the narrow constraints within which we normally care. Each family, he muses, is "drawn inward within their little shells of rooms," isolated from all of the other families. "None can care," he writes, "beyond that room; and none can be cared for, by any beyond that room" (54). A terrifying account of human life under these conditions follows, beginning with one joyless act of procreation, and culminating with another. Subjectivity also becomes standardized and anonymous. "How can it be," Agee asks at the end of this bleak passage, "that a child can take on the burden of breathing; and how through so long a continuation and cumulation of the burden of each moment one on another, does any creature bear to exist, and not break utterly to fragments of nothing: these are matters too dreadful and fortitudes too gigantic to meditate long and not forever to worship" (56–57).

Although a division in the text occurs here, the word "worship" is followed by a colon[23] rather than a period, linking this passage to the next one. Despite the fact that Agee's disquisition on the family functions to depersonalize that social unit, it begins with a very specific example, the Gudger family. Now he returns to it, in all of its concrete particularity. He not only thinks about the seven bodies sleeping on the other side of the wall but is assimilated to them. In the process, he loses his bodily frame of reference, and—with it—his ego.

> [I]t is not only their bodies but their postures that I know, and their weight upon the bed or the floor, so that I lie down inside each one as if exhausted in a bed, and I become not my own shape and weight and self, but that of each of them . . . so that I know almost the dreams they will not remember, and the soul and body of each of these seven . . . as if it were music I were hearing, in voice in relation to the others . . . and as one organism, and a music that cannot be communicated: and thus they lie in this silence, and rest. (58)

This time, Agee's out-of-body experience is generative of more than the intoxicating joy with which he elsewhere associates it. It also enlarges his capacity to care. Through its agency, Agee is able to span the seemingly unbridgeable distance separating himself from the Gudgers. Through its mediation, the quotidian also becomes sacred; the mundane sounds of a sleeping family metamorphose into the music of the spheres. Finally, Agee's recorporealization makes it possible for the seven members of the Gudger family to reconnect with the desires they have been obliged to renounce. When occupying their bodies, he is able to remember what they have forgotten: their own dreams.

Significantly, it is much more the bodies of the female sleepers than those of the male sleepers to which Agee is attracted. His descriptions of Annie Mae, Emma, and Louise are infinitely more detailed and tender than those of George, Junior, Bart, and Squinchy Gudger. This will be a continuing feature of *Let Us Now Praise Famous Men*. Agee consistently cares more about the female members of the Gudger, Ricketts, and Woods families than he does about the male members. The passage in which he describes the bodies of Annie Mae, Emma, and Louise makes crystal clear that it is because of their sexuality that he finds their bodies more inviting. It is also only a few pages later that Agee will begin imagining erotic relations between himself and Emma. For the moment, however, he remains in precisely that state of erotic suspension that he will later celebrate:

> I know that they rest and the profundity of their tiredness, as if I were in each of these seven bodies whose sleeping I can almost touch through this wall. . . . Annie May's, slender, and

sharpened through with bone, that ten years past must have had
such beauty . . . and the body of Emma, her sister, strong, thick
and wide, tall, the breasts set wide and high . . . not yet those of
a full woman, the legs long thick and strong; and Louise's green
lovely body, the dim breasts faintly blown between wide shoulders, the thighs long, clean and light in their line from hip to
knee, the head back steep and silent to the floor, the chin high-
est, and the white shift up to her divided thighs. . . . (57–58)

In the passage in which Agee describes the period of time when he was free
to examine the contents of the Gudger house, he also manages to sustain
this exalted state of consciousness. After spelling out the similarities between what he is doing now and what he did when he was alone in his
grandfather's house, he emphasizes the saving differences. "There is here
no open sexual desire, no restiveness, nor despair," Agee writes, "but the
quietly triumphant vigilance of the extended senses before an intricate task
of surgery" (137). Significantly, he also characterizes the Gudger house as
a "tabernacle upon whose desecration I so reverentially proceed," a characterization that once again brings together the mundane and the divine, and
that turns upon an almost theological paradox.

In the much later section of *Let Us Now Praise Famous Men* in which
Agee first meets Louise, he is not so successful; reverence gives way to sexual desire. In the "On the Porch" section of that book, he also seems to
suggest that the "fall" into sexuality is not only perhaps unavoidable but
also frequently irreversible: "out of this violence of flesh . . . it is not possible many times to withdraw into the quieter sphere of apposition in which
the body, brain and spirit of each of you is all one perfectly focused lens and
in which these two lenses devour, feed, enrich and honor each other" (468).
However, in a series of extraordinary passages near the end of the book,
Agee works systematically backward from Eros to care.

In the passages in question, Agee recounts his sexual fantasies during
his journey back from Birmingham to rural Alabama. At the outset, these
fantasies are crudely instrumental; they provide scenarios into which presumably any female body could be slotted. "I knew I very badly wanted, not
to say needed, a piece of tail," he writes (375–76). He then remembers that
he is close to the place where he earlier saw a prostitute, and he paints a detailed mental picture of what it would be like to go to bed with her. But even
before Agee sees the prostitute, he dismisses this thought. He dispenses
equally quickly with the possibility of sleeping with Estelle, a woman with
"lavender and inappeasable eyes," who also works in the area (376).

As Agee continues driving, he sees many empty porches, a sight that precipitates in him a recollection from his childhood years of lying face down on his grandfather's porch with an erection, striking the floor with "murderous anger and despair" (380–81). A moment later, though, he recoils from these emotions; he thinks of all of those whom he has injured, and wishes that he had never been born (384). After lunch, Agee's sexual fantasies assume a much more sublimated form. Now the girl with whom he imagines himself spending time is neither a "whore" nor a "bitch," but a girl with whom he has just established "physical intimacy," and with whom "much [is] still exploratory." Their desultory caresses are often interrupted by conversation, leading to a "serious and honorable joy" (384). For the first time, Agee also creates a link between his erotic imaginings and the larger political project of *Let Us Now Praise Famous Men*. The heavy atmosphere in which he and the girl lie is permeated with a sense of the "damned south," with its "miles and hundred of miles, millions and millions of people" (383).

With the last of Agee's fantasies, he finally reaches the goal toward which he has been heading during his entire journey back from Birmingham: the moment before desire has become overtly sexual. The woman about whom he now dreams is someone with whom he shares places, music, and films, and whom he worships (390). The South looms even larger in this passage—first in the guise of the imprisoned Confederate soldiers whom Agee has seen in photographs, and who are always evoked for him by the words and music of "tramp, tramp, the boys are marching"; and then in the guise of those very different prisoners who constitute their contemporary equivalent: the multitude of "patient, ignorant, ruined" tenant farming families, with their "pitiably decorated little unowned ship[s] of home" (390–92).

As I mentioned earlier, Agee suggests that at the moment prior to sexuality we are poised equidistant between belief in God and knowledge of his nonexistence. Religious references and biblical passages abound in *Let Us Now Praise Famous Men*, almost always functioning to thematize something like a "mundane rapture" or a "quotidian divinity."[24] The passage where Agee invokes the tenant farming families in their totality appears at first to have nothing to do with these paradoxical states. However, it ends with a peroration that dramatizes for us exactly what it means simultaneously to have faith in God and to know that he does not exist:

> on the stone of this planet there is a marching and resonance of
> rescuing feet which shall at length deliver you freedom, joy,
> health, knowledge like an enduring sunlight. . . . And whether

> this shall descend upon us over the steep north crown I shall
> not know, but doubt: and after how many false deliverances
> there can be no hopeful imagining: but that it shall come at
> length there can be no question: for this I know in my own soul
> through that regard of love we bear one another. . . . (392)

There is no reason to believe that the poor will ever be given their daily bread, nor that the meek will inherit the earth, Agee tells us here. Yet these things must be. Since it is no longer possible to place any credence in Christianity's redemptive scenarios, it is love alone that gives us the strength to hope in the face of hopelessness. It is also love alone that provides the agency through which the impossible will become possible. And although the flower of love unfolds only in the radiant light of the spirit, it springs out of the same soil as the basest sexual desire. It may even grow for a while upon the same stalk.

At the end of *Let Us Now Praise Famous Men*, immediately before Agee quotes the text from which its title is drawn, he asks us to visualize two images. The first image is of Squinchy Gudger nursing in his mother's arms. His hands are "blundering at the breast blindly, as if themselves each were a new born creature, or as if they were sobbing, ecstatic with love" (441). The second image is of Ellen Woods, asleep on the porch floor. "Completely at peace," she lies on her back, with her knees "flexed upward a little and fallen apart, the soles of the feet facing" (442). The first of these word-pictures comes closer than any passage I have ever read to depicting a state of pure desire, within which all human potentiality lies dormant. Agee does not hesitate to locate this potentiality at its bodily source: the child's genitals. Lying against his mother's body, we learn, Squinchy is "many things in one, the child in the melodies of the womb, the Madonna's son, human divinity sunken from the cross at rest against his mother, and more beside, for at the heart and leverage of that young body, gently, taken in all the pulse of his being, the penis is partly erected" (442).

The second of Agee's word-pictures emphasizes not so much the radical ambivalence of desire—the diverse forms that it can take—as the hope that lies latent within in. Once again the infantile genitals occupy the center of the image, giving new meaning to Agee's cherished idea of a moment immediately prior to sexuality. "It is as if flame were breathed forth from" Ellen's vulva, he tells us, "and subtly played about it: and here in this breathing and play of flame, a thing so strong, so valiant, so unvanquishable, it is without effort, without emotion, I know it shall at length outshine the sun" (442).

NOTES

1. I draw heavily here on Freud's discussion of the super-ego in *The Ego and the Id*, 28–59.

2. I develop this argument at much greater length in Chapter 1 of my forthcoming *Flesh of My Flesh*, this time in relation to the Bush Administration and the Christian Right.

3. The names used by Agee in *Let Us Now Praise Famous Men* are pseudonyms.

4. For an account of the tortuous publication history of *Let Us Now Praise Famous Men*, see Hersey, "Introduction."

5. The 1939 edition of *Let Us Now Praise Famous Men* contained thirty-one photographs. The 1960 edition, which was authorized by Evans, contained twice as many. Evans eliminated some of the original photographs in the later edition and added many others.

6. Indeed, Barson suggests that *Let Us Now Praise Famous Men* is primarily a portrait of the artist as a young man (71–88).

7. Stott writes, "there is nothing candid in Evans's best photographs, and little of the exposé; he does not glimpse but frankly, interminably, stares. His subjects are conscious of the camera, of its manipulator, and of the unknowable audience behind it. They are not taken off guard; on the contrary, they have been given time to arrange and compose themselves for the picture. . . . Evans does not 'expose' the reality he treats, he reveals it—or better, he lets it reveal itself" (268–69).

8. Unfortunately, Evans did not always adhere to the principles I have just elaborated. He excluded from *Let Us Now Praise Famous Men* a photograph of the Gudger family that shows them as they would most want to have been seen, because it is at odds with the book's emphasis on the misery of tenant farming life. See on this point King 223.

9. In "The Origin of the Work of Art," Martin Heidegger writes: "All works [of art] have [a] thingly character. What would they be without it? . . . There is something stony in a work of architecture, wooden in a carving, colored in a painting, spoken in a linguistic work, sonorous in a musical composition. The thingly element is so irremovably present in the artwork that we are compelled rather to say conversely that the architectural work is in stone, the carving is in wood, the painting in color, the linguistic work in speech" (*Basic Writings* 145).

10. See Barson: "Often [Agee] implies a comparison between his eye and that of a camera, clearly an influence of the similarity he saw between film form and the graphic qualities of the works of Blake and Joyce" (74).

11. Lowe also notes the simultaneity of singularity and relationality in *Let Us Now Praise Famous Men* (106).

12. In the second "On the Porch" section of *Let Us Now Praise Famous Men*, Agee explicitly differentiates his realism from that of the naturalists. The work produced by the latter is at its best "never much more than documentary." Agee seeks, on the other hand, to bring reality to the level of music and poetry (237).

13. For a fuller discussion of how this metaphor works in *Hiroshima, Mon Amour*, see my essay "La passion du signifiant."

14. It is with respect to the project of appropriation that Agee finally breaks company with Evans. Whereas the writer does not hesitate to make the tenant farming families his own, the photographer entertains a more attenuated relationship to them. Stott describes Evans's project very precisely, by contrasting it not to Agee's but rather to Edward Hopper's appropriations. "A number of Evans's finest pictures . . . recall Edward Hopper's paintings of city buildings and streets," he writes. "But there is a difference. Hopper's buildings are *his*. . . . In contrast, the things of Evans' world are only lent to him for a moment. He may manage to prolong the moment indefinitely, make it transcendent; but the things are not changed thereby" (288).

15. We are vulnerable to this kind of *méconnaissance* because the ego is no ordinary object. It is, rather, as Jean Laplanche suggests (66), an object masquerading as a subject.

16. For a much fuller account of the ideas elaborated in the last few pages, see my *World Spectators*.

17. It is on the occasion of discussing hearing that Agee clarifies the relation between seeing and the other senses. "The ear," he writes near the end of *Let Us Now Praise Famous Men*, "always needs the help of the eye" (464).

18. "*Manque-à-être*" is a phrase coined by Lacan to designate the subject's lack of being, a lack that is the basis of desire.

19. Madden suggests that Agee's desire may be masochistic in some more fundamental way (34).

20. For two rather different accounts of sexuality in the text, see, on one hand, Wagner-Martin, on the other, King and Spiegel. Wagner-Martin reads *Let Us Now Praise Famous Men* as "the romance of the wearily wasted Annie Mae or her surrogates and the well-placed voyeuristic narrator, James Agee" (45). For King, the book is a family romance, but one that follows a declining rather than an ascending trajectory (229); Agee makes the Gudgers his desired family. Spiegel provides a much more detailed version of the same argument, concluding that *Let Us Now Praise Famous Men* turns upon Agee's "passionate kinship" with George Gudger.

21. See William Shakespeare, *Sonnet 129*.

22. We are, of course, the recipients of this letter. By underscoring the epistolary form of this section of *Let Us Now Praise Famous Men*, Agee once again reminds us that his book will realize itself or fail to realize itself within us.

23. For a discussion of the colon, which is Agee's favorite form of punctuation, see Ohlin 91–92.

24. Many of Agee's critics have commented on the religious references and Biblical quotations in *Let Us Now Praise Famous Men*. See, for instance, Wensberg 417–18; Kramer 38; Madden 38–40; Lowe 103–104; Moreau 191–97; and Stott 308–309. For the most part, these critics do not take account of the ambivalence of Agee's relationship to Christianity. Walker Evans is instructive on this topic. Agee's Christianity was "a punctured and residual remnant," he writes in "James Agee in 1936"; it was an "ex-Church, or non-Church matter. . . . All you saw of it was an in-grained courtesy, an uncourtly courtesy that emanated from him towards everyone" (*Let Us Now Praise Famous Men* xliv).

WORKS CITED

Agee, James, and Walker Evans. *Let Us Now Praise Famous Men*. 1941. Boston: Houghton Mifflin, 1988.

Barson, Alfred T. *A Way of Seeing*. Amherst: U of Massachusetts P, 1972.

Freud, Sigmund. *Civilization and its Discontents. The Standard Edition of the Complete Psychological Works of Sigmund Freud*. Vol. 21. Trans. James Strachey. London: Hogarth, 1961. 64–145.

———. "Creative Writers and Day-Dreaming." *The Standard Edition*. Vol. 9. London: Hogarth, 1959. 141–53.

———. *The Ego and the Id. The Standard Edition*. Vol. 19. London: Hogarth, 1961. 12–66.

———. *Group Psychology and the Analysis of the Ego. The Standard Edition*. Vol. 18. London: Hogarth, 1955. 69–143.

Hanisch, Carol. 1968. "The Personal Is Political." *Women and Social Movements in the United States, 1600–2000*. <http://scholar.alexanderstreet.com/download/attachments/2259/Personal+Is+Pol.pdf?version=1>.

———. "New Introduction" to "The Personal Is Political." 2006. *Women and Social Movements in the United States, 1600–2000*.

Heidegger, Martin. *Basic Writings*. Ed. David Farrell Krell. San Francisco: Harper, 1977.

Hersey, John. *Hiroshima*. New York: Vintage, 1989.

———. "Introduction." *Let Us Now Praise Famous Men*. Boston: Houghton Mifflin, 1988. xx–xxxviii.

King, Richard. *A Southern Renaissance: The Cultural Awakening in the American South, 1930–1955*. New York: Oxford UP, 1980.

Kirstein, Lincoln. "Introduction." *American Photographs*. Ed. Walker Evans. New York: Museum of Modern Art, 1988.

Kramer, Victor A. *James Agee*. Boston: Twayne, 1975.

Lacan, Jacques. *The Seminar of Jacques Lacan, Book VII: The Ethics of Psychoanalysis, 1959–60.* Trans. Dennis Porter. New York: Norton, 1992.

Laplanche, Jean. *Life and Death in Psychoanalysis.* Trans. Jeffrey Mehlman. Baltimore, MD: Johns Hopkins UP, 1976.

Lowe, James. *The Creative Process of James Agee.* Baton Rouge: Louisiana State UP, 1994.

Madden, David. "The Test of a First-Rate Intelligence: Agee and the Cruel Radiance of What Is." *James Agee: Reconsiderations.* Ed. Michael A. Lofaro. Knoxville: U of Tennessee P, 1992. 32–43.

Moreau, Geneviève. *The Restless Journey of James Agee.* Trans. Miriam Kleiger and Morty Shiff. New York: William Morrow, 1977.

Nietzsche, Friedrich. *The Gay Science.* Trans. Walter Kaufmann. New York: Vintage, 1974.

———. *The Will to Power.* Trans. Walter Kaufman and R. J. Hollingdale. New York: Vintage, 1968.

Ohlin, Peter H. *Agee.* New York: Ivan Obolensky, 1966.

Saussure, Ferdinand de. *Course in General Linguistics.* Trans. Wade Baskin. New York: McGraw Hill, 1966.

Stott, William. *Documentary Expression and Thirties America.* New York: Oxford UP, 1973.

Silverman, Kaja. "La passion du signifiant: La notion d'apparence dans *Hiroshima, Mon Amour.*" *Où en est l'interprétation de l'oeuvre d'art?.* Ed. Régis Michel. Paris: Ecole Nationale Supérieure des Beaux-Arts, 2000. 125–50.

———. *World Spectators.* Stanford: Stanford UP, 2000.

Spiegel, Alan. *James Agee and the Legend of Himself.* Columbia: U of Missouri P, 1998.

Tindall, George Brown. "The Lost World of Agee's *Let Us Now Praise Famous Men.*" *James Agee: Reconsiderations.* Ed. Michael A. Lofaro. Knoxville: U of Tennessee P, 1992. 21–31.

Wagner-Martin, Linda. "*Let Us Now Praise Famous Men*—and Women: Agee's Absorption in the Sexual." *James Agee: Reconsiderations.* Ed. Michael A. Lofaro. Knoxville: U of Tennessee P, 1992. 44–58.

Wensberg, Erik. "Celebration, Adoration and Wonder." *The Nation.* 191 (1960): 417–18.

6

F. Scott Fitzgerald, Psychobiography, and the Fin-de-Siècle Crisis in Masculinity

This chapter argues that a crucial task for psychoanalysis in the new millennium is to help us chart the complex dialectic between psychic and historical levels of determination in the making of expressive culture. I take as my subject the missed encounter between modernist studies and the new histories of American manhood. My central question is why these fields have yet to engage each other fully, despite their evident disciplinary overlap—despite, for example, the increased recent interest in masculinity among scholars of modernism,[1] or the fact that historians of manhood have shown the years 1890–1920 (i.e., something like the modernist period) to be *the* crucial years in the emergence of modern gender (Bederman; Kimmel; Rotundo). This failure to meet has resulted, I suggest, from a methodological lacuna. Or, to put the case more affirmatively: the divide can be fruitfully overcome only by pursuing a specific methodological opening, namely, the development of a revitalized and historically sensitive psychobiography.

In pursuing this opening, my guiding assumption is that a method attentive to the deepest strata of psychic life is crucial to generating demonstrable claims about the relation between historical forces and aesthetic innovation. Such an assumption runs counter to the recent tendency among historically minded literary critics to read historical forces off the surface of literary texts—as if those forces were immediately legible as causes within the literature itself. My argument, in contrast, is that if we are to do more than assert a causal link between (for example) modernist formal inventions and the social transformations that gave rise to modern manhood—if we are to trace the mediations by which those transformations were experienced subjectively, and at the requisite psychic depth for them to shape aesthetic choices—we need to turn our attention to an author's childhood and infantile experiences.[2] We need to understand those transformations not just as

147

objective, external phenomena that impacted adult authors whose gender identity was fully formed. We must try as well to examine how they were lived by a given author's parents, as well as how this parental experience was (often unconsciously) communicated to the child.

If those of us committed to the study of literature continue to desire psychoanalysis, then, it is perhaps because only psychoanalysis can illuminate those nodal points of experience where the psychic and the social intersect. It can do so, however, only if we at once reassert the validity of psychobiographical inquiry and avoid the pitfalls of conventional psychobiography. The method I have in mind aims precisely to counter the solipsism and crude ahistoricism by which conventional psychobiographers have tended to find the same story (classically, an Oedipal one) in all their chosen subjects. The story I tell does indeed have its Oedipal turns; but I assume throughout that the Oedipus complex becomes the dominant way of forming gender only under specific historical conditions—conditions that, as John Demos has shown, were precisely those prevailing in the United States at the turn of the twentieth century. A psychobiography of the kind I propose will thus of necessity be one alert to the ways in which its own procedures are implicated in the story it tells. Because the theory and techniques of psychoanalysis were developed by analyzing *modern* men and women, psychoanalysis may be a theory of modern subjectivity rather than of subjectivity as such, and its mode of inquiry may be best suited to analyzing the phenomena of modernity.

This is emphatically not to claim that psychoanalysis is just a "discourse" that produces a deep subjective realm that it then appears to discover—and that it helps unwittingly to discipline. Such a view has become fashionable in recent efforts to historicize psychoanalysis.[3] Those subscribing to it tend to see each intelligible instance of an era's speech (art, advertising, social theory, advice manuals) as equally performative and identically coercive; they equate the description of new phenomena with their ideologically motivated "invention," deriding all of an era's self-understandings as pretenses of objectivity, forms of illegitimate transcendence that assume an "outside" to the history one inhabits. For me, this way of seeing things is politically crippling and phenomenologically falsifying. One need not be forced to choose between seeing historical actors as completely immersed in discursive currents for which they serve as unwitting conduits or seeing them as transcending their historical embeddedness to reflect upon their moment from a chimerical outside. One can choose, instead, to believe that people inhabit their historical moment in specific ways that, depending on their particular histories and capacities, enable them to conceptualize and reflect critically upon some phenomena while fully immersing them in others. On this understanding, psychoanalysis is perhaps best understood as both a product of its inventor's era (with some of its attendant blindnesses) *and* a uniquely trenchant theory for understanding the forms of subjectivity—especially of gendered subjectivity—of that very age.

My analysis focuses on F. Scott Fitzgerald partly because the feminist scholarship concerning him is in a sufficiently embryonic stage that merely tracing his biography in gendered terms is of considerable interest.[4] The case of Fitzgerald also, however, speaks in unusually compelling ways to the specific desire for analysis to which I have referred. It helps us see with special clarity the benefits of fusing historical and psychoanalytic methodologies. The benefits in this case include above all the unearthing of an *ambivalence* toward modern manhood that the historians of manliness rarely record, and the exposure of an historical density to "private" fantasy that even the most sophisticated psychological readings of Fitzgerald's life have obscured.

I

I begin with three historians of manhood: E. Anthony Rotundo, Michael Kimmel, and Gail Bederman. The first two authors weave broadly compatible narratives about the emergence of modern manliness in the United States, narratives similar enough to allow me to describe them together. I then proceed to complicate those histories by examining the distinctiveness of Bederman's account, before suggesting that her exploration, too, has limits that my reading of Fitzgerald seeks to redress.

The crucial elements uniting the stories told by Rotundo and Kimmel are that masculinity was *in crisis* during the years 1890–1920, and that this crisis is best understood as a breakdown in gendered roles that had been largely naturalized in the middle years of the nineteenth century. Manhood, these writers argue, was characterized in that earlier period by a dynamic interplay of qualities that would separately have been seen as a gendered binary. On one hand, to be a man meant to "make oneself" in the capitalist marketplace—to achieve economic autonomy, self-sufficiency, and ownership of productive property. The qualities that enabled such success were an aggressive assertiveness and competitive vigor thought of as innately male. Successful manhood was imagined, in other words, as the realization of an instinct for domination that was rooted in the male body, the expression of which could alone enable the economic and psychic autonomy so central to American conceptions of success.

On the other hand, this aggressive competitiveness was viewed with suspicion for its threat to social cohesion. Were it given full rein beyond the manly sphere of work, the dominative will would make social order impossible to maintain. This instinct therefore had to be countered by a range of softer virtues—moral compassion, self-restraint, emotional sensitivity. These virtues were thought to be natural to women in the same way that competitive aggression was thought of as natural to men; the virtues could, in fact, be transmitted to men only by women in the domestic sphere. The division of spheres was in this sense a mechanism for socializing men by giving them a place to develop their compassionate interiors—to cultivate feelings and dispositions that could not be safely indulged at work but were indispensable to men's roles as citizens, fathers, and husbands. "From this point of view, the social fabric was torn every day in the world and mended every night at home," writes Rotundo. "Men's sphere depleted virtue, women's sphere renewed it" (23).

Around the turn of the century, however, a range of developments disturbed the relative stability of this division. These developments primarily had to do with transformations in the economic sphere, where the promise of autonomous self-making was increasingly thwarted by a monopoly capitalism that reduced men to dependents in a large bureaucratic structure. "The number of salaried, nonpropertied workers (virtually all white-collar) multiplied eight times between 1870 and 1910," writes Rotundo. "Twenty percent of the total male work force was white-collar by 1910" (248). This new kind of employment "offered neither autonomy nor ownership of productive property" (Gorn 192). The result was a sense of dependence and disempowerment that many men described as emasculation. Kimmel quotes one observer, for example, who claimed that to "'put a man upon wages is to put him in the position of a dependent' . . . that the longer he holds that position, the more his capacities atrophy and 'the less of a man . . . he becomes.'" Similarly, Anthony Ludovici "observed the 'steady degeneration of men' brought on by the 'spectacle of men working at tasks which every woman knows she could easily undertake'" (84).

According to Kimmel and Rotundo, American men responded to this disempowerment in a range of related ways. There was, to begin with, a discursive shift: a move away from the term *manhood*, defined in opposition to *boyhood*, and toward the term *masculinity*, defined in opposition to *femininity* (Kimmel 119–20; Bederman 16–18). What made one a man now was less that one had successfully grown up than that one was persuasively not a woman—a shift that bespoke a heightened need to police the borders between male and female identities. (This need was intensified by first-wave feminists' claims to the sexual and political rights of men, as well as by the emergence of gay subcultures whose "inverts" raised the visible specter of a "femininity" lurking in all men [Cott; Chauncey].) More significant than this discursive transformation was a wholesale revaluation of the gendered division of spheres so central to nineteenth-century life. The "civilizing" virtues of women were now rewritten as emasculating dangers, forces that turned boys into sissies and threatened the "feminization of American culture." Men, accordingly, sought to expel the "feminine" within them while embracing as positive traits those attributes that had previously been coded ambivalently—primal male force, instinctual vitality, aggression, and bodily strength (Rotundo 253–55). This response entailed in part what Kimmel has called "the consumption of manhood": the vicarious identification, through sports and other consumer activities, with older, more autonomous, and more artisanal forms of manhood. For "Just as the realm of production had been so transformed that men could no longer anchor their identity in . . . the market, [they] created new symbols, the consumption of which 'reminded' men of that secure past, evoking an age before identity crises, before crises of masculinity—a past when everyone knew what it meant to be a man and achieving one's manhood was a given" (Kimmel 119).

It is precisely here, however, that the difference between Bederman's account and these others is instructive. Her book seeks in part to problematize the assumption behind the statement just quoted—namely, that the manhood fin-de-siècle men had difficulty achieving was *the same* as that "given" to those preceding them. Rather than treating manhood as a transhistorical category inhering within male bodies, that is, Bederman sees it as an effect of ideological processes that render it both fluid and internally contradictory (10). Her goal in defining it in this way is to emphasize that the meanings of manhood are subject to constant rearticulation; while the various significances a society ascribes to it are inescapable for any given individual at any given historical moment, the social need to reiterate those meanings, along with the way some of them collide with each other, opens a space for agency and change. It thus becomes possible to think of people as actively engaged in reshaping manhood: as self-consciously altering or challenging previously hegemonic definitions by highlighting aspects normally hidden by the naturalizing effect of gender ideology.

In the United States at the turn of the twentieth century, Bederman contends, those who effected this redefinition did so especially by articulating questions of manhood with those of white supremacy. Challenges to middle-class male legitimacy and power led many middle-class men and women to "turn . . . from gender to a related category—one which, like gender, also linked bodies, identities, and power. That category was race" (20). This articulation of gender with race generated two distinct kinds of strategies for buttressing male power. On one hand, those engaged in this process sought to distinguish the manhood of whites from that of "primitives" by emphasizing the white man's greater degree of cultural and technological complexity, his capacity for bodily and emotional self-restraint, and the highly developed differentiation between him and white women. This in essence naturalized the Victorian version of "manliness" as moral control over one's dominative instinct, as well as the nineteenth-century division of gendered spheres. On the other hand, "middle-class white men adopted a contrasting strategy and linked powerful manhood to the 'savagery' and 'primitivism' of dark-skinned races, whose *masculinity* they claimed to share" (22). Here the "darker races," precisely because they had yet to feel the softening effects of "civilization," provided an invaluable resource for the middle-class remaking of manhood, embodying a projected virility that could save white men from the unmanning effects of their own civilization.

This is one of several examples of the contradictions entailed in suturing male dominance to white power through the discourse of civilization. Part of what makes Bederman's book appealing is that its concepts are flexible enough to explain a variety of such responses, to link yet differentiate a range of efforts to effect this crucial suture. And yet her treatment has limits as well. The crucial one for me concerns the claim that there was not really a "crisis" in masculinity during these years at all. Bederman's rationale here is that manhood is always in a state of being more or less rapidly remade, and that the concept of a "masculine crisis" tends to obscure this insight. "[T]o imply that masculinity was in crisis," she writes, "suggests that manhood is a transhistorical category or fixed essence that has its good moments as well as its bad, rather than an ideological construct which is constantly being remade" (11). Such a statement is useful in that it warns us against a priori assumptions about what a given society means by "manhood." The problem is that it excludes the possibility of *ever* talking about a crisis in masculinity. It suggests that to be historical about gender is to speak of it as "constantly being remade" *instead of* "in crisis." Such an insistence makes it hard to distinguish between historical moments in which the need to remake manhood is widely felt with affective urgency and those in which it is not. One need not have recourse to an "essence" of manhood in order to make this distinction; all one has to do is demonstrate that a period's dominant definition of manhood felt exceedingly tenuous and hard to achieve, for historically specifiable reasons, and for a sufficiently large group of people. Bederman's own account amply demonstrates that this was true in the period that concerns her.

I want to make it clear that I am not especially invested in "crisis" as a historical category. Though I'm inclined to think it useful in this context, Judith Allen is right to note that we rarely speak of a "crisis in femininity," and this fact alone suggests a need for caution when employing the term. My point is rather that, in what counts as one of the best discussions of manhood in this period, an emphasis on discursive structures has obscured the affective dimensions of historical experience, absorbing internal, psychic conflict into discursive contradictions—and this despite a professed desire to reclaim the capacity of individuals to shape those very discourses. I'm suggesting that if we are to account for how and why individual men came to feel both the need and ability to remake manhood, we need a model more attentive to their internal lives while still responsive to the social and discursive materials out of which those lives are made. We need, in short, a method that traces the mutually shaping interaction between social/discursive forces, on one hand, and psychological interiority, on the other. In turning now to F. Scott Fitzgerald, my chapter seeks to model such a method.

II

One thing one finds in discussing Fitzgerald is that neither the problem of his gender formation nor that of his creative vocation can be understood outside the category of loss. In a late autobiographical sketch entitled "Author's House" (1936), he had this to say: "Three months before I was born my mother lost her other two children, and I think that came first of all . . . . I think I started then to be a writer" (*Afternoon* 184).[5] The statement suggests, at the most basic level, the foundational role of loss in the author's sense of his creative life. It indicates that loss was for him an originary and generative principle, the womb not merely of individual acts of expression (i.e., his novels and stories) but of artistic identity itself. Loss is here what "came first of all," the event that "started" Fitzgerald as a writer, and from this there follows the corollary proposition that without loss there would have been, for Fitzgerald, no impulse or reason to create at all.

The loss the passage mentions is of a quite peculiar kind, however. Not a deprivation directly experienced, it is, rather, one that Fitzgerald thinks of himself as *inheriting*. In this sense, one could think of it in the terms Mitchell Breitwieser has suggestively used, as a kind of psychic specter or ghost, a transgenerational "phantom" transmitted unconsciously to Fitzgerald by his mother, Mollie.[6] The young Fitzgerald incorporated this phantom through a process of receptive intuition; he internalized it as if by osmosis in that early, preoedipal intimacy with the mother that approximates to fusion, and which in this case entailed the "sharing" of a loss Fitzgerald had never experienced. The result was that his earliest self cohered around an absence he could not grieve. "[T]he inheritor of mourning is doomed to an inability to mourn," writes Breitwieser, ". . . not because the requisite knowledge is too awful but because it is nonexistent" (50). The self can never fill the hole of a loss that isn't its own; it can neither relinquish what it has not known nor find an adequate substitute for it, and Fitzgerald would thus come to spend his life in a doomed search to cure the insatiable longing produced by internalizing someone else's grief.

This process seems in Fitzgerald's mind to have had an incipient gender component. He speaks of his sisters' death as a loss for his *mother*, not his parents. His internalization of her grief thus suggests the incorporation of a mournful femininity at the very core of his being—a sense of being mixed up with his mother that was intensified by the intrusive protectiveness she exhibited toward him as a child.[7] Furthermore, as Jonathan Schiff has recently shown, Fitzgerald's parents conceived of him partly as a substitute for the dead sisters, in ways that led them unconsciously to associate him with—and to encourage him to try and be—a girl (40–41). It does not seem fortuitous in this context that the parents named him after not only a distant (if famous) ancestor (Francis Scott Key, composer of "The Star Spangled Banner") but also after one of his dead sisters. Louise *Scott* Fitzgerald was reincarnated as Francis Scott Fitzgerald, who always insisted on being called "Scott" (Schiff 31) as though at once to defend against the feminizing dangers of "Francis" ("Frances") *and* to pay a tacit homage to the girl whose loss was entombed within him.

What emerges from this preoedipal history is thus a set of psychic associations that link up creativity, unmournable loss, and an internalized femininity. This cluster of associations would profoundly shape Fitzgerald's later negotiations of his manhood and of the crisis in masculinity. It led him to identify with and even romanticize the forms of manhood displaced by that crisis, forms that seemed to him both lyrically "feminine" and marked by indelible loss. To see exactly how this worked, we need to turn to the Oedipal moment within his gender formation—that is, to his relationship with his father. The central interest of this relationship is that it served as a site of interchange between the psychic and the social; it's the place, that is, where Fitzgerald consolidated his gender identity by internalizing *both* the emergent imperatives of modern masculinity *and* a particular, highly idiosyncratic version of the residual manhood it displaced. This internalization produced a collision between two incompatible forms of manhood—a conflict that was grafted onto and exacerbated by Fitzgerald's earlier, preoedipal internalization of a mournful femininity.

The manhood Fitzgerald's father represented is crucial to understanding this process. As the author's biographers have often noted, Edward Fitzgerald was a belated son of the Southern aristocracy;[8] he embodied what we might call a *regionally specific* ideal of manliness that differed significantly from the national manhood described by Bederman, Kimmel, and Rotundo.[9] This regional ideal was both aristocratic and genteel; it included forms of aesthetic languor and an identification with failure and defeat; it entailed affective responsiveness and an emphasis on self-expression, which came together in the Civil War tales that Edward loved to tell his son; and it stressed the importance of sartorial elegance, breeding, and good manners, especially the charms of conversation and of social grace and ease (Le Vot 5–7, 9, 12, 17; Donaldson 1–10).

This aristocratic manhood was marked by inadequacy from the start. Edward's identification with it made him a social and gendered anachronism, since, as a number of scholars have indicated, the "softer" attributes of the Southern gentleman came increasingly to be seen as effete within an emergent gender order that valued uninhibited expressions of virility (Kimmel 76–77). Because the money in Fitzgerald's family came from his mother's side, moreover, the air of antebellum unmanliness was fused to an explicitly financial inadequacy. This inadequacy was intensified and more fully gendered by the shape of Edward's professional career. For here, the father fell victim to the structural transformations whose effects on masculinity in this period I have described. Having earlier moved West in the name of his economic self-making, he lost his wicker-furniture manufacturing business to a financial panic in 1898. He then became a salaried employee—a salesman—for one of the new national corporations, Procter & Gamble. In 1908 he lost this job as well, and moved with his wife and son back to St. Paul, Minnesota, where they were supported by Mollie's family for the rest of their lives.

That Fitzgerald felt his father's professional losses keenly is clear from an interview he gave in 1936. "Dear God," he remembers thinking on the day Edward was fired by Procter and Gamble, "please don't let us go to the poorhouse; please don't let us go to the poorhouse." In the same interview, he recalls returning the money his mother had just given him to go swimming (Bruccoli and Bryer 296). Such anxiety and self-sacrifice would perhaps be natural in a child of any age. But from a psychoanalytic perspective, the dates of these professional reversals are especially significant.

The first (the failure of the furniture business) occurred when Fitzgerald was around two-and-a-half years old—roughly when the Oedipus complex, as a sociofamilial mechanism for producing gendered identity, is at least provisionally "resolved." This is the age at which the male child becomes for the first time a "masculine" child, completing the familially directed labor of negotiating his difference from the mother and identifying himself with the father. The second reversal happened when Fitzgerald was twelve; this, according to Freud and others, is the period of the child's emergence from latency, the moment at which he acquires a newly genital organization of sexual drives and a heightened awareness of the meanings of genitality—of the social requirement to become a father, to engage in the social reproduction of fatherhood.

Edward's *social* humiliations, in other words, took place at moments when the norms of modern gender formation required of his son a particularly focused *psychic* identification with the father. The demands of Oedipal development would thus have raised the specter of a specific double bind: internalizing the father as psychic "imago" meant also internalizing his social emasculation. Or, to put this slightly differently: at the very moments when Fitzgerald's masculinity was Oedipally consolidated through identifications with Edward, he also internalized a knowledge of that manhood's social unviability. He incorporated a lost, *residual* manhood and internalized it as *inadequate*. His father's manhood, having thus been internalized, would henceforth be figured as a lost ideal to which one should aspire, at the same time that Fitzgerald subjected it to deidealization and disparagement.

We can see this pattern in action by turning to an unpublished essay Fitzgerald wrote on the occasion of his father's death. Here he recalls with fondness the responsibility that Edward took in forming his identity. The central lesson of this formation concerned the importance of honor and "good manners," and it's clear from this essay and other comments that this was a lesson Fitzgerald valued. ("[M]y generation of the radicals and breakers-down," he wrote in 1938, "never found anything to take the place of the old virtues of work and courage and the old graces of courtesy and politeness" [Turnbull 50].) Nevertheless, the essay goes on to indicate that his father "came from tired old stock with very little left of vitality and mental energy." It thereby figures the paternal legacy as meager, inadequate, marked by depletion—beneficent gentility bleeding insensibly into emasculated enervation. This latter association is further confirmed by comments Fitzgerald made elsewhere, most notably in the interview mentioned a moment ago. There he said that the day Edward lost his job he "came home . . . a completely broken man. He had lost his essential drive, his im-maculateness of purpose. He was a failure the rest of his days" (Bruccoli and Bryer 296). To call his father a "failure" here is to judge him against the emergent style of manhood, which valorized this "essential drive" as the expression of a primordial maleness whose loss ("He had lost . . .") would leave one defenseless against the emasculating dangers of modernity.

I'm suggesting we read the ambivalence toward Edward's manhood as equally Fitzgerald's ambivalence toward his own, and that this second ambivalence resulted from the specific confluence of psychofamilial and so-cial forces in his gender formation. By clinging to his aristocratic style of masculinity as an alternative both to "Marketplace Manhood" and to the emergent code of virility; by embodying this alternative masculinity as something lost, romantic, and lyrically appealing; by "failing," finally, in precisely the ways and at precisely the moments he did, Edward be-queathed to his son a manhood that Oedipal exigencies and filial feeling led Fitzgerald to internalize but that was at the same time "etched" with social failure and "defeat."[10] The solution Fitzgerald fashioned to this dilemma drew on the preoedipal inclinations and dynamics analyzed earlier. Before turning to that solution, however, it's important to fold in a further com-ponent of the manhood Fitzgerald internalized in this process.

III

That component is, of course, race. This is a category that could hardly fail to play a part in Edward's Southern manhood and, therefore, in the con-struction of his son's.[11] André Le Vot has written elliptically about the rel-ative *in*significance of the category in Fitzgerald's ideal of Southernness. The South of Fitzgerald's imagination, he writes, was "Not Faulkner's vi-olent and bloody Deep South, but the more cultivated and cosmopolitan, more delicate and romantic land of Poe, the moderate South of Maryland, in its origin a royal land, a Catholic land. In a sense he associated the North with the masculine spirit of conquest, the South with the feminine spirit of a quest for happiness, more intuitive, closer to things, to the elements" (9). I take the primary distinction here to be between that part of the South in which the commitment to slavery was fierce and socially constitutive and that in which it was less fierce and socially marginal or incidental. There is undoubtedly some truth in this distinction. Maryland was, indeed, a rela-tively moderate slaveholding state in the years of Edward's upbringing, at least in the sense that a comparatively small number of its families owned slaves. But Edward's identification with the South's Lost Cause is likely to have meant that his notions of manhood included some sense of white supremacy, of white entitlement to the "culture" and "cosmopolitanism" made possible by black labor.

Certainly, Fitzgerald's writings on the South suggest not merely that his attachment to Southernness included an adherence to some troubling racial stereotypes, but that this adherence was intertwined with his gender ambivalence in crucial ways. Here, for example, from his 1920 story "The Ice Palace," is a passage set in the Georgia countryside:

> [Sally Carrol] let the savory breeze fan her eyes and ripple the fluffy curls of her bobbed hair. They were in the country [where] tall trees . . . sent sprays of foliage to hang a cool welcome over the road. Here and there they passed a battered negro cabin, its oldest white-haired inhabitant smoking a corncob pipe beside the door, and half a dozen scantily clothed pickaninnies parading tattered dolls on the wild-grown grass in front. Farther out were lazy cotton-fields, where even the workers seemed intangible shadows lent by the sun to the earth, not for toil, but to while away some age-old tradition. . . . And round the drowsy picturesqueness, over the trees and shacks and muddy rivers, flowed the heat, never hostile, only comforting, like a great warm nourishing bosom for the infant earth. (51–52)

Without analyzing this passage at length, we can at least note that the "pickaninnies" and other "inhabitants" of the "negro cabins" are narratively reduced in it to mere landscape, to one among many elements making up the "picturesque" quality of the scene; and that this "drowsy," "comforting" picturesqueness intimates a recovery of fusion with the mother: "a great warm nourishing bosom for the infant earth." These latter details confirm Le Vot's sense that the South had a specifically feminine association for Fitzgerald—indeed, in this case, a maternal one. That association can be read back into Fitzgerald's biography to suggest that he thought of his father's Southern manhood as in some ways beneficently feminine, in touch with something elemental and maternal that Fitzgerald wanted to value. At the same time, the idealization of elemental femininity is here bound up with a casual racism by which African Americans are equally elementalized, assimilated to an "infant earth" enveloped by the atmospheric "bosom" of the South.

This casual, nostalgic racism could at times give way to something more ominous. In a letter to Edmund Wilson upon returning from his first trip to Europe, for example, Fitzgerald wrote:

> The negroid streak creeps northward to defile the nordic race. Already the Italians have the souls of blackamoors. Raise the bars of immigration and permit only Scandinavians, Teutons, Anglo Saxons + Celts to enter. . . . I think it's a shame that England + America didn't let Germany conquer Europe. It's the only thing that would have saved the fleet of tottering old wrecks. My reactions were all philistine, anti-socialistic, provincial + racially snobbish. I believe at last in the white man's burden. We are as far above the modern Frenchman as he is above the negro. Even in art! (Bruccoli 46–47)

Part of the interest of this passage concerns the way it participates in the pervasive discourse of civilization to which Bederman has called attention. As in the previous quotation, Fitzgerald associates blackness with the primordial and elemental. Here, however, he imagines these less in terms of an idyllic proximity to nature/the mother than as an irresistible, primitive force that sweeps through and "defiles" all races "above the negro," depriving them of civilized culture ("Even art!") and threatening them with total destruction ("the . . . tottering old wrecks" must be "saved").

This process appears to have little to do with the spread of people of African descent. It seems, rather, as if Fitzgerald encountered in Europe a breakdown of social hierarchies (he responds "anti-socialistically") and an artistic/cultural decline that in his mind *meant* racial blackening: a creeping of the "negroid streak" that gives presumably once-white Italians "the souls of blackamoors." Within this logic, the loss of cultural or civilized prominence is itself a degeneration into blackness, since civilization is by definition non- or even anti-"negroid" ("Scandinavians, Teutons, Anglo Saxons + Celts"). It (civilization) is also, moreover, vigorously anti-feminine. The Teuton's masculine, martial intervention could alone have halted the universal spread of this primitivizing blackness. The association of blackness with femininity is thus at once here less explicit and more disturbing than before: to be civilized is to be Nordic, Teutonic, Anglo Saxon, Scandinavian—*and also to be robust and manly.* The civilized are those whose masculine prowess enables them to dominate, expel, or staunch the threat of a feminine and primitivizing darkness.

This tension between a romanticized and an abjected view of blackness suggests an adult ambivalence toward racial otherness that mirrors Fitzgerald's ambivalence toward femininity and the "feminine" masculinity he associated with his father—and with himself. Where did this racial ambivalence come from? How was it psychogenically related to the familial influences I have analyzed and, especially, to the Oedipal relations that mediated for Fitzgerald his first encounter with the crisis in masculinity?

To answer these questions, it's helpful to return once more to the language of Fitzgerald's essay on his father. There he writes that Edward "came from tired old stock with very little left of vitality and mental energy." His father's masculine decline, in other words, is in part a racial matter: a question of his "stock" being "tired," of his bearing the legacy of a lost genetic "vitality"—terms that Bederman has amply shown to have had racial connotations in this period. By linking this formulation to the passages just analyzed, one might then speculate the following: the manhood bequeathed to Edward Fitzgerald embodied for his son not merely an ideal of civilized manhood but an ideal of civilized white manhood. This manhood relied implicitly on "dark" racial others to define itself. It was, however, by Edward's generation, a manhood socially marked by failure: enervated, emasculated, ontologically used up. In the newly emergent culture, this enervation had a racial as well as a gendered significance. To internalize Edward as paternal ideal was thus to incorporate not just a gendered but also a racial inadequacy. Or, to put this another way: in being feminized in his son's eyes, Edward was also "blackened." His loss of masculine "drive" and "purpose" signaled the degeneration of his "stock" and a concomitant incapacity to resist the defilement his son would later describe: to prevent the creeping into his whiteness of the "negroid streak" that slavery, with its rigid racial hierarchies, had sought to keep at bay.

Fitzgerald's ambivalence toward his father's manhood was thus intensified along two axes. Having internalized the modern standard of virility and linked that virility to "Nordic" supremacy, he felt a defensive need to repudiate the racial implications of his paternal inheritance. But because he also associated Nordic vigor with a capitalist modernity hostile to the "feminine" demands of the imagination, the taint of race would become one sign of a *beneficent* masculine failure to meet the gendered demands of modernity. Such a failure could alone propel authentic self-expression, since it endowed one's expressive acts with the lyrical, elegiac beauty that Fitzgerald thought of as intrinsic to failure. The author would thus repeatedly figure the form of manhood he wished to embody as feminine, lyrically expressive, and/or racially impure, while fusing these to a male identity whose misogyny and racism stood in some tension with this figuration. The contradictions entailed in this fusion led him to see the identity he yearned for as lost yet deferred into an indeterminate future—a strategy that drew on his preoedipal sense of a loss no object could fill, and one that posed considerable problems to his adult efforts to claim a masculine identity through marriage and work.

IV

It would not be hard to trace the persistence of this pattern throughout Fitzgerald's life; I offer such an account in the longer work from which this essay is drawn. Here, however, for reasons of space, I want to focus on the period of greatest interest and most severe psychic conflict, the one beginning in the summer of 1918 and ending in April 1920. This period encompassed the two key events of Fitzgerald's early adulthood: his choice of vocation and his marriage. Both of these required of him the assumption of a self definitively masculine and white. Work and marriage were, moreover, the central institutions through which such white manhood had traditionally been consolidated.

But the social transformations described earlier had rendered these arenas problematic. The domain of work had increasingly become one that men experienced as emasculating; it was neither sufficiently affirming of male skills and bodily strength nor sufficiently rewarding of competitive ruthlessness. Nor was the increasingly diversified (if still racist) workplace any longer an arena in which white men could reliably confirm their racial superiority. Marriage, meanwhile, proved less and less able to confirm men's sense of male dominance and entitlement. The economic and political gains of feminism placed new strains on men's intimacies with women, not least of which were the need to negotiate the dangerous appeal of female sexual autonomy and the wound to chivalry and paternalism caused by women's claims to equality.

These strains in the arenas of work and intimacy meant that Fitzgerald's initiation into manhood was coincident with his most directly personal experience of the crisis in masculinity. His response to and mechanism for dealing with that crisis were by this time highly developed. They entailed an ambivalence toward both the lost and the newly emergent forms of male identity; the fantasmatic construction of a manhood combining elements from both forms; and the deferral of that manhood's assumption in light of its psychic unviability. The need to manage his adult initiation through social institutions in crisis, however, seems to have led to a significant shift in these strategies as well. With very few exceptions, his letters and diary entries from this period abandon the effort to grapple directly with the problem of racial identity.[12] It's as if the gendered pressures of these events absorbed his psychic energies so fully that race and the problem of "darkness" dropped out of his psychic field altogether. The analysis I offer thus focuses primarily on the categories of gender and sexuality. I shall also be concerned, however, with the way race continued to shape Fitzgerald's choices at a deeper, more unconscious level. This unconscious determination is most evident in his choice of love object (a Southern belle) and in the content of some of his earliest writings (stories of the Civil War).

Taking his courtship and marriage first, then: Zelda appears to have figured for Fitzgerald as a female counterpart to the fusion of emergent and residual gender elements he sought in his own identity. At one level, she was a traditional Southern belle. Her father, Anthony Sayre, was an unprosperous but solidly respectable Southern gentleman, a judge in the Alabama Supreme Court and a son of the Montgomery *Post*'s longtime editor; her mother, Minnie, was the daughter of a Kentucky senator, and had herself dabbled in literary and artistic pursuits before her marriage. Zelda was raised by both her parents to cultivate beauty and charm—but little else; her education didn't extend beyond high school, since the goal of a young Southern woman in this period was not to *do* much of anything but to be the object of multiple adoration. By the time Fitzgerald met her in the summer of 1918, she had largely achieved this goal. Her fame as a beauty had spread through much of the respectable society of Alabama and Georgia, and she was in more or less constant demand at local dances and fraternity parties.

But partly with the encouragement of her mother, Zelda combined these conventionally feminine attributes with the more daringly reckless and "unfeminine" qualities of a New Woman. She drank and smoked and bobbed her hair; she had premarital sexual affairs (one account has her losing her virginity at fifteen); she made it clear that she wouldn't play the role of submissive housewife; and she displayed a fierce independence that she herself characterized as an "inclin[ation] toward masculinity" (qtd. in Meyers 46)—an inclination that on occasion led Fitzgerald, and more often his biographers, to accuse her of a selfishness that ruined him. The respectability of her family seems to have served as a buffer for this unconventionality, which may well have ruined the reputation of girls less socially protected. Thus, Zelda would later write, in the extraordinary autobiographical novel she composed while institutionalized in the 1930s, that she (or her fictional alter ego) was "two simple people at once, one who wants to have a law to itself and the other who wants to keep all the nice old things and be loved and safe and protected." What enabled this combination was the social position of her father, whose impervious respectability led her to describe him as a "living fortress" (qtd. in Mizener 75 and Meyers 44).

The combination of a residual femininity with a modern, antipatriarchal defiance was appealing to Fitzgerald in part because it spoke to both sides of his quarrel with modern manhood. Zelda's conventionally feminine characteristics inspired in him a desire for possession, a yearning to demonstrate his manhood by attaining her. Thus, for example, he wrote from New York in February, 1919: "DARLING HEART AMBITION ENTHUSIASM AND CONFIDENCE I DECLARE EVERYTHING GLORIOUS THIS WORLD IS A GAME AND WHILE I FEEL SURE OF YOU[R] LOVE EVERYTHING IS POSSIBLE I AM IN THE LAND OF AMBITION AND SUCCESS AND MY ONLY HOPE AND FAITH IS THAT MY DARLING HEART WILL BE WITH ME SOON" (Bruccoli 22). Fitzgerald wrote this telegram while trying to find a way to support Zelda financially, and the yoking together of courtship and professional aspirations is crucial. To "feel sure of [Zelda's] love" is to feel limitless "confidence" and "enthusiasm," to be certain of one's capacity for manly success in the field of work. Indeed, Fitzgerald's anticipation of possession leads him to experience his professional efforts as nothing more than a "game": something at once pleasurable ("everything glorious") and capable of being mastered ("Life was something you dominated if you were any good," as he put it later [*Crack-Up* 69]). "Everything is possible . . . in the land of ambition" precisely because of this implicit "faith" that Zelda will soon be his, as work and the prospect of heterosexual possession mutually reinforce each other to allow for an anticipatory experience of accomplished manhood.

But Zelda's emancipation as a New Woman, especially her sexual independence, complicated this desire for possession by giving her a "masculine" autonomy to which Fitzgerald played the role of a passively "feminine" object of desire: the one who desperately wanted to be chosen, rather than the one doing the choosing. The dearth of his letters to her that survived from this period make this claim harder to demonstrate directly. It's clear, however, that Fitzgerald's early identification with femininity was called forth and embodied in strikingly literal ways during his first forays into romance. In a well-known incident at Princeton, for example, he dressed up as a showgirl for a student play he wrote called *The Evil Eye*, even posing for a remarkably convincing publicity still. Back in St. Paul the following winter, he went further: "He [tricked] the students at the local college by attending a school ball, in company with his old friend Gus Schurmeier, dressed in his Princeton transvestite costume. The illusion was perfect. Young men crowded around the unknown belle, the daring and provocative beauty who shocked people by smoking in public and lifting her skirt to pluck a compact from her garter" (Le Vot 52; see also Mellow 36–37). The evident delight he took in these incidents, along with the persuasiveness of his gendered mimicry, suggests an identification with femininity whose depth had its roots in the earliest psychic dynamics discussed earlier.

The testimony of college girlfriends, moreover, indicates that Fitzgerald lacked a conventionally masculine ardor, despite the avidity with which he pressed his suit. He wasn't "a very lively male animal," Fluff Beckwith would later write; he lacked the qualities that made other men "aggressive and physically satisfying" (qtd. in Donaldson 52). Though this statement alone may not quite indicate a feminine gender identification, in combination with his cross-dressing experiments it suggests a fairly strong urge toward a conventionally feminine passivity and lack of sexual initiative.

More direct evidence can be gleaned from Zelda's letters to Fitzgerald during their courtship. At one point, in discussing their arguments, she describes herself as "very calm and masterful" and him as "emotional and sulky"—a description whose inversion of traditional gender roles would have been clear to both of them, and one that indicates something more ominous than playful for Fitzgerald in such inversion (Bruccoli and Duggan 51). Another letter complains that Fitzgerald writes to her too eagerly and too often, and so suggests his anxious uncertainty and need to have her demonstrate her love. Finally, in the same letter, Zelda chides her lover for repeatedly writing to her that he now understands why they used to keep princesses locked up in towers (Bruccoli and Duggan 43). The complaint suggests that Fitzgerald's experience of disempowerment at Zelda's hands had led him to fantasize a toxic possession that would reestablish conventional hierarchy and put Zelda back in her "proper" place.

But whether Fitzgerald experienced his identification with femininity as pleasurable or dangerous, what's key is that Zelda's own gender ambiguity intensified his contradictory impulses toward virile manhood, on one hand, and a more passive, emotionally expressive, and receptive masculinity, on the other. This contradiction was no doubt disquieting; to satisfy one aspiration within it would be to thwart the other, at least in the binarized gender universe to whose dictates Fitzgerald was subject. Even as he experienced his courtship as urgent to his sense of manliness, then, he also came to feel it as something whose consummation had to be deferred if he was to avoid an outbreak of open hostilities between contradictory impulses.

The mechanism for securing this deferral was in fact ready to hand. It consisted, first, in the fact that Zelda was herself a substitute object, that Fitzgerald found in her a replacement for the recently lost Ginerva King. (Ginerva was Fitzgerald's first real love, and he experienced her, too, as fundamentally unattainable, an almost transcendental object whom he loved primarily in absentia and whose worth was enhanced by the male rivalries in which she entangled him.) There was in this sense built into his love an element of disconsolate distance from the start, by which Zelda would never be the object he most wanted. More crucially, the qualities that made her an attractive replacement also facilitated Fitzgerald's urge to forestall full possession of her. Both her autonomy as a New Woman and her class position as a belle rendered her distant, aloof, and inaccessible in a way that made her seem lost from the start and led Fitzgerald to desire her through an identification with her numerous suitors. "Proxy in passion," he once wrote in his *Notebooks;* and again: "Feeling of proxy in passion strange encouragement" (nos. 466 and 765). Fitzgerald wanted Zelda in part *because* other men courted her. His experience of these men as "proxies" suggests that he sought to resolve his gendered conflict by identifying with the role of lover, that his love was as much about "being" (the socially privileged and implicitly white male lover) as "having" (the socially desirable and equally white beloved). If the man here is he who gets the girl, then getting *this* girl by way of *these* proxies would be for Fitzgerald a way to approximate a manhood at once aristocratic and white.

But because to get the girl was in this case to activate an urge to be possessed by her, the proxies served the further function of keeping such manhood at a deferred remove. For to love by proxy is, of course, to defer one's love interminably. It's to interpose another between the male self and its incarnation no less than between that self and its object, and so to guarantee that such love be structured not just by the beloved's unavailability, but also by a distance between the lover and "himself" (the ideal to which he aspires). The place where Zelda and Fitzgerald first met thus has a deeply symbolic significance: a country club dance in Montgomery, Alabama, is precisely the sort of place where Zelda would be coveted by men whom Fitzgerald could idealize, since those men would embody the aristocratic whiteness, gentility, and status so central to his idealizations—and yet so hard for him to assume except in the mode of mimetic rivalry.

It's unsurprising in this light that Fitzgerald orchestrated his courtship in such a way that he both literally lost Zelda before getting her and came to experience her as unattainable, even after their marriage. In June 1919, after an apparent misunderstanding in which Zelda sent Fitzgerald a note addressed to a rival suitor, he caused a scene that led her to break off their engagement. Scribner's acceptance of *This Side of Paradise* in September 1919 emboldened him to try again, and the couple were soon engaged once more and, within a year, married. The breakup left a permanent class and gendered scar, however. Years later, when he recounted this period of his life in "The Crack-Up," Fitzgerald described the romance as follows:

> It was one of those tragic loves doomed for lack of money, and one day the girl closed it out on the basis of common sense. During a long summer of despair I wrote a novel instead of letters, so

it came out all right, but it came out all right for a different person. The man with the jingle of money in his pocket who married the girl a year later would always cherish an abiding distrust and animosity toward the leisure class—not the conviction of a revolutionist but the smouldering hatred of a peasant. In the years since I have never been able to stop wondering where my friends' money came from, nor to stop thinking that at one time a sort of *droit de seigneur* might have been exercised to give one of them my girl. (*Crack-Up* 77)

The description has an extraordinary resonance in the context I've been elaborating. If some of its details are factually questionable, it nevertheless speaks a deep truth about Fitzgerald's romantic experience. Most basically, this truth has to do with the intertwining of manhood with loss and the insistence upon deferred possession. Fitzgerald may at one level have "got the girl" in marrying Zelda. But at another, the passage suggests that it was not really *he* who got her, nor did he really get *her* at all. It wasn't he who got her because the person who married her was "a different person" from the one who wanted her in the first place; loss of the beloved thus turns out to entail a self-loss so profound that, if one survives it, he does so only through a reconstruction that leaves the old self irrevocably behind. And Fitzgerald didn't really "get her" either, since his marriage was haunted from the start by a sense of masculine and class illegitimacy; if money and loss have made Fitzgerald a different man altogether, they've thereby enabled a romantic possession that isn't his by right—and so the girl never properly belongs to him, but could at any time be "taken" by one of the socially powerful rivals from whose attention, as we have seen, she derives her value in the first place.

V

This pattern of deferred identity and thwarted possession brings us finally to the problem of Fitzgerald's vocation. The history of that problem is the history of his repeated efforts to exit the structure of deferred incarnation by claiming a masculine identity through work. But it is also the history of his sense that the only viable identity for him was one that fused the modern, virile style of manhood with a residual gentility and receptivity that the modern world disparaged as feminine. The place of writing within this pattern can be grasped by turning again to the "Author's House" essay with which I began.

There, Fitzgerald speaks of his sisters' death as one explanation for what "made [him] a fiction writer instead of a fireman or a soldier" (*After-noon* 184). The statement suggests that becoming a writer was a way to achieve manhood without conforming to its conventional contours. The writer is, at one level, on a continuum with the "fireman" and the "soldier," since the very juxtaposition of terms is intended to indicate a relation between work and male identity. But the writer is also *less* manly than the others in that (1) his work does not entail the physical courage and risk that define these professions as masculine; and (2) the writer's identity as writer is founded in that history of loss and incorporated femininity to which the reference to his sisters points. Fitzgerald would thus come, throughout his career, to experience his creativity as something feminine dwelling within him. "[L]ike most people whose stuff is creative fiction there is a touch of the feminine in me," he wrote to Mencken (Bruccoli and Duggan 421). Or again, to Laura Guthrie: "I don't know what it is in me or that comes to me when I start to write. I am half feminine—at least my mind is" (qtd. in Kerr 406). Both statements suggest that writing was a way to keep faith with his earliest identifications with femininity, as well as with that part of his father that the crisis in masculinity had led him to see as feminine.

Fitzgerald's ambivalence toward this femininity was, however, profound. His efforts at conventional work in this period can be seen in part as efforts to escape that internal "touch of the feminine"—and thus to delay the full assumption of writing as a vocation. I want to focus on what seems to me the most decisive of these endeavors. Between February and July of 1919, Fitzgerald wrote advertising copy for the Barron Collier agency in New York. His purpose in doing so was in part to achieve the kind of financial success that would enable him to support Zelda. Fitzgerald's letters convey next to nothing about how this job felt to him, but a later essay called "My Lost City" (1932) indicates the complexly gendered meanings that this excursion into the workforce held for him, as well as the conflicted character of Fitzgerald's attempt to negotiate those meanings.

The essay suggests, to begin with, that the work intended to facilitate heterosexual manhood had also an emasculating effect. "When I got back to New York in 1919 I was so entangled in life that a period of mellow monasticism in Washington Square [i.e., a life like the one Edmund Wilson was leading] was not to be dreamed of. The thing was to make enough money in the advertising business to rent a stuffy apartment for two in the Bronx. The girl concerned had never seen New York but was wise enough to be rather reluctant" (*Crack-Up* 25). This need to work to support "the girl" colors Fitzgerald's entire experience of New York in this period. The work itself is on one hand imagined as masculinizing; that is, it's contrasted with the implicit unmanliness of "mellow monasticism": with a manhood defined by celibacy and a homosocial withdrawal from the demands of heterosexual life, rather than direct "entangle[ment]" in it. But on the other hand, the terms in which this opposition is couched make it clear that the manly option is in some central ways unmanning. Not only does Fitzgerald figure the marriage this work would enable as stultifying and unglamorous ("a stuffy apartment for two in the Bronx"); he also thinks of the need to work in the name of love as an emasculating constraint rather than something freely chosen. From 1917 to 1919, he writes, "I had as much control over my own destiny as a convict over the cut of his clothes" (*Crack-Up* 25). This is in part a reference to his life as a soldier—as a man subject to the beck and call of a government at war. But given that it also encompasses his stint of work in New York, the statement suggests that Fitzgerald experienced his work for love as a loss of male freedom, a compromising of his autonomy and his capacity to choose, and that his yearning for "mellow monasticism" represents a masculine protest against this unmanning form of labor.

We need then to grasp in what this protest—this longing for "mellow monasticism"—consists. In another portion of the essay, Fitzgerald links it directly to the life Wilson was leading in New York around 1916, a life whose symbol was the Greenwich Village apartment Wilson shared with two other men: "[T]hat night, in [Wilson's] apartment, life was mellow and safe, a finer distillation of all that I had come to love at Princeton. The gentle playing of an oboe mingled with city noises from the street outside, which penetrated into the room with difficulty through great barricades of books; only the crisp tearing open of invitations by one man was a discordant note" (*Crack-Up* 25). Once again, desirable manhood is figured here as a fusion of hard and soft elements. The masculine meaning of the apartment is clear when Fitzgerald describes it as a "man's world" (*Crack-Up* 24)—a world of men to which he escapes in response to the loss of a girlfriend. But this "man's world" is defined less by virility or success in business than by elegance, sensuous receptivity, and bohemian refinement. The elegance includes a capacity to mute the busy solicitations of the world while keeping one responsive to them. And it includes the promise of sallying forth into that world, the tearing open of invitations suggesting an experience of being wanted amid the glamor and sparkle of metropolitan life.

When we add that the life here imagined is also the life of the writer, the full extent of Fitzgerald's ambivalence becomes clear. Conventional work enabled for him the assumption of heterosexual masculinity, but both it and the life to which it gave access felt unmanning and constrictive to him. The life of the writer then offered an escape from these constraints through the camaraderie of a "man's world," but the monasticism thus produced was at once devitalized and dangerously homosocialized by the lack of hetero-sexual entanglement. How can we be surprised, in this light, if Fitzgerald tried to escape the circle by combining both aspirations—by imagining writing itself as the route to a financial success that would enable the as-sumption of heterosexual manhood? In a letter to Max Perkins (his editor at Scribner's) dated August 16, 1919, he wrote: "I asked you the chances of an early publication [for *This Side of Paradise*] . . . because I want to get started both in a literary and financial way" (Bruccoli 30–31). Or again, in his re-sponse to Perkins's acceptance letter: "Would it be utterly impossible for you to publish the book Xmas—or say by February? I have so many things dependent on its success—including of course a girl—not that I expect it to make me a fortune but it will have a psychological effect on me and all my surroundings" (Bruccoli 32). Both passages indicate that Fitzgerald fused the writer with the man of business in an effort to resolve the contradictions I've described. Both suggest that his desire for success as a writer was inti-mately bound to a desire for wealth, since wealth alone would save him from the dreariness of the two-room flat in the Bronx, enabling him to gain pos-session of Zelda and then to approximate, in New York proper, the life of refined homosocial community through which he aspired to escape the unmanning dangers of marriage and conventional work.

The precariousness of such a solution is not far to find, however. It's perhaps most evident in Fitzgerald's extraordinarily gendered ambivalence toward writing as a *profession*—that is, toward writing for money. For if, on one hand, the financial success achieved through writing enabled him to marry Zelda—and so to achieve at least momentarily a secure sense of het-erosexual manhood—on the other, he repeatedly equated supporting Zelda with the need to write "trash" for money, and with a profligate waste of his talent that's the psychic equivalent of castration. Thus he wrote to his daugh-ter toward the end of his life: "When I was your age I lived with a great dream. The dream grew and I learned how to speak of it and make people lis-ten. . . . Then the dream divided . . . when I decided to marry your mother . . . even though I knew she was spoiled and meant no good to me. . . . I was a man divided—she wanted me to work too much for *her* and not enough for my dream" (Bruccoli 363). Zelda becomes here not the glittering prize and proof of true manliness but the stultifying agent of distraction and inner di-vision, whose need for money compromises one's manhood and deforms the creative impulse. Because of her, Fitzgerald must work for money instead of

his "dream"; because of her, he's "a man divided" between an authentic artistic impulse and a need to prostitute that impulse in the name of popular success—in the name of what he calls, in another letter, the "trashy imaginings"
of his short stories (Bruccoli 67). That he indeed felt this as prostitution is
clear from a range of comments he made. "[T]he *Post* now pay the old whore
$4000. a screw," he wrote in 1929. "But now its [*sic*] because she's mastered
the 40 positions—in her youth one was enough" (Bruccoli 167). Or again,
from the *Notebooks*: "My mind is the loose cunt of a whore, to fit all genitals"
(no. 1390). The beneficent femininity of creative aspiration is here rewritten
as something monstrous once it's subordinated to the profit motive—a sub-
ordination that Fitzgerald and his friends consistently associated with
Zelda.[13] Though the second statement lacks the reference to popular writing
contained in the first, it's linked to the other by the figure of the whore and
in fact suggests that Fitzgerald experienced the profession of art as an abjectly
feminizing receptivity through which one conforms to the exploitative demands of the capitalist marketplace. The "mind" stretches and makes itself
"fit" the "genitals" of those who pay for its services.

The dangers of such a feminization drove Fitzgerald ever further into
the male camaraderie that was the other side of his compromise—and that
of course produced problems of its own. "If it wasn't for Zelda I think I'd
disappear out of sight for three years," he wrote in 1921. "Ship as a sailor or
something + get hard—I'm sick of the flabby semi-intellectual softness in
which I flounder with my generation" (Bruccoli 48). The escape from
Zelda's devitalizing powers, which the passage links to the modern world's
"flabbiness" and "semi-intellectual softness," is here a "hardness" derived
from the company of men and the vigorous masculine demands of sailing.
Or, to put it slightly differently, Fitzgerald imagines the return to a pre-
modern, artisanal homosocial community as a counter to the debilitating
effects of a capitalist marketplace that renders one soft, flabby, lacking in
intellectual vigor. The dangers of this escape, however, emerge almost immediately. In a notebook entry that apparently refers to Hemingway, he
wrote: "I really loved him, but of course it wore out like a love affair. The
fairies have spoiled all that" (no. 62). The male camaraderie of a writerly
community seems here to risk a homosexualization that requires one to
break the bonds of male love, and the "fairy" then stands as both a projection of Fitzgerald's yearnings for homosocial connectedness, *and* as the figure for a modernity that codes those yearnings unacceptably unmanly.

From here it's only a very short step to the expressions of effemino-
phobia and homophobia that pepper Fitzgerald's notebooks and letters. He
at one point in the 1920s planned an article entitled "Sissy America"; it was

to deal with the feminizing effect of American women on American men, or, as he put it in a wire to his agent, Harold Ober: "A BITTER AND SENSATIONAL ARRAINMENT [*sic*] OF CONTEMPORARY MALE" (qtd. in Mellow 299–300). More seriously, his comments about gay men range from the chilling statement that homosexuality is "natures [*sic*] attempt to get rid of soft boys by sterilizing them" (*Notebooks* no. 1320) to relatively crude homophobic dismissals[14] to more explicit denunciations of gay writers as bad writers *because* gay: "He had once been a pederast and he had perfected a trick of writing about all his affairs as if his boy friends had been girls, thus achieving feminine types of a certain spurious originality. (See Proust, Cocteau and Noel Coward.)" (*Notebooks* no. 905). If writing for money and for Zelda emasculates you by dividing you into an authentic (male) artist and a writer of (feminine) "trash," this statement suggests that male camaraderie raises equally serious problems for creativity. Precisely because such camaraderie poses the danger of homosexualization ("The fairies have spoiled all that"), and because that homosexualization is felt as an assumption of abjected femininity, Fitzgerald attacks the "touch of the feminine" at the heart of his creative life. He seeks, that is, to expunge the feminine component of creativity by projecting it onto gay men, while simultaneously recoding it as the deformation of a prior, more masculine expressive impulse—a deformation that produces work whose "spurious originality" consists in the mixture of masculine and feminine that Fitzgerald valued yet found so disturbing.

The result of the double danger I'm describing is that the effort to fuse writing to financial success is marked by the same forms of deferral I have traced in other domains. "One by one my great dreams of New York became tainted," Fitzgerald writes in "My Lost City." "The remembered charm of [Wilson's] apartment faded with the rest when I interviewed a blowsy landlady in Greenwich Village. . . . I wandered through the town of 127th Street, resenting its vibrant life; or else I bought cheap theatre seats at Gray's drugstore and tried to lose myself for a few hours in my old passion for Broadway. I was a failure—mediocre at advertising work and unable to get started as a writer. Hating the city, I got roaring, weeping drunk on my last penny and went home. . ." (26). The ellipses at the end are Fitzgerald's, and they matter. Immediately following them comes his description of a magical, triumphal return to New York "six months later," when "the offices of editors and publishers were open to me, impresarios begged plays, the movies panted for screen material." Elided in such a description is the entire history of courtship I've described: a broken engagement, a first novel, a marriage. Elided is the fact that Fitzgerald responded to his professional "emasculation" in the same way he responded to losing Zelda: that is, by writing a novel. And in this case as in that one, the apparent success that followed from that response entombed within it the loss and perpetual deferral of a sense of accomplished manhood. Fitzgerald thus goes on to say about his triumphal return to the city: "I remember riding in a taxi one afternoon between very tall buildings under a mauve and rosy sky; I began to bawl because I had everything I wanted and knew I would never be so happy again" ("My Lost City" 28–29). Loss is here so fully lodged at the heart of romantico-professional triumph that the very experience of present accomplishment opens onto vistas of desolation. For one enchanted transitory moment, Fitzgerald seems to have experienced himself as the kind of man he wanted to be—a man precariously holding together his conventionally masculine and feminine elements. But that experience of integration receded repeatedly into a past he would spend his life trying to recover, while also projecting it as an impossible, unattainable future identity.

NOTES

I'm grateful to Bill Anthes, Pamela Barnett, Allen Miller, Seth Moglen, Mark White, and SUNY Press's anonymous reviewers for suggestions that improved this essay. Thanks as well to the College of Liberal Arts at the University of South Carolina and the Research Center in American Modernism at the Georgia O'Keeffe Museum for funding that helped me complete it.

1. On Pound, see DuPlessis; on Stevens, Lentricchia; on Eliot, Koestenbaum; on Fitzgerald, Kerr; and on Faulkner, Porter.

2. Izenberg argues persuasively for such an approach in the context of Continental modernism.

3. See Pfister, who nowhere engages Freud's writings in the body of his chapter, but whose terms indicate that he thinks psychoanalysis shares the blame for "inventing" "the psychological."

4. Among Fitzgerald's biographers, Donaldson and Le Vot are most alert to issues of gender.

5. Schiff shows that the second-eldest sister in fact died ten months before the author's birth (21).

6. Breitwieser derives the idea of a transgenerational phantom from Abraham and Torok.

7. Mellow (11–24) and Schiff (35–36) note the author's maternal identifications.

8. Edward "was descended . . . from Scotts and Keys who had been in this country since the early seventeenth century and had regularly served in the colonial legislatures" (Mizener 1).

9. Le Vot makes a compelling case for seeing the opposition between East and West in Fitzgerald's fiction as a redaction of a more primal opposition between North and South (9).

10. The phrase "etched by defeat" is Le Vot's (13).

11. On race in Fitzgerald, see Nowlin and Gidley.

12. The problem of race erupts instead in Fitzgerald's fiction of this period (Nowlin 418–25).

13. For assertions by Fitzgerald's friends that Zelda was bad for his work, see Mellow 143.

14. See especially *Notebooks* nos. 1241 and 386.

WORKS CITED

Abraham, Nichola, and Maria Torok. "Notes on the Phantom: A Complement to Freud's Metapsychology." *The Shell and the Kernel: Renewals of Psychoanalysis.* Trans. Nicholas Rand. Chicago: U of Chicago P, 1994. 171–76.

Allen, Judith A. "Men Interminably in Crisis?: Historians on Masculinity, Sexual Boundaries, and Manhood." *Radical History Review* 82 (2002): 191–207.

Bederman, Gail. *Manliness and Civilization: A Cultural History of Gender and Race in the United States, 1880–1917.* Chicago: U of Chicago P, 1995.

Breitwieser, Mitchell. "Fitzgerald, Kerouac, and the Puzzle of Inherited Mourning." *Symbolic Loss: The Ambiguity of Mourning and Memory at Century's End.* Ed. Peter Homans. Charlottesville: UP of Virginia, 2000. 43–61.

Bruccoli, Matthew J., ed. *F. Scott Fitzgerald: A Life in Letters.* New York: Touchstone, 1995.

—— and Jackson R. Bryer, eds. *F. Scott Fitzgerald in His Own Time: A Miscellany.* Kent, OH: Kent State UP, 1971.

—— and Margaret M. Duggan. *Correspondence of F. Scott Fitzgerald.* New York: Random, 1980.

Cott, Nancy F. *The Grounding of Modern Feminism.* New Haven, CT: Yale UP, 1987.

Chauncey, George. *Gay New York: Gender, Urban Culture, and the Making of the Gay Male World, 1890–1940.* New York: Basic, 1994.

Demos, John. "Oedipus and America: Historical Perspectives on the Reception of Psychoanalysis in the United States." *Inventing the Psychological: Toward a Cultural History of Emotional Life in America.* Eds. Joel Pfister and Nancy Schnog. New Haven, CT: Yale UP, 1997. 63–78.

Donaldson, Scott. *Fool for Love: A Biography of F. Scott Fitzgerald.* New York: Dell, 1983.

Douglas, Ann. *The Feminization of American Culture*. New York: Knopf, 1977.

DuPlessis, Rachel Blau. "Propounding Modernist Maleness: How Pound Managed a Muse." *MODERNISM/Modernity* 9.3 (2002): 389–405.

Fitzgerald, F. Scott. *Afternoon of An Author: A Selection of Uncollected Stories and Essays*. Princeton, NJ: Princeton UP, 1957.

———. *The Crack-Up*. Ed. Edmund Wilson. New York: New Directions, 1945.

———. "Death of My Father." Appendix. *The Apprentice Fiction of F. Scott Fitzgerald*. Ed. John Kuehl. New Brunswick, NJ: Rutgers UP, 1965.

———. "The Ice Palace." *The Short Stories of F. Scott Fitzgerald: A New Collection*. Ed. Matthew J. Bruccoli. New York: Scribner, 1989.

———. *The Notebooks of F. Scott Fitzgerald*. Ed. Matthew J. Bruccoli. New York: Harcourt Brace Jovanovich, 1978.

Gidley, Mark. "Notes on F. Scott Fitzgerald and the Passing of the Great Race." *American Studies* 7.2 (1973): 171–81.

Gorn, Elliott J. *The Manly Art: Bare-Knuckle Prize Fighting in America*. Ithaca, NY: Cornell UP, 1986.

Izenberg, Gerald. *Modernism and Masculinity: Mann, Wedekind, and Kandinsky through World War I*. Chicago: U of Chicago P, 2000.

Kerr, Frances. "Feeling 'Half-Feminine': Modernism and the Politics of Emotion in *The Great Gatsby*." *American Literature* 68.2 (1996): 405–31.

Kimmel, Michael S. *Manhood in America: A Cultural History*. New York: Free Press, 1996.

Koestenbaum, Wayne. *Double Talk: The Erotics of Male Literary Collaboration*. New York: Routledge, 1989.

Lentricchia, Frank. "Patriarchy Against Itself: The Young Manhood of Wallace Stevens." *Critical Inquiry* 13.4 (1987): 742–89.

Le Vot, André. *F. Scott Fitzgerald: A Biography*. Trans. William Byron. New York: Doubleday, 1983.

Mellow, James R. *Invented Lives: F. Scott and Zelda Fitzgerald*. Boston: Houghton Mifflin, 1984.

Meyers, Jeffrey. *Scott Fitzgerald: A Biography*. New York: HarperCollins, 1994.

Mizener, Arthur. *The Far Side of Paradise: A Biography of F. Scott Fitzgerald*. Boston: Houghton Mifflin, 1949.

Nowlin, Michael. "F. Scott Fitzgerald's Elite Syncopations: The Racial Make-up of the Entertainer in the Early Fiction." *English Studies in Canada* 26 (2000): 409–43.

Pfister, Joel. "On Conceptualizing the Cultural History of Emotional Life in America." *Inventing the Psychological: Toward a Cultural History of Emotional Life in the United States.* Eds. Joel Pfister and Nancy Schnog. New Haven, CT: Yale UP, 1997. 17–59.

Porter, Carolyn. "*Absalom, Absalom!*: (Un)Making the Father." *The Cambridge Companion to William Faulkner.* Ed. Philip M. Weinstein. Cambridge: Cambridge UP, 1995. 168–96.

Rotundo, E. Anthony. *American Manhood: Transformations in Masculinity from the Revolution to the Modern Era.* New York: Basic, 1993.

Schiff, Jonathan. *Ashes to Ashes: Mourning and Social Difference in F. Scott Fitzgerald's Fiction.* Selinsgrove, PA: Susquehanna UP, 2001.

Turnbull, Andrew, ed. *The Letters of F. Scott Fitzgerald.* New York: Dell, 1963.

Part Four

Psychoanalysis and Sexuality

7

Desiring Death

Masochism, Temporality, and the Intermittence of Forms

DOMIETTA TORLASCO

> *To the bow is given the name of life and its work is death.*
> —Heraclitis, *Fragments*

I

"Vienna, 1957"—time and space made specific, punctual, firmly interlocked in a caption that appears on the screen at the beginning of Liliana Cavani's film *The Night Porter*. The Soviet troops have recently departed, and the city where the bourgeoisie portrayed by painter Gustav Klimt had once lived an elegant and decadent life is now trying to forget, to wipe out the past and begin again as if, only in the previous decade, a crime against the human community had not been committed.[1] The inscription is superimposed on the visual track as a man in black coat, hat, and umbrella enters the front door of the Hotel zur Oper. He is Max (Dirk Bogarde), the night porter and messenger of the guests' secret desires, and the threshold he has just crossed is the limen between clean, translucent, orderly streets and shadowy, labyrinthine, intensely private interiors—the chronological time of public discourse and the convoluted time of memory. I return to *The Night Porter* now, in a time of severe cultural and political crisis, to linger on this threshold between linear and circular time and, mindful of its historical implications, ask the question of death and desire—of desire as desire for death. In what way is the desire of analysis that the film both portrays and performs, that is, dramatizes in the diegesis and enacts in the relationship to the spectator, also inevitably a desire for death? Does the threshold between chronology and convoluted time that Max has traversed also function as the limen between a domain in which death "takes place," realizing itself as annihilation of the other, and a sphere in which death is simultaneously "already behind" and "still ahead," prevented from occurring by a repetitive and always incomplete shattering of the self? How can the refusal to bind together, the tendency to undo connections that characterizes the death drive, be used to reject standard forms of memory and resist the oblivion realized through the assimilation of marginal perspectives?

Their encounter in the hotel lobby is at once fortuitous and inevitable. Lucia Atherton (Charlotte Rampling) is returning from a night at the opera with her conductor husband; Max has just taken up his place behind the front desk. As they recognize each other, it is already time to part. Yet the inexorable return to the scene of the crime that united them has been set in motion. Their brief exchange of glances is indefinitely prolonged by a series of flash-like scenes, scraps of color and sound that begin to appear intermittently after they retire to their respective quarters. Directly dependent upon each character's conceptual and perceptual point of view, the flashbacks expose the time and place of their first encounter. They are in a concentration camp: Max is a Nazi officer who poses as a doctor to take sensational pictures of the prisoners; Lucia is the girl who soon becomes his favorite model. At all times, in the recollected past, the two figures are opposed according to the poles of passivity and activity—Max is filming and shooting a revolver; Lucia is being filmed and shot at. It is only the following night, when they see each other at the opera, that a disturbance is introduced into a seemingly orderly pattern. As the camera moves back and forth between them, almost miming the tension secreted by their bodies, and Lucia turns around to meet Max's piercing look, a slow process of reversal and contamination begins.

I am interested in tracing the forms through which this revolution in the field of vision and violence occurs—in documenting the perceptual transactions that enable the scopic drive and the sadomasochistic drive, here indissolubly linked by the early connection between camera and gun, to realize their circular, loop-shaped structure. The appearance of such a structure, as Jacques Lacan emphasizes in *The Four Fundamental Concepts of Psychoanalysis*, coincides with nothing less than the constitution of the drive itself.[2] According to Lacan, the drive comes into existence in so far as the subject makes herself the object of another vision or will—makes herself seen or tormented by the other. Indeed, the subject qua subject of desire emerges exactly at this juncture, when both the departure and the end of the drive are inscribed on her own body, in a turning around that indicates not self-enclosure but openness to the other. Only by exposing herself to the gaze and soliciting its effect, that is, by becoming an exhibitionist, does the voyeur assume her desire to see. Similarly, the experience of pain is accessible to the sadist only after she has transferred to the other the role she wanted for herself, that is, after she has become a masochist. "What is involved in the drive," Lacan writes, "is *making oneself seen* (*se faire voir*). The activity of the drive is concentrated in this *making oneself* (*se faire*) . . ." (195). The reversal or return constituting the circuit of the drive involves a confusion between passivity and activity rather than a simple shifting around of positions—the drive is most active in its passive form. The vicissitudes to which Max and Lucia will submit themselves belong under the sign of this partial, impure drive.

In "Masochism and Subjectivity," Kaja Silverman argues that *The Night Porter* illustrates the extent to which passivity marks not only the female but also the male subject. While Lucia's victimization repeatedly coincides with her being visually exposed, the gaze that subjugates her is shown to be in excess of any actual male look. By aligning the violating gaze with the camera, the film suggests that vision originates in a site of radical alterity, that is, in an impersonal viewpoint from which Max himself is barred. Later on, when Lucia dances in front of Nazi officers at the concentration camp, what we are offered is an elaborate mise-en-scène displaying the autonomy of the gaze—an act of voluntary exhibitionism that disarticulates the equation of male subjectivity and scopic mastery. Indeed, Silverman claims, Max's pleasure is not the pleasure of mastery, the sadistic position being only a privileged vantage point from which the subject can enjoy a profoundly masochistic pleasure. "Max," she writes, "is fascinated not with his own cruelty, but with Lucia's pain. In fact he identifies with that pain" (5). It is in the space opened by this interpretation that I will interrogate Max and Lucia's return to a scene in which the line dividing victim and executioner is irremediably blurred, where the oppressed becomes oppressor and the oppressor is in turn oppressed—the area of radical ambiguity that Primo Levi has named the "gray zone." However, as I follow their obstinate and defiant return, I will question the assumption that masochistic pleasure belongs to the present and to the recollected past, as if these were two interconnected but ultimately distinct dimensions, focusing instead on the disrupted temporality that governs the film's affirmation of masochism. The reciprocal contamination of passivity and activity that *The Night Porter* delineates is also a contamination of past, present, and future.

In *The Freudian Body*, Leo Bersani articulates a theory of masochism that, by problematizing the relation between narrative and form, allows us to conceive of this radically heterogeneous temporality. While analyzing the reliefs from the neo-Assyrian palaces at Nineveh, Bersani recognizes the traces of "a work of art of considerable brutality, a work in which [. . .] a form of violence perhaps inherent in narrativity is indulged in and yet also countered by a certain 'violence' of form" (67). The relief representing the lion hunt compels our eyes to rush toward and arrest at the point of most extreme violence, where a horseman's spear penetrates the open mouth of a lion. Yet, Bersani notices, "this anecdotal climax is ambiguous" (68). After a pause, our eyes continue to move in multiple directions, along the lines of force generated by a play of irreconcilable forms. Far from suggesting a state of repose, these forms are themselves endowed with the most dynamic energy—a mobile, unfocused violence that is able to oppose the destructiveness that seems to characterize the narrative impetus, diffusing its intensity and scattering it all over the scene. According to Bersani, this destructuration expresses a kind of "subversive passivity" that does not deny violence but prevents it from reaching a moment of annihilating intensity. "Catastrophe," he writes, "is produced when violence stops, when the dislocations provoked by desire's mobility seek, as it were, to take place, to have a place, to become attached to particular objects and, in so doing, to destroy them" (70). Such a deadly aggressiveness would coincide with a permanently arrested perception, a state of petrification affecting the seer and the seen alike—it would bring about the expiration of our desire to see as well as the depletion of the visible. Here, however, relations and forms challenge the identity of even the most conventional figurative elements—in the relief representing the lion fight, Bersani observes, a curve is simultaneously an abstract line, the bar of a cage, and a section of the lion's body—thus articulating patterns of repetition that undermine the triumph of "catastrophic violence."

Under the spell of this admirable analysis, I return to the relief from the lion hunt and find myself looking at the scene of an impossible death—a catastrophe that cannot take place, that is denied a place by a subversive arrangement of forms. Caught in an excited oscillation, a back and forth movement between different figures, I can neither see the whole scene at once nor diligently follow its unfolding from one side to the other. Instead, I perceive multiple pictures—fragments of variable extension and indistinct contour that appear in a pulsating, disorderly manner. I become the subject of a vision that is not only "agitated, erratic" (78) but also intermittent—the subject of a strange rhythm. Emerging from the interval that separates the storyline and the formal play—the interstice Bersani identifies but leaves unexplored—these visual fragments refuse to be ordered according to the rules of chronology and causality, and yet suggest an enduring narrative movement. They relate to each other in a convoluted manner, as if they were the flashbacks or flashforwards of a moment that does not fully exist in itself, a missing time that appears only in the almost identical repetitions it produces.

As a result, the violence of the impact between the flesh and the spear is dispersed throughout the surface, returning—without ever being completely realized—in each and every one of the visual fragments I see, even those that do not directly contain its representation. Unlike catastrophic violence, this aggressiveness cannot be left behind, relegated to a time that has completely passed, nor can it be exhausted by the narrative denouement.

Together with Max and Lucia, the spectator of *The Night Porter* also experiences an attraction toward a scene—the scene of a new and unprecedented crime—that cannot stop returning, in the ambiguous zone between narrative and form, to the detriment of a scene that could finally be mastered. Could we then distinguish, following theorists like Bersani and Jean Laplanche, between a desire for death that aims at reaching a state of immobility, a condition of inorganic stillness, and a desire that repeatedly refuses to orient itself teleologically, striving for a death that is always "already behind" and "still ahead"? Under which conditions does this other temporality of death come into view? What is at stake in conceptualizing the death drive as a principle of masochistic excitement, rather than as a principle of discharge? By analyzing the film's flashbacks, I will show that the intermittent appearance of closely related forms generates configurations in which the present can no longer be isolated from past and future, thus internally fracturing the crime scene and indefinitely prolonging its duration. It is by virtue of this rhythm that the spectator is made to experience, together with the characters, a desire for death in the future anterior that functions as an antidote to the annihilation of the other. In its traumatizing impact, such a desire is also productive of images that would not otherwise be visible—images relegated to oblivion when the crime scene is reduced to a single, punctual occurrence.

II

When Lucia decides not to follow her husband on his concert tour and remains in Vienna, fragments of memory start emerging again. She sits in the darkness of a Loos bar and a close-up of her face is interrupted by another scene—they are in the camp's hospital, Max has inflicted a wound on her arm and is kissing it. Later, in an antique store, a pink dress captures her attention, and flashes of an almost identical garment materialize—they are in the barracks, Max is slipping the dress on her semi-naked body and adjusting it. Both montage sequences still gravitate around Lucia's point of view, yet the compositional pattern as well as the rhythm governing the alternation between past and present generate an identificatory process that ultimately questions the identity and self-possession of everyone at stake. I linger on the sequence and its intricate formal arrangement in the light of Bersani's suggestion: "A psychoanalytic criticism, far from seeking keys to the hidden wishes and anxieties 'behind' the text, would be the most resolutely superficial reading of texts. It would trace the continuous disappearing and reappearing of relations and forms" (110). On the right side of the screen, standing firm and fully clothed as she fondles the pink dress, Lucia assumes in the diegetic present the position that Max occupies in the recollected past. However, such a position is both intermittent and ambiguous—it exists only between past and present, in the slit opened by the pulsation of closely related visual forms. As I watch Lucia vanish there, at the right edge of the frame, where Max is appearing, and see her resurface on the left as a much younger woman, I realize that any position made available by the film represents an impossible point of anchorage for characters and spectator alike.

After Lucia secretly moves into Max's apartment, a modest residence in a peripheral Viennese neighborhood, the sequence revolving around the pink dress repeats itself through new and familiar forms. The spatial arrangement is meticulous, Lucia standing again on the right and Max occupying the portion of the screen reserved for Lucia as a girl. This time, however, identification and its vicissitudes are further complicated by the simultaneous appearance of three figures—Max, Lucia, and Lucia's specular image. Facing a full-length mirror, her back turned to the spectator, Lucia holds the dress up against her body and smiles with complicity, while Max intently observes not the static reflection but the woman in flesh and blood as she performs the part once imposed upon her. A strange temporality pervades the scene. I meet Lucia's eyes returning my look from the glaring surface of the mirror and do not know whether she is an emanation of the past or a creature of the present. The tension between temporal dimensions that had previously emerged through the rhythmic structure of montage is now inscribed in the frame's spatial configuration: Lucia is here between present and past, the double of the woman that she will have been. Then, as if to intensify the effect of temporal ambiguity, the scene from the camp returns, and Max is there again, on the right, wearing his Nazi uniform and slipping a pink dress on the girl who is facing him. Throughout the sequence, past and present become visible only in their mutual dependence, the past in the camp now containing traces of what will have been, the present in the apartment marked by a memory that is already other for its having been remembered. What the operation of montage—the vibration of forms between frames and within the frame—gives birth to is a time that is single and yet fragmented, fluid and yet internally punctured—a time that is repeated, interfered with, and multiplied from within. As I watch the characters trade and confuse each other's identity, I cannot locate myself in a pure and autonomous present any more than I can secure a simply active position.

That a disarticulation of well-established coordinates has occurred through character identification calls for closer attention. Among the most reliable assets of classical cinema, so-called secondary identification or identification with the characters has been under attack for rendering the cinematic apparatus invisible and promoting the spectator's insertion into normative gender, class, and race positions.[3] According to Stephen Heath, the alignment between spectator and character realizes the conversion of the screen's "space" into a narrative "place," thus reaffirming a perspectival arrangement that maintains the subject in a centered and immobile position, imprisoned by a desire for imaginary plenitude. Feminist theorists like Ann Friedberg and Mary Ann Doane also denounce the ideologically pernicious influence of secondary identification, namely, its capacity to reduce difference and assimilate otherness in support of the existing power structure. However, in her work on political cinema, Kaja Silverman argues that identification does not inherently and automatically serve the dominant order—that, on the contrary, it is endowed with a unique potential for subversion. Because the Imaginary register is constitutive of our subjectivity not once and for all but over and over, throughout infantile as well as adult life, identification represents not only an irreducible operation but also a privileged vehicle for psychic and social transformation. I will turn to her work as it promises to shed light on the complex scenario we encountered in *The Night Porter*, where identification functions not in the service of cinematic suture[4] but on behalf of the cut or wound that is exposed, exploring its texture and redefining its contours.

In *The Threshold of the Visible World*, drawing on French psychoanalyst Henri Wallon and German philosopher Max Scheler, as well as on several early film theorists, Silverman proposes to conceptualize cinematic identification as potentially excorporative or "heteropathic," rather than unavoidably incorporative or "idiopathic."[5] The distinction is of the utmost importance. If the latter variety is predicated upon the ego's thirst for sameness and unity—a thirst that only the murderous assimilation of another self can temporarily satisfy—the former one preserves an unbridgeable distance between the subject and the other, allowing a process of seduction into difference to take place. The spectator who identifies according to an exteriorizing logic abandons her own corporeal coordinates—her sensational ego and the specular image to which she is bound by a proprietary relationship—and adventurously goes exploring the other's bodily framework.[6] A passage from Béla Balázs's *Theory of Film* further elucidates the kind of "transport or abduction" that cinematic identification is capable of realizing:

> In the cinema the camera carries the spectator into the film picture itself. . . . Although we sit in our seats . . . we do not see Romeo and Juliet from there. We look up to Juliet's balcony with Romeo's eyes and look down on Romeo with Juliet's. Our eye and with it our consciousness is identified with the characters in the film, we look at the world out of their eyes and have no angle of vision of our own. We walk amid crowds, ride, fly or fall with the hero and if one character looks into the other's eyes, he looks into our eyes from the screen, for, our eyes are in the camera and become identical with the gaze of the characters. They see with our eyes. (48)

While occupying a confined place in the movie theater, the spectator who watches a filmed version of Shakespeare's *Romeo and Juliet* is transported into the picture through a creative use of cinematic technology—the changing distance between spectator and scene, the division of a scene into shots, the variation of angle, perspective and focus, the close-up, and montage.[7] In a self-expropriating move, she leaves her own look behind and adopts the characters' perspective, shifting from one character to the other even when this entails, as Silverman points out, a traversal of gender lines.[8]

The extent to which the identificatory process can entail a disruption of the self's integrity is illustrated by a short story, which Scheler employs as an allegory about heteropathy and idiopathy and Silverman discusses to underscore the primacy of the corporeal dimension:

> A white squirrel, having met the gaze of a snake, hanging on a tree and showing every sign of a mighty appetite for its prey, is so petrified by this that it gradually moves towards instead of away from the snake, and finally throws itself into the open jaws. . . . plainly the squirrel's instinct for self-preservation has succumbed to an ecstatic participation in the object of the snake's own appetitive nisus, namely "swallowing." The squirrel identifies in feeling with the snake, and thereupon spontaneously establishes corporeal identity with it, by disappearing down its throat.[9]

As Silverman points out, the white squirrel perceives and behaves according to an excorporative model. She is the heteropath who relinquishes her own bodily boundaries, submitting herself to the shape of another. The snake, on the contrary, approaches difference with an indomitable appetite for incorporation, a desire that finds literal expression in the dynamics of ingestion. She is the idiopath who, all the incongruent elements having been absorbed, can finally reaffirm an autonomous and coherent identity.

Through a multifaceted use of montage, *The Night Porter* not only performs but also foregrounds the process of abduction described by Balázs—it puts heteropathic identification on display, presenting us with characters that are themselves repeatedly engaged in ecstatic perceptual transactions. As a result, the bodily ego that the spectator comes to assume, whether it is Max's or Lucia's, is not an individual, discrete entity but a constellation or assemblage of heterogeneous traits—gestures and affects that take shape in between different characters. By virtue of its dazzling montage, the film also rewrites Scheler's story—a story that dramatizes, together with the procedures of identification, the relentless work of the death drive, exposing its masochistic as well as sadistic components. The squirrel can identify heteropathically because her "instinct for self-preservation" has yielded to a desire for "ecstatic participation" that coincides with the radical unbinding or de-forming of her own bodily coordinates, while the snake identifies idiopathically by letting aggressiveness fulfill itself through the dissolution of the other's bodily envelope.[10] Yet, our analysis has shown, Max and Lucia could not be symmetrically aligned with the allegorical figures of squirrel and snake, at least not in any static and inflexible manner. Not only do they rhythmically exchange positions, taking turns in assuming the roles of predator and prey, they also perform the same primordial scene repeatedly and incompletely, always stopping before the end, always interrupting their reciprocal and deadly attraction before the climax is reached. In the story, whether the emphasis falls on the squirrel's unconditional surrender or on the snake's triumphant attack, the death drive operates as a principle of discharge and annihilation—it forces death to realize itself in the present, to take place as catastrophe. In the film, where Max and Lucia create a play of forms without narrative resolution—a performance unfulfilled by death—the death drive functions as a principle of masochistic excitement, inducing desire not to expire but to circulate in between the anticipation and the postponement of death.[11] The time of the death drive is here a time out of joint, in which death will have always taken place— a circular time that offers no escape but also no instantaneous release. The implications are far-reaching. Since "the drive, the partial drive," Lacan reminds us, "is profoundly a death drive" (205), such a convoluted time is also what marks the very emergence of the subject, in the looping around, the always missed coincidence between seeing and being seen, tormenting and being tormented.

One sequence above all enacts the suspended play I have just sketched. Attentively, I follow its intricate movement. Wearing Max's sweater, a slip, and a child's shoes that are too small for her—once more, a figure showing the traces of multiple identities—Lucia abruptly runs to the bathroom and locks the door. Inside, the camera registers a moment of hesitation, then her deliberate gestures. She seizes a bottle of perfume and shatters it on the floor, right in front of the door, turns the key and swiftly steps back. Max, who has been pounding on the door trying to force his way in, all of a sudden encounters no resistance and finds himself stepping on the broken glass—he smiles in response, taking visible pleasure in the pain he is experiencing. Then, as he lightly lifts his wounded foot, Lucia slides her hand underneath. They stare at each other, and Max steps down on it, causing the glass fragments to penetrate deeper into his own flesh, while simultaneously piercing her fingers and palm. Now it is Lucia's turn—she smiles with the same intensity. It is during this prolonged and fragile exchange that masochistic enjoyment seizes both of them, not at the same time, but at intervals too short to be detected. Because they move back and forth between activity and passivity, never occupying any permanent single position, each one of them can identify excorporatively without being incorporated and destroyed by the other. Here, the identificatory process undergone by the snake and the squirrel remains incomplete, coming to coincide with the assumption of the other's shape in a time that is not the present—producing not the dissolution of one bodily ego for the sake of another, but a reciprocal subversion of forms. After the film's last flashback shows Lucia delicately kissing Max's chest, we are given yet another interlacing of hands and feet, as the two lovers wash the blood off each other's wounds. We have now fully entered a domain in which the death drive could be dissociated from unfulfilled masochistic excitement only at the expense of life itself.[12] It is not by sheer coincidence that the sequence closes with Max's realization that they are under surveillance and will soon be under siege.

III

As she wanders through the hotel's underground corridors, during the time that precedes her decision to move into Max's apartment, Lucia becomes the spectator of a most peculiar reunion. Gathered around a large table are Max and his friends, all former Nazis, and they are intently discussing the preliminaries of an upcoming hearing. The group comprises Hans Vogler (Gabriele Ferzetti), who is addressed as "professor" and displays psychoan-

alytic expertise; Klaus (Philippe Leroy), who claims authority on investiga-
tive and legal matters, having access to the government's files on war crim-
inals; Bert (Amedeo Amodio), a homosexual dancer who used to perform
for them in the camp; and two alleged business men. In a severe parody of
the Law and the Freudian cure, what they are planning is alternatively referred to as "trial" or "group analysis," the end and the means being considered the same—the removal of guilt through meticulous confession. All
members of the group have already endured this process and, as a result,
gained a sense of liberation from the past, together with the entitlement to
resume honorable professions. All except Max—the last one on the list, he
is accused of living "as a church mouse," having chosen to carry out an obscure job in a society that strives to rebuild its lost glory. In front of his
peers, Max criticizes the process's therapeutic effectiveness as well as its
morality, and shows signs of resistance in submitting to it, especially now
that a witness for the prosecution has come back from the dead. He has yet
to inform the others about such unexpected return, fearing not his conviction but the witness's demise. He knows very well that, under the group's
rules, every defendant is eventually acquitted but that, for him to remain
innocent, the evidence that has been painstakingly collected is to be destroyed or, in Klaus's words, "filed away." That is, papers and photographs
are to be burnt, and living witnesses assassinated. We observe the scene
from Lucia's viewpoint, as she stands behind the ajar door, in a zone of im-
perfect darkness. When she runs away, glimpses of her perturbed
demeanor are intercut with Max's expressions.

In her article on *The Night Porter*, Silverman underscores that the
group, as a whole, is firmly positioned on the side of the ego, performing the
inhibitive and defensive functions proper to it. According to the rules of the
secondary process, the group uses language to bind the unpleasurable affect
generated through recollection and increase its own cohesiveness. Max and
Lucia, on the other hand, allow their perceptions and actions to occur under
the dominance of the primary process, refusing to bind or "translate" the exciting pain of recollection into a culturally enforced, stable, and homogeneous representation of life. The distinction is crucial to my argument on
temporality and the death drive. When death is envisioned according to a
model of catastrophic violence, as an event that realizes itself in the present,
the death drive is not opposed but ultimately conducive to the binding and
consolidating of the ego. In the case of the group, desiring death becomes
the ultimate expression of narcissism, not the condition of its diffusion—it
sanctions the imaginary coherence Lacan attributes to the ego, at the expense of the subject's relation to the signifier.[13] The danger posed by Max

and Lucia coincides here with the introduction of another temporality—theirs is a desire for death in the future anterior, a shattering force that radically undermines any aspiration to the mastery and destruction of the other. Significantly, these two conflicting interpretations of the death drive shape the way in which memory is conceived and practiced at the personal as well as collective level. The group, while pursuing death as annihilation, is set to implement an erasure of forms—to methodically produce oblivion as "that which effaces . . . the signifier as such.[14] Max and Lucia, on the contrary, submit themselves to masochistic transactions that repeatedly avoid death—the attainment of death, its taking place—thus preserving the play of signifiers from dissolution. In its strange and threatening fecundity, their fascination with a death out of joint engenders the possibility not only to remember but also to remember along lines that are not traced beforehand.

Despite the pressure exercised by the group, Max will not give up Lucia. For him, what is at stake is neither confession nor the removal of guilt. If he works at night, hiding like a church mouse, it is because he experiences "a sense of shame in the light"—shame, not guilt, is the affect that constitutes his being. Similarly, Lucia will not seek refuge in the authorities investigating her disappearance. She continues to remain with Max "of [her] own free will," even when the professor and his friends put them under armed surveillance, severing all communications between the apartment in which they hide and the outside world. Until one night, exhausted by confinement and lack of food, they prepare for their last performance. They leave the apartment—Max in full Nazi uniform, Lucia in pink dress and white shoes—and drive away, knowing they will be trailed. At dawn, they stop on a majestic modern bridge. While walking toward the scene's vanishing point, their backs turned to the spectator, they are executed in unhurried succession. Their bodies occupy the screen for a few moments, then the film ends. The fulfillment of the group's desire for catastrophic violence, this last scene is left to mark the coincidence between narrative climax and eclipse—the evacuation of exciting pain and the final disappearance of forms. If the crime scene returning in Max and Lucia's masochistic play is radically split, multiplied, spread over time—the past becoming the effect of the moment it produces, the future which it will have been—the crime scene willed by the group has precise spatial and temporal boundaries. It can be examined, solved, and eventually archived, that is, filed away. Against the heterogeneous, creative memory affirmed by the couple's desire for death in the future anterior—a desire that has thoroughly permeated the film's enunciative strategies—the denouement imposed by the group coincides with nothing less than the effacement of vision. Oblivion—that which effaces the signifier as such—is here the accomplishment of analysis (group analysis, individual analysis, cultural analysis) as normalizing procedure, the discourse of those who hold power at the expenses of the subversive creativity (and the very life) of those who stand at the margins. The erasure of desire as such.

NOTES

1. In her introduction to the Italian edition of the screenplay, the director explicitly adopts the term "crime scene" when speaking of the victim's return to the concentration camp. Cf. Cavani vii. Arendt, too, reminds us that the London Agreement of 1945 for the first time defined the deportation, enslavement, and extermination of a civilian population as "crimes against humanity."

2. Cf. Lacan: "What is fundamental at the level of each drive is the movement outwards and back in which it is structured. It is remarkable that Freud can designate these two poles simply by using something that is the verb. *Beschauen und beschaut werden*, to see and to be seen, *qualen* and *gequalt werden*, to torment and to be tormented. This is because, from the outset, Freud takes it as understood that no part of this distance covered can be separated from its outwards-and-back movement, from its fundamental reversion, from the circular character of the path of the drive" (178).

3. Film theorists distinguish between "primary" and "secondary" identification—identification with the apparatus versus identification with the fictional characters. See, for instance, Metz.

4. The concept of suture has been pivotal in understanding the relation between cinematic signification and the viewing subject. Theoreticians of suture claim that classical cinema employs the cut, which at once divides and links shots, to conceal the operations of the enunciation and promote secondary identification. Thus lured into the film's fictional world, the spectator experiences, at least intermittently, a sense of coherence and plenitude. Regarding the multifaceted theory of suture, see Dayan; Heath, "Notes on Suture"; Miller; and Oudart. All these articles are discussed in Silverman, *Subject of Semiotics*. On *Night Porter*'s repeated foregrounding of the "cut," at the level of both diegesis and enunciation, see Silverman, "Masochism and Subjectivity" 5.

5. Freud's notion of identification as incorporation is here opposed to Wallon's theorizing of identification according to an excorporative logic. The terms "idiopathic" and "heteropathic" originally appear in Scheler's work.

6. See Silverman's chapter on "the bodily ego" in *Threshold*, which begins by quoting Freud's famous sentence, "the ego is first and foremost a bodily ego," and goes on to explore theorists such as Lacan, Wallon, and Fanon.

7. Balázs enumerates cinema's specific devices in the chapter entitled "A New Form-Language."

8. Silverman reads this last statement as a clear though marginal return to incorporative identification. I believe we could also understand the identification here described as internal to the abduction that has already take place. If, at the very end, the viewer's own parameters of embodiment seem to prevail again, we might imagine that the look she is now lending to the characters differs from the one that initiated her to the cinematic spectacle, having been transformed by the spectacle itself.

9. The story is drawn from Schopenhauer and quoted in Scheler 21–22.

10. On the opposition between the bodily ego as a bound/binding form and the death drive as unbinding force, see Laplanche: "Opposite the ego, a binding, vital form, the *death drive* is the last theoretical instance serving to designate a logos that would necessarily be mute, were it to be reduced to its extreme state . . . the conflict between ego and drive, between defense and 'wish fantasy,' is neither the sole nor the ultimate form of the opposition between *binding* and *unbinding*. At the unconscious level, within the fantasy—at least if it is considered as something other than 'pure' free energy—there must be indeed another more fundamental polarity: life drive and death drive, interdiction and desire" (126).

11. I here refer to masochism as inherently sexual and governed by exciting pain. Cf. Bersani: "in *Beyond the Pleasure Principle* Freud violently manipulates the notion of repetition in order to propose in the death instinct a nonsexual masochism, *a masochism from which exciting pain has been wholly evacuated*" (62).

12. See Bersani: "Masochism is both relieved and fulfilled by death, and to stop the play of representations perhaps condemns fantasy to the climatic and suicidal pleasure of mere self-annulment" (27).

13. Weber argues that the death drive constitutes "just another form of the narcissistic language of the ego" (168) and gives voice to "the need for another form of repetition, to counterbalance that of the death drive (as repetition of the same)" (188).

14. See Lacan: "*Oblivium* is that which effaces—effaces what? The signifier as such. Here we find again the basic structure that makes it possible, in an operatory way, for something to take on the function of barring, striking out another thing. This is a more primordial level, structurally speaking, than repression . . . this operatory element of effacement is what Freud designates, from the outset, in the function of the censor" (27). For an interpretation of the death drive in relation to Lacan other than the one I have pursued in this work, see Žižek. His text posits an intimate connection between the death drive and *das Ding* as "the real-traumatic kernel in the midst of the symbolic order," that which "enables us to conceive the possibility of a total, global annihilation of the signifier's network" (135).

WORKS CITED

Arendt, Hannah. *Eichmann in Jerusalem: A Report on the Banality of Evil*. London: Penguin, 1992.

Balázs, Béla. *Theory of the Film: Character and Growth of a New Art*. Trans. Edith Bone. New York: Dover, 1970.

Bersani, Leo. *The Freudian Body: Psychoanalysis and Art*. New York: Columbia UP, 1986.

Cavani, Liliana. *Il Portiere di Notte*. Torino: Einaudi, 1974.

Dayan, Daniel. "The Tutor Code of Classical Cinema." *Movies and Methods: An Anthology*. Ed. Bill Nichols. Berkeley: U of California P, 1976. 438–51.

Derrida, Jacques. *The Post Card: From Socrates to Freud and Beyond*. Trans. Alan Bass. Chicago: U of Chicago P, 1987.

Doane, Mary Ann. "Misrecognition and Identity." *Cine-Tracts* 3.3 (1980): 25–32.

Freud, Sigmund. *Beyond the Pleasure Principle. The Standard Edition of the Complete Psychological Works of Sigmund Freud*. Vol. 18. Trans. James Strachey. London: Hogarth, 1955. 17–64.

Friedberg, Anne. "A Denial of Difference: Theories of Cinematic Identification." *Psychoanalysis and Cinema*. Ed. E. Ann Kaplan. New York: Routledge, 1990. 36–45.

Heath, Stephen. "Notes on Suture." *Screen* 18.4 (1977/78): 48–76.

———. *Questions of Cinema*. Bloomington: Indiana UP, 1981.

Lacan, Jacques. *The Four Fundamental Concepts of Psychoanalysis*. Ed. Jacques-Alain Miller. Trans. Alan Sheridan. New York: Norton, 1998.

Laplanche, Jean. *Life and Death in Psychoanalysis*. Trans. Jeffrey Mehlman. Baltimore: Johns Hopkins UP, 1976.

Levi, Primo. *The Drowned and the Saved*. Trans. R. Rosenthal. New York: Random, 1989.

Miller, Jacques-Alain. "Suture (elements of the logic of the signifier)." *Screen* 18.4 (1977/78): 29–34.

Metz, Christian. *The Imaginary Signifier: Psychoanalysis and the Cinema*. Trans. Celia Britton, Annwyl Williams, et. al. Bloomington: Indiana UP, 1977.

Oudart, Jean-Pierre. "Cinema and Suture." *Screen* 18.4 (1977/78): 35–47.

Scheler, Max. *The Nature of Sympathy*. Trans. Peter Heath. Hamden, CT: Archon, 1970.

Silverman, Kaja. "Masochism and Subjectivity." *Framework* 12 (1980): 2–9.

———. *The Subject of Semiotics*. New York: Oxford UP, 1983.

———. *The Threshold of the Visible World*. New York: Routledge, 1996.

———. *World Spectators*. Stanford: Stanford UP, 2000.

Weber, Samuel. *The Legend of Freud*. Minneapolis: U of Minnesota P, 1982.

Žižek, Slavoj. *The Sublime Object of Ideology*. London: Verso, 1989.

8

Sadistic and Masochistic Contracts in Voltaire's *La pucelle d'Orléans* and Graffigny's *Lettres d'une Péruvienne*; or, What does the Hymen Want?

Sharon Diane Nell

> *un milieu, pur, de fiction*
> —Mallarmé, *Mimique*

According to Luce Irigaray, the hymen, conventional sign of virginity, is the boundary that separates womanhood (pure exchange value) and motherhood (use value). As a virgin, a woman "is nothing but the possibility, the place, the sign, of relations between men. In herself, she doesn't exist: the simple envelope covering the stakes of social circulation" (Irigaray 181). The transition from Woman to Mother, Irigaray tells us, involves the transgression of that envelope—the transgression of the hymen. But is the hymen a limit that is really that easy to transgress?

In Lacan's formulation, the answer to this question is no, and from two perspectives. Sade, for example, teaches us not *how* to transgress but how *to try* to cross the boundary between self and other: "Ne peut-on dire . . . que Sade nous enseigne, en tant que nous sommes dans l'ordre d'un jeu symbolique, *une tentative* de franchir la limite, et de découvrir les lois de l'espace du prochain comme tel?" ["Can one not say . . . that Sade teaches us, in so far as we are in the order of a symbolic game, *an attempt* to cross a limit, and to discover the laws of the space of the neighbor (fellow man) as such?"] (Lacan, *L'éthique* 232; my emphasis). To Lacan, the Christian "golden rule" imperative—love your neighbor as yourself—is a sadistic command. For loving my neighbor gets in my way: it erects a barrier between me and my enjoyment (Lacan, *L'éthique* 229). It also entails getting too close (too "proche") to the void of "me" mirrored in the neighbor (the "prochain"), and loving the neighbor too much, so much that I, the sadist, attempt to destroy her. But no matter how hard the sadist tries to cut the victim into pieces (Lacan, *L'éthique*

237), she is not to be destroyed and in fact does not change at all (Lacan, *L'éthique* 238). The reiteration of destructive violation in Sade and its lack of consequences (or effectiveness) are, therefore, part of the laws of the other's space and of the symbolic game of sadism.

On the other hand, in Irigaray's explanation of the function of virginity, the woman is an empty sign—an idea reflected in Lacan's theories about what is usually thought of as the opposite of sadism: masochism. To Lacan, courtly love manifests a masochistic pattern. The Lady of courtly love is an empty signifier that produces other empty signifiers: she is "a kind of automaton which utters meaningless demands at random" (Žižek, "Courtly Love" 151). She is a "black hole" in the Symbolic, the Thing that can be circled, but only at a distance. In the game of masochism, the rule is that the hymen is an impermeable barrier whose transgression must be infinitely and repeatedly delayed.

In sadism, therefore, the transgression of the boundary must be reiteratively attempted; however, these repeated attempts to transgress are doomed to have no effect. The masochistic pattern has a different structure, but the outcome is the same: the masochist repeatedly circles the limit, but cannot approach too closely. The laws of these two games overlap with a common contractual interdiction: in neither is anything allowed to happen. Sadism and masochism therefore rehearse in different ways a crucial aspect of the literary form known as the ancient Greek novel, whose characteristic convention, according to Mikhail Bakhtin, is that "nothing happens" (Bakhtin 89–90). In this context, literary convention is a type of fiction as well as a kind of contract: the conventions of ancient Greek romance entail specific expectations.

Crucial in the double game of sadomasochism is the position and function of the hymen and more generally what Freud terms "the riddle of femininity" and "the enigma of women" ("Femininity" 116). Like the "Desire of the Analysts," the title of this volume, my essay's central question— "What does the hymen want?"—is predicated on a double meaning and theorizes the hymen as both subject and object. My question is, of course, an ironic reformulation of the famous question attributed to Freud: "Was will das Weib?" (qtd. in Lacan, *L'éthique* 18). Playing on the English word "want," I am simultaneously asking "what is the hymen's desire?" and "what does the hymen lack?" just as Freud decried the opaqueness of feminine desire (questioned in fact its very existence) and at the same time pointed out the castration of the female body ("Femininity" 116, 112). It is true that both of my questions are counterintuitive—the reader may well ask "how can an inanimate object desire?" and "how can a concrete object lack anything?"—but these questions imitate Lacan's own counterintuitive strategies. As we shall see, moreover, the hymen can wield power in ways that are reminiscent of subjects, and, in efforts to define and theorize it, it is seen as lacking to such an extent that it does not even exist.

Of Freud's question, Lacan remarked in 1959, "Sommes-nous là-dessous beaucoup plus avancés?" ["On this point, have we advanced much?"] (Lacan, *L'éthique* 18). As a feminist critic, it is my desire to try to "advance" this question today. This chapter will therefore appropriate the tools of the analyst(s) in order to explore the ways in which female sexuality, in the form of the hymen, both is done to and done by fictional women. It will compare two eighteenth-century narrative texts whose ideologies and discourses struggle over the fiction, convention, and contractual nature of women's virginity. In one of the narratives, the mock-heroic epic *La pucelle d'Orléans*, Voltaire explores and transgresses the legendary conventions associated with Jeanne d'Arc. The *philosophe* depicts the adventures of a Jeanne whose selection by the Divine and designation as *pucelle* bind her contractually to retain her virginity for one year so that France will win the war against the English; the enemy, however, continually attempts to transgress her hymen through rape and thus endeavors to break her virginity contract. The narrative in *La pucelle* exhibits the symptoms of sadism outlined above and at the same time displays elements of the ancient Greek novel in which "nothing happens."

The second narrative, Françoise de Graffigny's epistolary novel, *Lettres d'une Péruvienne*, while also endeavoring to prevent anything from happening, stages a masochistic relationship. Graffigny's heroine, the Peruvian princess Zilia, is torn from her home and her vocation—that of Virgin of the Sun and fiancée of the future Incan king—by the Spanish; her adventures, however, lead her to France, intellectual enlightenment, and an independent life. Her French suitor, the Chevalier Déterville, creates for himself the position of slave while portraying Zilia as a demanding and unreasonable mistress. He "circles" Zilia, but, because of the structure of masochism, is unable to approach her too closely, even though he claims that he so desires. In order to contextualize historically the conflicting viewpoints in these two narratives, we will first investigate the problem of the hymen in the philosophical, legal, and medical discourses of the eighteenth century.

IN SEARCH OF THE HYMEN

As it is depicted in the eighteenth-century *Encyclopédie*, female virginity poses both physiological and ethical problems. The Chevalier de Jaucourt, who is listed as author of many of the virginity-related articles in the *Encyclopédie*, deplores the importance men place on physical virginity:

> Men . . . jealous of liberties of all kinds, have always attached
> great importance to all they believe they could possess exclusively
> and first; it is this kind of madness which has transformed the vir-
> ginity of maidens into a real being. Virginity, which is a moral
> being, a virtue which only consists in purity of the heart, has be-
> come a physical object, in which all men take an interest. . . .[1]

In this citation, whose sentiments Jaucourt attributes to Buffon, physical virginity is depicted as a fiction, a fantasy that men experience because of their
desire to have the woman exclusively and to have her first. But the hymen,
the conventional sign of virginity, is not universally present, Jaucourt insists:
it is not a real being, but a moral one. A masculine "madness" to see and
document the hymen, moreover, has led men to develop social conventions
that force women to submit to humiliating physical examinations, which
Jaucourt calls "des usages, des cérémonies, des superstitions" ["customs, ceremonies, superstitions"] (Jaucourt, "Virginité" 17:327), and which are
nothing less than "deflowerings." Jaucourt wants to have virginity both
ways, for, despite his distaste for these superstitious practices (and his explicit wish to keep certain things unseen and silenced), he manages to overcome his reticence at causing women to blush long enough to catalogue the
various (theoretical) morphologies of the hymen, which he calls "this delicate membrane of indeterminate shape which is found or is not found in the
conduit of modesty" (Jaucourt, "Hymen" 8:392).

Jaucourt states that it is not possible to identify the hymen as a sign of
virginity: its universal presence is "imaginary and frivolous" ("Hymen" 8:393).
When it does exist, moreover, the hymen, like the uterus, is monstrous[2]—it is
too present. The hymen can prevent coitus and childbirth but not menstrual
flow or conception. Moreover, the flow of blood that is the accepted sign of a
young woman's virginity (at the moment of its destruction) is yet another
point of instability, according to Jaucourt. If a young girl has sexual relations
with a man for the first time before puberty, she will not bleed. Later, during
puberty (which, Jaucourt claims, causes the reproductive organs to grow), she
will bleed as easily *as if* she were a virgin. If sexual relations stop for a time and
begin again, she will bleed again (Jaucourt, "Virginité" 17.327–28). Thus, virginity and the physical signifiers that are associated with it are points of what
Thomas DiPiero calls "morphological instability" (185). Since it can be broken, regrow, and be broken again, the hymen is a sign of unruly female flux,
like menstruation (Clément 57). To Jaucourt it is *both* the signifier of virginity and of its loss (deflowering). It is a mark, an undecidable boundary that at
once separates the untouched from the touched and reveals that the difference
between the two is illusory and fictional.

Moral virginity or, in Jaucourt's words, "a virtue which only consists in purity of heart," can also pose problems. Both sexes desire equally, and a woman's modesty can cause her to be more desirable: "Desires veiled by shame only become more seductive" (Jaucourt, "Pudeur" 13.553). Natural law, however, does not allow unrestrained contact between the two equally desiring sexes and requires the stabilization of women's unstable bodies: "The woman's austere duties derive from the fact that a child must have a father. . . . Nature willed it thus" (Jaucourt, "Pudeur" 13:553). But since Woman's unruly hymen is what Shari Benstock, following Jacques Derrida, calls "an internal limit of undecidability" (119), will these "austere duties" suffice to regulate her body? It is clear that Jaucourt is participating in a highly anxious discourse about the hymen and its relationship to virginity. We now turn to medicine and the law for concrete and material instantiations of the discourse.

The Chevalier de Jaucourt's impulse to see and document the hymen while at the same time disavowing his desire to do so corresponds to medical and juridical practice in the eighteenth century. According to these two domains, it was imperative to establish Woman's physical integrity by examining her genitals. This examination, known as "la visite feminine" ("the feminine visit"), functioned in several ways from antiquity to the eighteenth century: men, particularly powerful men, utilized it to determine the virginity of potential brides, while women requested it in order to prove either prenuptial purity or their husband's impotence (Darmon 160–62).[3] The result of these visits? Documentation which, as Jaucourt states, establishes in textual form both virginity and its loss: she may have been a virgin before the examination, but because of the examination itself (during which she was often penetrated by phallic objects and her desires awakened), she emerges "corrompue et gastée" ("corrupted and ruined") (Anne Robert qtd. in Darmon 191).

One fact at least is established by the "visit": this is a female, if fragmented, body. Furthermore, the narrative of the examination demonstrates the position of the hymen with regard to mutually implicated products of Lacan's Symbolic: reality, texts, and Law. The documentation of the "visit" recounts how the body is marked, but it also participates in marking the body: "Language casts sheaves of reality upon the social body, stamping it and violently shaping it" (Wittig, "The Mark of Gender" 4). What was previously amorphous is now a structured and delimited "body." Discerning and naming the hymen causes it (the hymen) to be produced: moreover, the hymen, now a signifier, posited in language and acting as the "mark of gender," forces the body "to come into being" (Butler, *Gender Trouble* 8). In Lacanian terms, the Real ("the pulsing [. . .] presymbolic substance" [Žižek, *Looking Awry* 14]) has been inscribed and structured by symbolic reality: "'Reality' is the field of symbolically structured representations, the outcome of symbolic 'gentrification' of the Real'" (Žižek, "In His Bold Gaze" 239). Reality, a symbolization of the Real and as such what Fredric Jameson calls "the political unconscious," is an ideological screen of signifiers that mediates between the Real and us (35).

We have no access to the Real as such, Lacan tells us, because once we write or talk about it, it enters into the Symbolic through language and becomes "reality." But reality, like gender, language, and the Law—all manifestations of the Symbolic—is not something that we formulate for ourselves. Indeed, Lacan states that "language with its structure preexists (to) the entrance that each subject makes there" (Lacan, "L'instance" 495). Reality preexists the subject as well: "(what we experience as) reality is not the 'thing in itself,' it is always-already symbolized, constituted, structured by symbolic mechanisms" (Lacan, "L'instance" 495; Žižek, "The Spectre of Ideology" 73). Reality, therefore, is not something that we do; rather, it is "done" to us:

> *[Le principe de réalité] ne fonctionne pas seulement au niveau de ce système par où le sujet, échantillonnant dans la réalité ce qui lui donne le signe d'une réalité présente, peut corriger l'adéquation du surgissement leurrant de la* Vorstellung *telle qu'elle est provoqué par la répétition au niveau du principe du plaisir. Il est quelque chose au-delà. La réalité se pose pour l'homme, et c'est en cela qu'elle l'intéresse, d'être structurée, et d'être ce qui se présente dans son expérience comme ce qui revient toujours à la même place.* (Lacan 91; my emphasis)

> [(The principal of reality) does not function only at the level of this system in which the subject, sampling in reality that which gives him the sign of a present reality, can correct the appropriateness of the deceptive sudden appearance of the *Vorstellung* such that it is provoked by repetition at the level of the pleasure principle. It is something beyond. *Reality is posited for man*, and it is in this that it affects him, to be structured, and to be that which presents itself in his experience as that which always returns to the same place.]

Reality is therefore not something that one chooses or constructs for oneself but a performative process: it is "posited" for subjects—it is a doing without a doer—and at the same time it is reiterative—it "always returns to the same place" (Butler, *Gender Trouble* 25; Miller, *Subjecting Verses* 9). On the other hand, reality is a "precarious" fiction of the Symbolic, "a fragile symbolic

cobweb that can at any moment be torn aside by an intrusion of the Real"
(Lacan, *L'éthique* 40; Žižek *Looking Awry* 17). In a similar way, the presence
or absence of the hymen—itself a function of the Symbolic—is precariously
hypothetical (Darmon 167). Yet, like reality, the "fragile symbolic cobweb"
that is the hymen is a symbol, a necessary, conventional fiction (Darmon
167). In other words, it is a text, what Jameson calls a "symbolic act" (77).

If reality is the performative symbolization of the Real, the Law is the
set of imperatives that the Symbolic imposes on reality. Moreover, the Law,
like reality and texts, is a kind of fiction: "the Law has the status of a sem-
blance; the Law is necessary without being true" (Žižek, "The Obscene Object of Postmodernity" 49). While the Law regulates reality, it also regulates
the circulation of the woman's body. Specifically, the inappropriate loss of
virginity (sex before marriage) as well as the inappropriate preservation
of virginity (male impotence after marriage) entail the transgression of the
marriage contract, "une fiction légale" ("a legal fiction"), a necessary and
conventional text that has emerged from patriarchal symbolic Law.[4] It is not
just the hymen's loss that is subject to regulation: indeed, as Nadine Bérenguier affirms, since her "austere duties" bind the virgin to preserve the intactness of her body, "[t]he prenuptial period, in principle extra-contractual,
is subject to the same contractual logic as the marriage for which it must
prepare" (Bérenguier 454). Just as a prediscursive "before the law" cannot
be located (Butler, *Gender Trouble* 2), the virgin is always already subject to
the symbolic contract. As we shall see later on, these contracts can be found
in two essential forms: sadistic and masochistic.

FICTIONAL BUT BINDING

On the surface, Voltaire's *La pucelle d'Orléans* and Françoise de Graffigny's
Lettres d'une Péruvienne seem very different: *La pucelle* is a narrative mock-
epic poem about Joan of Arc and *Lettres d'une Péruvienne* is an epistolary
novel about a Peruvian princess. Choosing to compare these two texts may
seem arbitrary;[5] however, Voltaire's poem and Graffigny's novel each tell
the story of the "austere" if fictional duties of enlightenment virgins.

Voltaire highlights the precarious fictionality of Jeanne d'Arc's legend
from the beginning of *La pucelle d'Orléans*. All the French noblemen in *La pucelle* laugh when Saint-Denis reveals his quest to find a virgin to save France
because they contend there are no virgins at all to be found (1.337).[6]
Nonetheless, Denis does discover his virgin, Jeanne, and documents the
presence of a hymen, and thus "fixes" her sex as female, with a "deflowering"
physical examination (2.401–23). Because of her size, her accoutrements and

weapons, Voltaire's Jeanne seems at first glance to be *de trop*, too visible, like Mary Russo's "unruly woman," a remnant of seventeenth-century amazonian "heroism" (Russo 213; DeJean 36).[7] In her armor, in a dress, or nude, she sticks out like a sore thumb, her too-present hymen seemingly projected onto the surface of her body and inviting penetration. In a sense, Jeanne's virginity constitutes a kind of phallic hymen that leaves her always already deflowered and always ready to penetrate and kill the enemy. In one comic episode, a nude Jeanne arrives at a convent in order to fight the English soldiers who are raping the nuns:

> *Jeanne était nue; un anglais impudent*
> *Vers cet objet tourne soudain la tête,*
> *Il la convoite; il pense fermement*
> *Qu'elle venait pour être de la fête.*
> *Vers elle il court et sur sa nudité*
> *Il va cherchant sa sale volupté.* (11.125–30; my emphasis)

[Jeanne was nude; an impudent Englishman suddenly turns his head toward *this object*. He lusts after her; he firmly thinks that she has come to take part in the celebration. He runs toward her and goes seeking his dirty pleasure on her nude body.]

Jeanne's virgin body is like a magnet: the would-be rapist seems violently compelled to attempt to penetrate "this object." Her body, inscribed as female by her physical examination, now appears to invite a "mark imposed by a [second] oppressor" (Wittig, "One Is Not Born a Woman" 311). Even as her body seems to invite penetration, however, Jeanne kills the soldier who tries to rape her and then goes on to kill all the English soldiers even as they rape the nuns: "chacun fut percé sur sa nonne / et perd[ait] l'âme au fort de son désir" ["each was pierced on his nun and [lost] his soul at the height of his desire"] (11.154–55).

Indeed, Jeanne incarnates undecidability: for the hymen "is positioned between the inside and the outside of the woman, consequently *between* desire and accomplishment" (Derrida, *La dissémination* 262; his emphasis). Moreover, her status as transvestite indicates what Marjorie Garber calls a "category crisis": "a failure of definitional distinction, a borderline that becomes permeable, that permits . . . border crossings from one (apparently distinct) category to another . . ." (17). Jeanne the virgin is always crossing, transgressing, penetrating borders in the name of purity. Jeanne's crossdressing—passing as a man—is in itself is a kind of transgression of the boundary between male and female. In addition, she crosses political boundaries. For example, immediately after Saint Denis provides her with biblical weapons for protection and a winged ass for transportation (2.214–45), he challenges her to imitate Ulysses and the Greeks of the Iliad and sneak by night into the tent of Jean Chandos, the brutal Englishman who will become her archenemy. Denis suggests that she kill Chandos while he sleeps, but Jeanne refuses: "je serai d'un courage bien bas / De tuer des gens qui ne combattent pas" ["my courage would be base indeed were I to kill those who do not fight"] (II.291–92). She does, however, enter the tent and leave her mark. Not only does she steal Chandos's sword and velvet breeches, she draws three fleur-de-lys on the buttocks of Chandos's "charming" page, who sleeps nearby (II. 304–23). Jeanne crosses from French to English camps, and while she claims to keep her noble mission pure by refusing to kill the enemy in his sleep, she leaves a humiliating trace of her visit (stealing Chandos's possessions and marking his servant on the buttocks).

Moreover, the documented existence of Jeanne's hymen proves that its presence does not guarantee virginity. We can argue, à la Derrida and Jaucourt, that she is deflowered by the collective gaze of the ecclesiastical authorities when she undergoes a "feminine visit," that is, when her uniqueness and difference from other women is documented (2.401–07). The physical examination leaves only a trace of her hymen: her duty to withhold "her flower" (Derrida, *Spurs* 38). It turns out that her "austere duty" to virginity and its potential transgression is meaningless in terms of the narrative structure of the poem: a poetry-writing contest in heaven between rival saints has already ensured the victory of the French (16:241–43). This trace of her hymen—her "duty"—is fictional, an empty signifier that points to the arbitrary and empty nature of the big Other and the Symbolic in general.

In a similar fashion, Graffigny's Zilia, whose duty to remain a virgin has been prescribed by the Peruvian patriarchal system, demonstrates the precarious nature of virginity. Indeed she has already been "deflowered" at the end of the *Lettres d'une Péruvienne* when she decides to preserve her virginity: for, at the beginning of the novel, she is taken by force from the Temple, a home she shares with the other Virgins of the Sun, and her difference as exotic Other is "unveiled." Zilia's body is not literally violated by her Spanish captors: they kill and kidnap but, at least according to Zilia, they do not rape. Nonetheless, as Jaucourt would agree, she is repeatedly deflowered, morally if not physically. Transferred to the French ship, for example, she must submit to the symbolically penetrating gazes of her new captors, but here again, she is not physically violated (Graffigny, *Lettres* 37). Later on, in Mme. Déterville's salon, she is exhibited in her Incan garb as a curiosity for the Parisians who laugh at and paw her (*Lettres* 67–68).

Moreover, a case can be made that Zilia's hymen, like Jeanne's, is projected externally; her hymen is figured not by her body, but by her *quipos*, the veil-like web of knots that Graffigny uses as a Pervuvian writing system. The *quipos* are doubly hymeneal: Zilia's knotted web is also a series of letters to her beloved (Benstock 119). Derrida notes the related etymologies of "hymn" (*hymne*) and "hymen": both words signify weaving and creating a text (Derrida, *La dissémination* 263). Thus, Zilia weaves "le mystérieux tissu de mes pensées" ["the mysterious weaving recording my thoughts" (Graffigny, *Letters* 22)] and at the same time she "sings" of her love for Aza:

> [C]es noeuds qui frappent mes sens, semble donner plus de réalité à mes pensées; la sorte de ressemblance que je m'imagine qu'ils ont avec les paroles, me fait une illusion qui trompe ma douleur: je crois te parler, te dire que je t'aime, t'assurer de mes voeux, de ma tendresse; cette douce erreur est mon bien et ma vie. (Graffigny, *Lettres* 36)

> [These knots strike my senses and seem to lend greater reality to my thoughts. The kind of likeness I imagine they bear to words gives me an illusion that tricks my pain, for I believe myself to be speaking to you, telling you that I love you, reassuring you of my devotion and tenderness. This sweet error is my one possession and my life. (Graffigny, *Letters* 37)]

Celebrating her love for Aza through weaving/writing recreates the past for Zilia: she sees him again for the first time and experiences again her love and emotion. Weaving/writing eliminates both the distance between Aza and Zilia and the distance between past and present. This moment of weaving/writing, therefore, constitutes a re-creation of the hymen:

> "Hymen" . . . signe d'abord la fusion, la consommation du mariage, l'identification des deux, la confusion entre les deux. Entre *deux*, il n'y a plus de différence, mais identité. Dans cette fusion, il n'y a plus de distance entre le désir . . . et l'accomplissement de la présence, entre la distance et la non-distance; plus de différence du désir à la satisfaction. (Derrida, *La dissémination* 258)

> ["Hymen" . . . sign first of all of the fusion, the consummation of marriage, the identification of the two, the confusion between the two. *Between* two, there is no longer any difference, but identity. In this fusion, there is no longer any distance between desire . . . and the fulfillment of presence, between distance and non-distance; no longer any difference from desire to satisfaction.]

Aza is present to Zilia as she weaves/writes about her love for him, and in this way she is able to "consummate" their love.

At the same time, however, these "letters" instantiate "a psychosexual trajectory of desire that creates *'correspondances'*" between Zilia and her beloved (Benstock 88). Indeed, while she keeps her *quipos* safe from the Spanish (Graffigny, *Lettres* 38), they circulate (in a limited fashion) to her fiancé, and are (temporarily) taken away from her by the French (Graffigny, *Lettres* 22, 37). Zilia's body continues to circulate—she is captured by the Spanish (letter 1), passes into French hands (letter 4), then arrives in France (letter 10), passes to the custody of Déterville's mother (letter 13), is sent to the convent (letter 18), and so on. But like Jaucourt's young girls who are able to regrow their hymens, Zilia is able to place these "relations"—the circulation of her *quipos* and her body—under erasure through weaving/writing her *quipos*.

Later on in the novel, however, when she has reached the "end" of the *quipos*, she fears that the erasure of distance between the two lovers is at an end:

> [J]e vois la fin de mes cordons, j'en touche les derniers fils, j'en noue les derniers noeuds, ces noeuds, qui me semblaient être une chaine de communication de mon coeur au tien, ne sont déjà plus que les tristes objects de mes regrets. L'illusion me quitte, l'affreuse vérité prend sa place, mes pensées errantes, égarées dans le vide immence de l'absence, s'anéantiront désormais avec la même rapidité que le temps. (Graffigny, *Lettres* 77)

> [I see the end of my cords drawing near. I am touching their last threads and tying their last knots. These knots, which seemed to me to be a line of communication linking my heart to yours, are already nothing more than the sad objects of my regret. Illusion is deserting me, replaced by the awful truth: my wandering thoughts, lost in the immense void of absence, will henceforth be reduced to nothing with the same speed as time. (Graffigny, *Letters* 79)]

When there are no more *quipos* left to weave, we see, with Derrida, the flip side of the hymen. Rather than signifying fusion, consummation, erasure of distance, it is now that which is "between": "the hymen . . . stands *between* the inside and the outside of woman, consequently between desire and its fulfillment. It is neither desire nor pleasure but between the two" (Derrida, *La dissémination* 262). Similarly, writing in French is initially alienating for

Zilia: "Il arrive souvent qu'après avoir beaucoup écrit, je ne puis deviner moi-même ce que j'ai cru exprimer" (Graffigny, *Lettres* 79) ["It often happens that after having written a great deal, I cannot figure out what I believed myself to be expressing" (Graffigny, *Letters* 81–82). Writing in French is an obstacle that stands *between* Zilia and her thoughts. By the end of the novel, she realizes that she writes for herself:

> *J'ai cru . . . que le seul moyen [d'adoucir mes inquiétudes] était de te les peindre, de t'en faire part, de chercher dans ta tendresse les conseils don't j'ai besoin; cette erreur m'a soutenue pendant que j'écrivais; mais qu'elle a peu duré! Ma lettre est finie, et les caractères n'en sont tracés que pour moi.* (Graffigny, *Lettres* 99)

> [I decided that the only way for me to ease my fears would be to depict them for you, to share them with you, to seek in your tenderness the counsel I need. This error sustained me while I was writing, but how briefly it endured! My letter is finished, and the characters composing it have been drawn solely for me. (Graffigny, *Letters* 103).]

Nonetheless, at the end of the novel, she affirms her intention to fulfill her "austere duties" as a Virgin of the Sun. She decides to remain true to Aza, the Incan prince to whom she was betrothed but who has converted to Catholicism, fallen in love with a Spanish noblewoman, and broken off the engagement. Although her French suitor, Déterville, wishes to marry her, Zilia decides to pretend that she is still Aza's fiancée.

Thus, at the novel's conclusion, enshrined in a European simulacrum of the Temple of the Sun with its reified versions of Peruvian virgins painted on the walls, Zilia clothes herself with Incan conventions, what Jaucourt calls "customs, ceremonies and superstitions," that are ultimately dead and meaningless (Jaucourt, "Virginité" 17:237). Furthermore, her decision at the end of the novel to continue performatively to act *as if* she remains betrothed to Aza constitutes a melancholic "incorporation" of his loss. This incorporation of loss through the perpetual performance of a lost Incan custom—that of being a Virgin of the Sun—while residing in a space (France) that continuously places the dead Incan civilization under erasure, conveniently allows her hymen to become the "'encrypted' . . . permanent residence" of the lost Incan culture (Graffigny, *Lettres* 166; Butler, *Gender Trouble* 87). These "dead" practices may enact a fiction, but they are not without a function and one that works to Zilia's advantage: like the Virgin Mary, Zilia, sole female survivor of the Incas, may be "alone of all her sex"

(Kristeva 244) but it is not her separateness from the French,[8] symbolized by her rejection from the Catholic nuns and her refusal to marry her French suitor (Graffigny, *Lettres* 81, 166), which cause her to suffer, but rather her separation from Aza, a separation from which she eventually derives pleasure (Graffigny, *Lettres* 163–44).

Indeed, her separateness from the French, her economic independence, and her initially "unwanted" but convenient liberty from Aza all allow her to maintain her position of undecidability and, ultimately, to retain her freedom. Zilia decides not to marry Déterville, an action that would have neutralized cultural difference. She refuses to suppress heterogeneity, to "briser la glace" ["break the ice mirror"]—or to lose her physical and cultural virginity; therefore, her never-consummated desire will be forever "mimed" (Derrida, *La dissémination* 258–59). In other words, Zilia's virginity will be performative: it will be the "reiteration of a norm or set of norms" (Butler, *Bodies That Matter* 12). She will continue to "cite" Incan virginity and, because of her status as Aza's (former) fiancée, and also because of her different cultural origin, she can claim that she has no choice, that her virginity is "done" to her (Butler, *Bodies That Matter* 13; *Gender Trouble* 25). Before she finds out that her betrothed has fallen in love with another woman, Zilia refuses to marry the Frenchman Déterville according to the following logic: he is not Incan; she is not French; chance has brought them together, not choice (Graffigny, *Lettres* 96). After Aza's unfaithfulness has been revealed, she vows to continue to act *as if* she is the Incan prince's bride: "Le cruel Aza abandonne un bien qui lui fut cher; ses droits sur moi n'en sont pas moins sacrés" (Graffigny, *Lettres* 166) ["Cruel Aza has abandoned a possession that was once dear to him but his rights over me are no less sacred for having done so" (Graffigny, *Letters* 172)]. The clever thing about Zilia's reasoning is that she will reiterate norms that are foreign to her French context: even Zilia herself acknowledges the unlikelihood for a young French woman to remain single indefinitely (Graffigny, *Letters* 165). Zilia manages to keep her position undecidable: she will never marry Aza but can claim perpetually to "be" his fiancée—not really single—all the while admitting to Deterville that "les douceurs de la liberté se présentent quelquefois à mon imagination" (Graffigny, *Lettres* 164) ["Freedom's great sweetness enters my imagination at times" (Graffigny, *Letters* 170)].

Zilia's manipulation of her *quipos* also demonstrates the undecidability of the hymen. Graffigny tells the reader in the novel's preface that, for the purposes of publishing her "memoirs," Zilia has translated the first part of the novel—the part supposedly written in the *quipos*—into French. Graffigny assures the reader that the same hand that knotted the veil-like web of *quipos* wrote the French version of these letters (Graffigny, *Lettres* 4). As Shari Benstock notes, after Jacques Derrida, "[t]he veil is not only a vestment, it also signifies the hymen that conceals and protects the female sexual organs" (185). Furthermore, Derrida associates the veil and hymen with style, the stylus, and writing (*Spurs* 36–38). Zilia's act translates her *quipos* into French, but since she also inscribes them in a different form (from Incan knots to European letters inscribed in ink on paper), she translates, or "carr[ies] over from one place to another" (Benstock 163). This reinscription of her story—her translation and transcription into French and into France—gives her the opportunity to control and revise her narrative and to tell it from an enlightened, European perspective. Her revisions can be seen as a regrowing or reinforcing of her hymen, putting under erasure the violation of the Temple of the Sun by the Spanish—and even putting under erasure the restricted liberty that she would have had had she remained in Peru—while retaining control over the circulation of her body within the foreign culture. Zilia thus utilizes the undecidability of the hymen to subvert a patriarchal order that wishes to put her into circulation on its terms. She is able to use her narrative to maintain the veil of the hymen intact, which keeps her body separate from European culture but allows her to continue her intellectual growth within the European context. At the same time, she forces the representatives of that culture, like Deterville, to circle around her.

The hymen and its absence are therefore undecidable and fictional in both *La pucelle d'Orléans* and *Lettres d'une Péruvienne*. Derrida states that both the hymen's function as "sign of fusion" and its position *entre* makes it an undecidable hinge point spatially as well as temporally: "With all the undecidability of its meaning, the hymen only takes place when it doesn't take place, when nothing *really* happens . . ." (*La dissémination* 262). A challenge to what we would think of as "normal" narrative development (where events succeed one another, where characters develop, etc.), the hymen can only happen when nothing happens. But the hymen "happens" in both *La pucelle d'Orléans* and *Lettres d'une Péruvienne* because both works draw elements from a narrative form that deals specifically with the virgin's body and in which "nothing happens," the narrative form that Mikhail Bakhtin calls the "Greek Romance Chronotope" (Bakhtin 151). In fact, both works reprise the "basic situation" of Greek Romance: two lovers meet at the beginning of the narrative, instantly fall in love but are quickly separated. Their paths may cross over the course of the novel, but the focus of the narrative is devoted to their separate adventures and their desire to reunite and marry. Bakhtin points out that, despite the presence of many adventures between the two anchoring moments—the simultaneous point of encounter and *coup de foudre*, and the final, marital union between the two characters— "nothing happens," the "gap" between them, according to Bakhtin, "is an extratemporal hiatus between two moments of biographical time" (89–90).

Crucial elements of this chronotope recur in our eighteenth-century texts. Bakhtin states that Voltaire parodies the "Greek Romance Chronotope" in *Candide*—and in a rather "tailored" way. Candide and Cunégonde meet and fall in love within the first few paragraphs of the novel, are instantly separated, and spend the entire novel endeavoring to reunite and marry (Bakhtin 90–91). In *La pucelle*, Voltaire "multiplies" this structure: eight characters, the members of four separated couples, try to reunite with their partners, although their efforts are thwarted by intervening adventures. In *Lettres d'une Péruvienne*, the epistolary model of Ovid's *Heroides* is combined with the "Greek Romance Chronotope" (DeJean 79). The narrative is related through letters written by the female protagonist to her fiancé: Zilia recounts how she meets and falls in love with her fiancé, Aza, but on their wedding day, evil Spanish soldiers massacre all the Incas except for Zilia and Aza, who are taken as separate hostages. From that point, the paths of the two characters diverge: Zilia ends up in France and Aza in Spain. Zilia's focus, the thing that keeps her alive, is her desire to reunite with Aza and marry him (an event that does not actually happen even though she decides to pretend as if it *has* happened).

The convention that "nothing happens" has crucial implications in Greek romance for virginity. Although, as in Achilles Tatius's *Kleitophon and Leucippe*, an example of Greek Romance, the male lover, Kleitophon, can have sexual experiences with other women during the interval between the separation of the lovers and their reunion, it is imperative that the betrothed retain her virginity. In the course of Achilles Tatius's narrative, for example, Leucippe is subjected to a variety of sadistic experiences that ritualistically do violence to her body as well as put her virginity in danger: because other men desire her, she is "sacrificed" (216), drugged (230), kidnapped and "beheaded" (236), sold into slavery by pirates (242), and threatened with rape (259).[9] The Priest of Artemis expresses his doubts that virginity can be retained in such circumstances with a telling elision: "you know as well as anyone that a girl trapped in such toils, no matter how she resists, is all too likely to have been—" (Achilles Tatius 273). Leucippe's virginity, in accordance with Artemis's role in the *rites de passage* of Greek maidens about to be married, is subsequently tested by the "syrinx," a "magic" flute crafted by Pan.[10] She passes the test and, in this way, her virginity is documented through a "magical" test, not a physical examination to establish the presence of the hymen. The end point of the narrative thus reached, Leucippe can now lose her virginity (Segal 89). But, in a sense, is this virginity not already lost? David Konstan points out that Melite, a married woman who has sex with Kleitophon, is able to pass her test of fidelity through a technicality (53). Furthermore, Charles Segal demonstrates the presence in the narrative of "two" Leucippes: "the pure Leucippe who survives intact and the image of a sexually initiated (violated) Leucippe from whom the heroine is carefully separated by acts of ritual or quasi-ritual sacrifice" (85). Because of these two images, we can suggest that Leucippe's status as virgin is undecidable and that, like Melite—through a technicality—Leucippe passes her test of virginity. If this is the case, furthermore, it points even more to the conventional status of virginity—that "nothing happens" sexually. Moreover, just as we have seen in the case of eighteenth-century virginity, the betrothed's "prenuptial period" (Bérenguier 454), characterized by her "austere duties" to preserve the intactness of her hymen, must follow the same contractual logic as that of the marriage itself. The documentation of Leuccippe's virginity, an ancient form of the "feminine visit," renders material and textual this contractual logic. We have already seen that the Law, reality, and texts are mutually implicated products of the Symbolic. Contracts, an expression of the Law, and literary conventions, textualized "symbolic acts," both entail binding expectations. While the legal contract binds parties to act in certain ways, the literary convention, "an agreement between the writer and his readers (or audience) which allows him [sic] various freedoms and restrictions" (Cuddon 155), requires a text to work in certain ways. I argue that the hymen is both a contract and a convention in *La pucelle* and *Lettres d'une Péruvienne*: Jeanne d'Arc and Zilia are bound by contracts to act in certain ways, and their narratives are required to follow the literary conventions of the ancient Greek novel.

    Joan of Arc's virginity is a convention of her legend; following this legend, Jeanne's virginity is documented at the beginning of Voltaire's poem. Presented to the king by Saint Denis, she invites the former to have her physically examined, and he does, in fact, have her maidenhead documented by ecclesiastical authorities:

> *Jeanne, écoutez, Jeanne, êtes-vous pucelle?*
> *Jeanne lui dit: ô grand sire, ordonnez*
> *Que médecins, lunettes sur le nez,*
> *Matrones, clercs, pédants, apothicaires*
> *Viennent sonder ces féminins mystères,*

Et si quelqu'un se connaît à cela,
Qu'il trousse Jeanne, et qu'il regarde là.
(Voltaire, *La pucelle d'Orléans* 2.401–07)

[Jeanne, listen, Jeanne, are you a maid? Jeanne replies: O great lord, order that doctors, glasses on their noses, matrons, clerics, pedants, apothecaries, come to probe these feminine mysteries; and if someone is well-versed in those things, let him pull up Jeanne's skirts and look there.]

This examination results in a literal contract: a "virginity certificate" ["un brevet de pucelle"] (2.420–23) and the mortals in Voltaire's poem believe her hymen must remain intact for the French to prevail in the war against the English. While this turns out not to be the case, the English and French mortals regard the "virginity certificate" as a contract between God and the French king. It is a contract with a time limit, however: she is bound to keep her "flower" for one year, at which point its supposed function will have been fulfilled. On the other hand, if, during this year, the terms of the contract are violated, Jeanne will lose her power and the English will win the war. To abide by the contract, Jeanne postpones sexual intercourse. Dunois, her would-be boyfriend, desires Jeanne, and vice versa, but both are willing to honor the terms of the contract: ". . . il savait qu'à son bijoux caché / De tout l'état le sort est attaché, / Et qu'à jamais la France est ruinée / Si cette fleur se cueille avant l'année" ["he knew that the fate of all the state was attached to that hidden jewel, and that France would be ruined forever if this flower were picked before the year was out"] (3.206–09).

In Graffigny's novel, Zilia's virginity and her rejection of the official marriage contract, while parallel to Jeanne's, are also conventions of seventeenth-century women's fiction (DeJean 88–89). And while the existence of a contract can be argued in *Lettres d'une Péruvienne*, Zilia undergoes no test to document her virginity. Rather, her strict containment in the Temple of the Sun and her very limited contact with men create the assumption that she is a virgin; however, one may well wonder (in a manner similar to that of the priest of Artemis in Leuccipe and Kleitophon) how, given her harrowing experiences, she has miraculously been able to avoid rape. Like Leucippe, she has been subjected to virginity-threatening "toils": she is violently removed from the Temple of the Sun during a horrific battle scene and then spends numerous days or perhaps even weeks with the brutal and potentially raping Spanish before her transfer to her kinder, gentler French captors. Moreover, on a more figurative level, her status as Virgin of the

Sun can be called into question since she dresses alternately in her traditional Incan garb (which denotes her status as Virgin) and the French *tenue* that Déterville gives her (Graffigny, *Lettres* 55).

Despite the lack of empirical proof of her virginity, it is possible to say that her virginity is documented and that a contract is established. Toward the end of the novel, Déterville, her suitor, and Céline, his sister, take Zilia to what seems to be an "enchanted" château. They divert her with charming rustic entertainments and ask her to sign a document, which in fact is the contract that makes this magic castle her possession. Céline asks her:

> *Ne pourriez-vous nous pardonnez de vous avoir procuré, à tout événement, une demeure telle que vous avez paru l'aimer et de vous avoir assuré une vie indépendente? Vous avez signé ce matin l'acte authentique qui vous met en possession de l'une et de l'autre.* (Graffigny, *Lettres* 150)

> [Could you not forgive us for having procured a dwelling for you, which in any event you would seem to like, and for having ensured you an independent life? This morning you signed an authentic contract putting you in possession of both. (Graffigny, *Letters* 154)]

Inside the house is a "cabinet" that recreates the Temple of the Sun in which Zilia grew up and which was "raped," or defiled, by the murderous Spanish invaders on her wedding day:

> *Les pavés du temple ensanglantés, l'image du soleil foulée aux pieds, des soldats furieux poursuivant nos Vierges éperdues et massacrant tout ce qui s'opposait à leur passage; nos Mamas expirantes sous leurs coups, et don't les habits brûlaient encore du feu de leur tonnerre, les gémissements de l'épouvante, les cris de la fuerue répandant de toutes parts l'horreur et l'effroi, m'ôtèrent jusqu'au sentiment.* (Graffigny, *Lettres* 19–20)

> [The bloodied paving stones of the temple, the trampled image of the Sun, raging soldiers chasing down our distraught Virgins and massacring all that stood in their way, our *Mamas* dying beneath their blows in clothes still burning from the fire of their thunder, and the groans of terror and cries of fury from every direction spreading horror and fear combined to take my very senses from me. (Graffigny, *Letters* 20)]

The violent "rape" of the Temple is erased in the enchanted château; however, painted on the walls of the *cabinet*, Virgins of the Sun are dressed as Inca princesses. Zilia remarks that "On . . . voyait nos Vierges représentées en mille endroits avec le même habillement que je portais en France; on disait même qu'elles me ressemblaient" (*Lettres* 152) ["In a thousand places . . . were representations of our Virgins wearing the same attire I had when I arrived in France. It was even said that they resembled me" (*Letters* 157)]. Thus, these texts (the contract and the wall paintings) serve to "fix" Zilia as a virgin, thus serving as *her* contract, *her* "virginity certificate," even as they are predicated on an initial "rape."

SADISTIC AND MASOCHISTIC CONTRACTS

La pucelle and *Lettres d'une Péruvienne*, thus, have in common the "Greek romance chronotope" structure as well as the hymen as convention and contract; however, the way in which their respective contracts are treated is radically different. In *La pucelle*, Voltaire creates a "sadistic" situation, while Graffigny's use of courtly love in his *Letters* is "masochistic." Slavoj Žižek, citing Gilles Deleuze, points out the asymmetry between sadism and masochism:

> In his celebrated study of masochism, Gilles Deleuze demonstrates that masochism is not to be conceived of as a simple symmetrical inversion of sadism. The sadist and his victim never form a complementary "sado-masochist" couple. Among those features evoked by Deleuze to prove the asymmetry between sadism and masochism, the crucial one is the opposition of the modalities of negation. In sadism we encounter direct negation, violent destruction and tormenting, whereas in masochism negation assumes the form of disavowal—that is, of feigning, of an "as if" which suspends reality. (Žižek, "Courtly Love" 152)

Moreover, Deleuze tells us, "the masochist draws up contracts while the sadist abominates and destroys them" (Deleuze 20).

To see how this works out in *La pucelle*, we have to consider a category of character that I have not yet mentioned, the "evil" Englishman, Jean Chandos, his henchmen, and other characters who try to rape the female characters in the mock-epic poem. The main occupation of Chandos and those of his ilk throughout the poem is to find Jeanne and rape her, thereby nullifying her celestial contract. While endeavoring to find Jeanne, the limitless lasciviousness of these characters targets any and all women who are encountered. While these efforts to deflower Jeanne never succeed, the King's mistress, the hyperfeminine Agnès Sorel (a comic, carnivalesque antivirgin) is raped numerous times. Although she attempts to create her own contract by swearing that she will become "an honest woman" and remain faithful to the King, she repeatedly either sleeps or desires elsewhere. Yet, like Sade's Justine and the betrothed of the ancient Greek novel, nothing ever really happens—Agnes's character and basic "innocence" remain intact. Jacques Lacan's assessment of Justine can be applied practically verbatim to Agnès Sorel: no matter how many trials she must endure, Agnès's desirable body and virginal character are "indestructible":

> the victim survives all ill treatment, she does not become debased even in her physical attractiveness to which the author's pen returns always with insistence, like all description of this kind—she always has the most beautiful eyes in the world, looks the most moving and the most touching. (Lacan, *L'éthique* 238)

In representing Jeanne d'Arc's hymen as essentially meaningless and Jeanne as ultimately sexual, Voltaire negates the value of all types of contracts (pledges, oaths, promises): the poem's narrator declares, "il ne faut jamais jurer de rien" ["one must never swear anything"] (6.130). We can also say that Voltaire wishes to pit against one another at least two aspects of the Thing, which Lacan links to the fascination with Woman (the Lady of courtly love and the femme fatale), the incestuous character of the maternal body, and the obscene "coordinates" of enjoyment (Žižek, "Courtly Love" 151; Žižek, *Looking Awry* 89; Žižek, *Enjoy Your Symptom!* 118; Lacan, *L'éthique* 65). On the one hand, Voltaire's narrative works to systematically demystify and desublimate objects that are elevated to the dignity of the Thing (the "impossible-unattainable substance of enjoyment" [Žižek, *Looking Awry* 84]), thereby demonstrating their nothingness: "This Thing, all the forms of which created by man belong to the register of sublimation, will always be represented by a void" (Lacan, *L'éthique* 155). Fascination with the Thing can only be maintained while the object is "in shadow": "As soon as we try to cast away the shadow to reveal the substance, the object itself dissolves" (Žižek, *Looking Awry* 84). This pattern is rehearsed in *La pucelle*. Although initially perceived as fascinating and exceptional, the poem's events reveal that Jeanne and Agnès are both just "ordinary" women who are incapable of sexual fidelity and whose bodies constantly risk penetration.[11]

On the other hand, sadistic characters like Jean Chandos embody another aspect of the Thing: the "radical evil" of *jouissance*, "the Thing which is 'too hot' to be approached closely" (Žižek, *Looking Awry* 161, 169). Jean Chandos is fascinating but also dangerously violent toward women. One of the indications that Chandos represents the dangerous abyss of *jouissance* into which particularly Jeanne and Agnès risk being drawn is the fact that the characters rarely meet him directly but are often in *indirect* contact with him. Agnès, for example, comes into contact with his clothes on two occasions. In another example of indirect contact, Agnès falls under the power of one of Chandos's agents, an "aumonier" or chaplain (6.278–89). This "scélérat" ("scoundrel") reacts to her with violence and unbridled lust. Despite her pleas and cries, the "aumonier" rapes Agnès (10.108–13). When Jeanne and Agnès come into direct contact with Chandos, it is a dangerous situation indeed. In Canto 3, a sexually stimulated Chandos tries to rape Agnès (3.348–50): "[P]ressé d'un aiguillon bien vif" ["Driven by a very sharp sting"], Chandos begins to undress Agnès so that he can both get his *culotte* back and have sex with her, while she, on the other hand, makes clear that he is forcing her to have sex: "non je n'y consens pas" ["no, I do not consent"] (3.373–75).

The abyss of *jouissance* that Chandos represents also threatens to invade the realm of the Symbolic. In canto 13, the French happen upon a group of English enemies, one of whom is Chandos. The warriors of the French troop draw lots to see who will fight the evil Englishman. The lot falls to Jeanne, but Chandos is not aware at first that he is fighting a woman. Initially, the two warriors seem equally matched, but soon Jeanne's inferiority in battle becomes apparent: she is just not as muscular and strong as Chandos (13.228–31): Jeanne falls to the ground, and Chandos sees that she is a voluptuous and seductive woman:

> *Le casque ôté, Chandos voit une tête,*
> *Où languissaient deux grands yeux noirs et longs.*
> *De la cuirasse il défait les cordons.*
> *Il voit, ô ciel! ô plaisir! ô merveille!*
> *Deux gros tétons de figure pareille,*
> *Unis, polis, séparés, demi-ronds,*
> *Et surmonté de deux petits boutons*
> *Qu'en sa naissance a la rose vermeille.* (13.241–48)

[When her helmet comes off, Chandos sees a head where two
large and long black eyes were languishing. He undoes the laces
of the breastplate. He sees—O heavens! O pleasure! O marvel!
Two big knockers of the same size—smooth, polished, separated, half-globes—and topped with the two little buds which
the red rose has at its birth.]

But in addition to her physical "charms," Chandos immediately sees the
political reasons for raping Jeanne: if she is no longer a virgin, she will lose
her power to win the war for France. Moreover, he will take pleasure in destroying the hymen that gives her this power: "j'aurai pour partage / Les
plus grands biens, la gloire et le plaisir" ["My part will be the greatest of the
spoils: glory and pleasure"] (13.265–66).

Moreover, Jeanne is not only an object elevated to the dignity of the
Thing, she is also "constructed" by Saint Denis, the representative of symbolic Law. Although Chandos is tempted by Jeanne's feminine features
(features that mark her as "woman-in-the-feminine" [Benstock 184;
201n22]), ultimately the reason that he tries to have sex with her is *so that*
she will no longer be able to fill the symbolic category of *pucelle*. By sexually assaulting Jeanne, he directly attacks Denis and the Symbolic. The author's aim, it would seem, is sadistic in nature: he desires the "direct
negation, violent destruction . . . tormenting" and the destruction of the
hymeneal contract (Žižek, "Courtly Love" 152). Ultimately, however,
Chandos can only *try* to transgress the hymen: at the crucial moment of
penetration, Saint Denis strikes him with impotence and Chandos is therefore unable to penetrate and deflower the maid of Orleans.

In contrast, the contract serves masochist ends in the *Lettres d'une
Péruvienne*. From this perspective, the affinity of Graffigny's novel with
courtly love and Zilia's elevation to the position of Lady becomes apparent.
From the moment that the Chevalier Déterville brings Zilia aboard the
French vessel, he treats her as deserving respect and veneration, while
positioning himself physically as subservient:

> *Il se met sur ses genoux fort près de mon lit, il reste un temps consid-
> érable dans cette posture gênante: tantôt il garde le silence, et les yeux
> baissés, il semble rêver profondément. . . . S'il trouve l'occasion de
> saisir ma main, il y porte sa bouche avec la même vénération que nous
> avons pour le sacré diadème.* (Graffigny, *Lettres* 38–39)

[He kneels quite close to my bed and spends considerable time
in that uncomfortable position. Sometimes he falls silent and,
eyes lowered, seems to be lost in a profound reverie. . . . If he

finds an opportunity to seize my hand, he applies his mouth to it with the same veneration we show for the sacred diadem. (Graffigny, *Letters* 39–40)]

Zilia's response to this strange behavior is to wonder if men in Déterville's culture worship women as goddesses. He may seem to "worship" her, but Deterville regards Zilia as "a feminine object devoid of all real substance" (Žižek, "Courtly Love" 151), since, before she learns his language, he teaches her to parrot back to him sentences in French that she does not comprehend: "Il commence par me faire prononcer distinctement des mots dans sa langue. Dès que j'ai répété après lui, *oui, je vous aime*, ou bien, *je vous promets d'être à vous*, la joie se répand sur son visage . . ." (Graffigny, *Lettres* 48, my emphasis) ["He starts by having me clearly pronounce some of the words of his language. As soon as I have repeated after him 'Yes, I love you' or 'I promise to be yours,' joy spreads over his face . . ." (Graffigny, *Letters* 49)]. For Déterville, Zilia, like the courtly Lady, "functions as a kind of 'black hole' in reality, as a limit whose Beyond is inaccessible" (Žižek, "Courtly Love" 152).

Déterville continues to revere Zilia throughout the rest of the novel, accepting the tasks she assigns him, no matter how arbitrary they may seem to him or how much pain they cause him. In particular, she asks him to help her reunite with her fiancé, Aza, although such a reunion will cause Déterville cruel torment:

> *Ah! c'en est trop, s'écria-t-il en se levant brusquement: oui, s'il est possible, je serai le seul malheureux. Vous connaîtrez ce coeur que vous dédaignez; vous verrez de quels efforts est capable un amour tel que le mien, et je vous forcerai au moins à me plaindre.* (Graffigny, *Lettres* 98).

> ["Oh, this is too much! Yes, if possible, I shall be the only un-happy one. You will come to know this heart you scorn. You will see of what efforts a love such as mine is capable, and I will force you at least to pity me." (Graffigny, *Letters* 102)]

But, although he continually laments Zilia's power, it is Déterville himself who progressively endows Zilia with power over the course of the novel—he turns over to her the Peruvian treasures that he had confiscated from the Spanish—*her* treasure, he claims. Déterville has the contract for Zilia's en-chanted castle drawn up and has the pictures of Virgins of the Sun, projec-tions of his narcissistic ideal, painted on the walls of the house's inner sanctum. These actions remind us, in Žižek's words, that

> [m]asochism . . . is made to the measure of the victim: it is the
> victim (the servant in the masochistic relationship) who initiates
> a contract with the Master (woman), authorizing her to humil-
> iate him in any way she considers appropriate (within the terms
> defined by the contract) and binding himself to act "according
> to the whims of the sovereign lady." ("Courtly Love" 153)

In the typical masochist "scene," the victim will maintain a "reflective distance" (Žižek, "Courtly Love" 154). Theatrically tearful scenes occur several times, during which Déterville bemoans his mistress's cruelty and
power: "De quel sang-froid vous m'assassinez! s'écria-t-il. Ah! Zilia! que je
vous aime, puisque j'adore jusqu'à votre cruelle franchise" (Graffigny, *Lettres* 97) ["'With what calm do you kill me!' he cried. 'Oh, Zilia, how I love
you, for I adore even your cruel honesty'" (Graffigny, *Letters* 100)]. In addition, there is an interesting moment when Déterville seems to step outside his "game" with Zilia—where he tells her "in a cold, businesslike way"
(Žižek, "Courtly Love" 154) that he could have given in to his desires and
had sex with her at any time:

> *Vous savez, Zilia, si je l'ai respecté cet objet de mon adoration. Que ne
> m'en a-t-il coûté pour résister aux occasions séduisantes que m'offrait
> la familiarité d'une longue navigation! Combien de fois votre inno-
> cence vous aurait-elle livré à mes transports, si je les eusse écoutés?
> Mais, loin de vous offenser, j'ai poussé la discrétion jusqu'au silence.*
> (Graffigny, *Lettres* 96)

> [You know whether I showed respect for the object of my ado-
> ration, Zilia. What did it not cost me to resist the seductive op-
> portunities offered me by the close quarters of a long sea
> voyage! How many times might your innocence have delivered
> you over to my transports of desire had I heeded them? But far
> from giving you offense, I pushed discretion to the point of si-
> lence. (Graffigny, *Letters* 100)]

From this perspective, then, the contract is Déterville's, not Zilia's.[12] What
is his desire? Officially, "to sleep with the lady," but what is really desired is
infinite deferral of the sexual act and the preservation of Zilia's status as virgin in order to perpetuate the masochistic relationship. This is precisely
the solution Zila articulates at the end of the novel: she will pretend, feign
to be a "Virgin of the Sun," in order to continue to inflict pain. Where is
Zilia's desire? Through this courtly love structure, we can say that, on the

one hand, Graffigny is able to appropriate and subvert the masculine fantasy of courtly domination so that her heroine can remain, like Artemis, unmarried and virginal.[13] On the other hand, Graffigny's heroine is unable to escape the legal logic of patriarchy, for she must remain subject to the prenuptial virginity contract.

<hr />

Ultimately, the answer to "What does the hymen want?" depends on whom you ask. To Shari Benstock and Jacques Derrida, the hymen is a fiction. Absent and permeable even in its visibility, its meaning is a construction of masculine "madness," both in the frivolity of giving it meaning (*La pucelle*) and in the impossibility of its existence (*Lettres d'une Péruvienne*). What does it desire? In the case of *La pucelle*, we can put agency in parentheses and look at the hymen as a performative "doing to" a subject rather than as a subject who does or as a physical object that exists. The hymen, in the form of the ultimate virgin, Jeanne d'Arc, performatively reiterates "a set of norms" that enact a compulsory heterosexual narrative (Butler, *Gender Trouble* 12–13). It wishes its own eventual destruction, not through the conventional means (burning at the stake), but through a heterosexual sex act that will eliminate "category crisis," render her gender culturally intelligible, and "fix" stable borders between the genders.

In Graffigny's novel, it is more difficult to dismiss the woman's agency because Zilia uses her hymen to subvert the patriarchal system: she manages to make her hymen's "wish" to remain intact the desire of the patriarchal system. Zilia's virginity is not "done" to her in the same sense that Jeanne d'Arc's is "done" to her, but it is performative all the same. It is a citational practice that reiterates the now dead and fictional norms of Incan culture. Interestingly enough, if we interrogate the hymen from the perspective of psychoanalysis, it is also a fiction, a manifestation of "reality." In Lacan's words, "the characteristic of pleasure, a dimension of that which enchains men, is completely found on the side of the fictive . . . what we call the symbolic" (Lacan, *L'éthique* 22). Jaucourt's notion of virginity as an undecidable "physical object" is revealed to be a fictional, if "binding," contract, an artifact of the Symbolic that can occur in either sadistic or masochistic contexts.

Have we "advanced" the question of Woman's desire by using the tools of the analyst? We have found unsurprisingly perhaps that a male writer in the Enlightenment systematically reduces woman to an object and denies her the possibility of desire and agency. But we have also interrogated a woman's text to help us begin to find an answer: Graffigny's heroine struggles for agency through the use of those same symbolic means that are used to subject her. The preceding pages have demonstrated that the hymen is a gap, the space that can only happen when nothing happens. Sadistic and masochistic contracts organize their legal requirements around it, but can never attain or destroy it. If the hymen is a metonymy for Woman, it demonstrates that she is not a "lack" but rather undecidability. While it does elude representation, the hymen is not the "horror of nothing to see": it is a "mark without a mark" (Irigaray 25; Derrida, *La dissémination* 262). Catherine Clément notes that women are the height of paradox: "on the side of *the* Law ["la règle"], since they are wives and mothers, and on the side of mentrual periods ["les règles"], natural disruptions" (18, my emphasis). Woman is order and disorder simultaneously; her hymen is a hinge point. Finally, while the hymen, like the Law, can "be done" to Woman, it can also be used by Woman to disrupt and subvert.

Contrary to Jaucourt, the "austere duties" in the two texts we have been discussing do not relate to reproduction but rather to power. In the case of sadism, Jean Chandos fulfills his sadistic "duty" in attempting to destroy the hymen. On the other hand, Zilia can claim rather cleverly that she is "only doing her duty" by abiding the terms of her masochistic contract with Déterville: she is contractually bound to tie his hands.

NOTES

1. All translations are mine, except where otherwise noted.

2. For a discussion of the *Encyclopédie*'s "monstrous" uterus and its relationship to hysteria, see Miller 50.

3. I would like to thank Philip Stewart for bringing Pierre Darmon's book to my attention.

4. This contract could be either explicit (as in the case of a marriage arranged by parents) or implicit (as in the case of a seduction) (Bérenguier 452).

5. Voltaire and Graffigny are linked by a traumatic historical event. During a stay at Cirey with Voltaire and Mme du Châtelet, Graffigny was accused by her hosts of clandestinely copying one of *La pucelle*'s cantos and sending it to her friend, François-Antoine Devaux (Graffigny, *Choix de Lettres* 20–25).

6. The references to the Voltaire text include both the canto number and verse number(s).

7. Joan DeJean situates the origins of "heroinism" in European literature in a different country (France) and much earlier than does the term's inventor, Ellen

Moers (122–24, 147); moreover, DeJean discusses manifestations of heroinism in politics (with the *femme forte* of the early seventeenth century), not only in amorous literature (DeJean 26, 78–79).

8. Zilia insists that her inability to love Déterville stems from her cultural difference from him "Vous n'êtes point de ma nation" (Graffigny, *Lettres* 96) ["You are not at all of my nation" (Graffigny, *Letters* 99)]. At the end of the novel, she maintains this cultural separation, although she professes to regret it (Graffigny, *Lettres* 166).

9. The violence that Leucippe must endure (particularly her evisceration when she is "sacrificed" and her beheading when she is "murdered" by pirates) brings to mind the ritual defloration that Freud discusses in "The Taboo of Virginity": penetrating her body through violence illustrates "the practice of rupturing the hymen . . . outside the subsequent marriage" (194).

10. Charles Segal interprets this ordeal in the following way: "Leucippe will be neither the sterile virgin who remains devoted to Artemis . . . nor the sexually intemperate girl who yields to desire and perishes a victim of Artemis' wrath" (89).

11. Ironically, Jeanne does wish for the eventual destruction of her hymen, but wants to fulfill the terms of her contract and have sex with Dunois (which does, in fact, happen at the end of the narrative).

12. This is interesting because other approaches—including ones I have written (Nell, "Un grand nombre"; Nell, "Qu'est-ce qu'une lectrice?")—have interpreted the signing of the contract as Zilia binding herself in marriage to Déterville. Indeed, Erin Isikoff has interpreted this signed document as a marriage contract between Zilia and Déterville (Isikoff 23).

13. "[A] literary life and a traditional marriage proved incompatible" in the seventeenth century (DeJean 4).

WORKS CITED

Achilles Tatius. "Leucippe and Clitophon." *Collected Ancient Greek Novels.* Ed. B. P. Reardon. Trans. John J. Winkler. Berkeley: U of California P, 1989. 170–284.

Bakhtin, Mikhail. *The Dialogic Imagination.* Austin: U of Texas P, 1981.

Benstock, Shari. *Textualizing the Feminine: On the Limits of Genre.* Norman: U of Oklahoma P, 1991.

Bérenguier, Nadine. "Le 'dangereux dépôt': virginité et contrat dans *Julie ou la nouvelle Héloïse.*" *Eighteenth-Century Fiction* 9.4 (July 1994): 447–63.

Butler, Judith. *Bodies That Matter: On the Discursive Limits of "Sex".* New York: Routledge, 1993.

————. *Gender Trouble: Feminism and the Subversion of Identity*. Rev. ed. New York: Routledge, 1999.

Clément, Catherine. "La coupable." *La jeune née*. Paris: Union générale d'éditions, 1975. 9–113.

Cuddon, J. A. *A Dictionary of Literary Terms*. Harmondsworth: Penguin, 1979.

Darmon, Pierre. *Le tribunal de l'impuissance: virilité et défaillances conjugales dans l'ancienne France*. Paris: Seuil, 1979.

DeJean, Joan. *Tender Geographies: Women and the Origins of the Novel in France*. New York: Columbia UP, 1991.

Deleuze, Gilles. *Presentation de Sacher-Masoch: le froid et le cruel*. Paris: Minuit, 1967.

Derrida, Jacques. *La dissémination*. Paris: Seuil, 1979.

————. *Spurs: Nietzsche's Styles/Eperons: Les styles de Nietzsche*. Trans. Barbara Harlow. Chicago: U of Chicago P, 1979.

DiPiero, Thomas. *White Men Aren't*. Durham: Duke UP, 2002.

Freud, Sigmund. "Femininity." *The Standard Edition of the Complete Psychological Works of Sigmund Freud*. Vol. 22. Ed. James Strachey. London: Hogarth, 1964. 112–35.

————. "The Taboo of Virginity." *The Standard Edition*. Vol. 11. Ed. James Strachey. London: Hogarth, 1957. 191–208.

Garber, Marjorie. *Vested Interests: Cross-Dressing and Cultural Anxiety*. New York: Routledge, 1992.

Graffigny, Françoise de. *Choix de Lettres*. Ed. English Showalter. Oxford: Voltaire Foundation, 2002.

————. *Letters from a Peruvian Woman*. Eds. Joan DeJean and Nancy K. Miller. Trans. David Kornacker. New York: MLA, 1993.

————. *Lettres d'une Péruvienne*. Eds. Joan DeJean and Nancy K. Miller. New York: MLA, 1993.

Irigaray, Luce. *Ce sexe qui n'en est pas un*. Paris: Minuit, 1977.

Isikoff, Erin. "The Temple, the Château and the Female Space: Nancy Miller's Overreading of Graffigny's *Lettres d'une Péruvienne*." *Dalhousie French Studies* 33 (1995): 15–26.

Jameson, Frederic. *The Political Unconscious: Narrative as a Socially Symbolic Act*. Ithaca, NY: Cornell UP, 1981.

Jaucourt, Chevalier de. "Hymen," "Pudeur," "Virginité." *Encyclopédie ou dictionnaire raisonné des sciences, des arts et des métiers*. 1751–772. *ARTFL Project*. Ed. Mark Olsen. 30 Aug. 2002. <http://duras.uchicago.edu/efts/ARTFL/projects/encyc/>.

Konstan, David. *Sexual Symmetry: Love in the Ancient Novel and Related Genres.* Princeton, NJ: Princeton UP, 1994.

Kristeva, Julia. "Stabat Mater." *Histoires d'amour.* Paris: Denoël, 1983. 225–47.

Lacan, Jacques. *Le séminaire de Jacques Lacan. Livre VII: L'éthique de la psychanalyse.* 1959–1960. Ed. Jacques-Alain Miller. Paris: Seuil, 1986.

———. "L'instance de la lettre dans l'inconscient ou la raison depuis Freud." *Ecrits.* Paris: Seuil, 1966. 493–528.

Mallarmé, Stéphane. *Oeuvres complètes.* Paris: Gallimard, 1947.

Miller, Paul Allen. "Floating Uteruses and Phallic Gazes: Hippocratic Medicine in the *Encyclopédie.*" *Intertexts* 2.1 (Spring 1998): 46–61.

———. *Subjecting Verses: Latin Love Elegy and the Emergence of the Real.* Princeton, NJ: Princeton UP, 2004.

Moers, Ellen. *Literary Women.* New York: Oxford UP, 1963.

Nell, Sharon. "Qu'est-ce qu'une lectrice? Les femmes et la possibilité de lire dans *La Princesse de Clèves* et les *Lettres d'une Péruvienne.*" *Lectrice d'ancien régime.* Ed. Isabelle Brouard-Arends. Rennes: Presses Universitaires de Rennes, 2002. 523–31.

———. "Un grand nombre de bagatelles agréables': Zilia vis-à-vis des divertissements du rococo." *Françoise de Graffigny, femme de lettres: Ecriture et réception.* Ed. Jonathan Mallinson. Oxford: Voltaire Foundation. 380–88.

Russo, Mary. "Female Grotesques: Carnival and Theory." *Feminist Studies, Critical Studies.* Ed. Teresa de Lauretis. Bloomington: Indiana UP, 1986.

Sade, Marquis de [Alphonse-Donatien]. *Justine.* Paris: Livres de Poche, 1973.

Segal, Charles. "The Trials at the End of Achilles Tatius' Clitophon and Leucippe: Doublets and Complementaries." *Studi Italiani di Filologia Classica.* 3rd ser. 2 (1984): 83–91.

Voltaire. *Les oeuvres complètes de Voltaire. La pucelle d'Orléans.* Vol. 7. Ed. Jeroom Vercruysse. Genève: Institut et Musée Voltaire, 1970.

Wittig, Monique. "The Mark of Gender." *Feminist Issues* 5.2 (1985): 3–12.

———. "One is Not Born a Woman." *Writing on the Body: Female Embodiment and Feminist Theory.* Eds. Katie Conboy, et al. New York: Columbia UP, 1997. 309–17.

Wright, Elizabeth and Edmond Wright, eds. *The Žižek Reader.* Malden, MA: Blackwell, 1999.

Žižek, Slavoj. "Courtly Love, or Woman as Thing." *The Žižek Reader.* Eds. Elizabeth Wright and Edmond Wright. Malden, MA: Blackwell, 1999. 148–73.

————. *Enjoy Your Symptom! Jacques Lacan in Hollywood and Out*. New York: Routledge, 1992.

————. "In His Bold Gaze My Ruin Is Writ Large." *Everything You Always Wanted to Know About Lacan (But Were Afraid to Ask Hitchcock)*. Ed. Slavoj Žižek. London: Verso, 1992. 211–72.

————. *Looking Awry: An Introduction to Jacques Lacan through Popular Culture*. Cambridge, MA: MIT Press, 1991.

————. "The Obscene Object of Postmodernity." *The Žižek Reader*. Eds. Elizabeth Wright and Edmond Wright. Malden, MA: Blackwell, 1999. 37–52.

————. "The Spectre of Ideology." *The Žižek Reader*. Eds. Elizabeth Wright and Edmond Wright. Malden, MA: Blackwell, 1999. 53–86.

9

Queer(ing) Pleasure

Having a Gay Old Time in the Culture of Early-Modern France

Pierre Zoberman

Whether same-sex desire was recognized as a defining identity trait or not in early-modern France—and indeed early-modern Europe in general—it gave rise to various representational, textual strategies. An inquiry into the distinctive place of desire in the life and representation of such figures as Monsieur,[1] a notorious sodomite, might help us determine the status of desire and pleasure in the culture of the period. In other words, I mean to explicate sexual mores (and more specifically, socially deviant sexual practices) in analytic terms, while complicating, questioning, and historicizing the suture between the analytic, the political, and the social. In the following pages, I will argue that, when trying to ascertain whether we can identify gay subtexts in seventeenth-century culture, and whether we can apply such contemporary categories as "gay" to the society of the *Ancien Régime*, we can draw on Lacan's analysis of uncompromising desire (as opposed to mundane resignation and the coming to terms with the demands and strictures of everyday life) most clearly formulated in *The Ethics of Psychoanalysis* to establish relevant criteria. In particular, Lacan's text can help us understand the status of this most striking prince of the blood as the *magnificent sodomite*. Monsieur, like to a lesser degree members of his circle when his presence temporarily frees them from the constraints of life at the King's court, engages in what seems, at least at first glance, to be free pleasure in a very broad sense (and this might be seen as not compromising where desire is concerned). It is tempting to suggest, however, that he also looks beyond the constant stream of pleasures and partial objects, with regard to which fulfillment can never be definitive, toward absolute fulfillment—a fulfillment that, as Lacan states about Antigone, can only be death.

On the other hand, the parallel I am implying between the radiance of Antigone—as the archetypal (tragic) character whose "no" allows her to enjoy an extraordinary death that ends all desire—and Monsieur cannot be maintained rigorously: Antigone, qua tragic character, does not have to worry about material considerations such as what things are worth in terms of petty, human exchanges; Monsieur is engaged in a concrete, social world, where desire takes as its objects elements whose costs can and must be estimated, and which, in order for fulfillment to take place, must be met. Even if Monsieur's life hints at a desire leading beyond the pleasure principle, it does so in the social world (i.e., through pleasure(s)), and this contradiction colors all accounts of the time.[2]

Monsieur has recently become something of a fashionable topic. And, as if to echo by anticipation the phrase "the desire of the analysts"[3] the agendas of those writing about him clearly color their output. In the 1950s, Daniel Marc, in a lecture at Arcadie, a pioneer gay cultural association and support group (Marc 1956), depicted Monsieur as an early version of a self-abasing drag queen, in a gesture one might characterize as retroactive iconization (so that Monsieur becomes a reference, a predecessor, understandable in modern-day terms, and thus to a certain extent an anachronism). Even though it lacks a sense of cultural contextualization, Marc's gesture is helpful in encouraging us to cast a more inquisitive glance at what we might term "the history of sexuality." More apologetically, Philippe Erlanger, in his biography of the King's brother, developed the theory of a plot to effeminize him so as to prevent him from causing for Louis XIV the kind of trouble his uncle, Gaston of Orléans, had made for Louis XIII—the official historian is clearly eager to explain away Monsieur's shocking deviance. Here, same-sex desire seems to have met with very specific desires on its analysts' part. Even Didier Godard's recent book, *Le Goût de Monsieur*, after a factual study of laws governing sodomy and the scope of repression in early-modern Europe—one of the most useful aspects of the book[4]—falls into a tangle of contradictions. He counters traditional, homophobic history by trying to demonstrate that, in the seventeenth century, there was no concept of sexual identity, that bisexuality (or, rather, sexual indeterminacy) was prevalent and unproblematic, and that there was no censure of discourse—in other words that homosexuality was not a taboo subject and did not carry social opprobrium, and that the social tolerance concerning homosexual practices extended beyond the high nobility.[5]

My own desire is neither to set up an icon nor to apologize for Monsieur's sexual mores (or possibly his gayness), but rather to look beyond the standard satirical texts in order to illuminate the status of a certain queerness in early-modern France. The following reflections were born of a series of considerations on the representation of Monsieur, in various contexts: in what I call the *royal text*, a network of cultural productions celebrating the King, where any hint, not only of homosexuality, but of anything that would not pertain specifically to Louis XIV's glory was erased;[6] in Saint-Simon's *Mémoires*,[7] with their bitter attacks against Monsieur's favorites; and in the *mondain* accounts[8] of his lavish fêtes, providing the unexpected source for the identification of what we might call gay subtexts. Contemporary readers knew all about Monsieur's sexual preferences and relationships with his minions. Such *knowingness* implied a matter-of-fact tolerance. It also meant that, in public texts like the *Mercure galant*, many things were only half expressed, hinted at, gestured to with a wink and nod. We are then looking for textual clues that may have turned portraits of people we know anecdotally to have been—to use current terminology—homosexuals into *homosexual portraits*.

I had to reject effeminacy as a defining factor per se: Saint-Simon does claim that, despite his military prowess and courage, Monsieur embodied all "the bad qualities of women," yet effeminacy, though viewed negatively and often hurled as a slur, did not necessarily entail an accusation of homosexuality.[9] Saint-Simon's ubiquitous recrimination is that Monsieur's "abominable taste" made the Chevalier de Lorraine, an ambitious and unprincipled member of the Guise family, his master.[10] It is tempting to see the upheaval of the "traditional," aristocratic order as proof of Monsieur's "gayness," especially since the same complaints had been voiced where Henri III was concerned, and Marlowe's *Edward II* provides a literary version of this subversion of the political hierarchy through same-sex desire.[11] Saint-Simon himself, however, has to acknowledge that Monsieur never loses sight of his position and is superlatively aware of rank. Moreover, his concern with the threat posed by homoeroticism to the traditional order only surfaces in connection with Monsieur. So it could only be a partial answer—in both senses of the word.

Finally, I developed the hypothesis that the pursuit of pleasure for the sake of pleasure, with no "ethical" value to redeem it, and no linguistic attenuation to explain or extenuate it, might function as a revealing sign. At first glance at least, here were people who seemed not to have shrunk from their desires. Thus, it is essential more fully to understand the place of *desire* and *pleasure* in the Ancien Régime—in society at large as well as in the individual lives and psyches of its members. So, I will proceed by first examining opposing manifestations and accounts of pleasure in the Ancien Régime, and then take my inquiry beyond, beyond, that is, both pleasure as immediate enjoyment, here and now (there and then) and beyond the potentially deceiving appearance of free pleasure. This, in turn, will help assess the push toward a psychoanalytical explanation for sociohistoric phenomena, and might be used as a testing ground for the validity and limits of such an approach.

In the end, then, the absolute pursuit of pleasure, the refusal to cede on desire even in the face of (and beyond) death, will serve as the guiding thread to my analysis. In many ways, this methodological decision reflects a recognition of the essential correctness of Foucault's position at the end of volume 1 of the *History of Sexuality* that we do not find liberation from the regime of sexuality and the categories of compulsory heterosexism in saying yes to "sex," but, just possibly, in an archeology of bodies and pleasures. Therefore, this might be a good testing ground for the possibility of responsibly asking new questions of the past, and the effectiveness for the study of past historical contexts of concepts that they could not articulate. While doing a history of Monsieur as "gay," "homosexual," or "queer" is in some ways an urgent task in any attempt to understand both seventeenth-century history and the genealogy of what it means to be and act queer in the new millennium, it may always fall short of the mark. But such is the nature of queer, which is less about asserting definitive truths than about asking questions. This terminology, while useful and necessary to establishing the stakes of Monsieur's absolute pursuit of pleasure, even beyond its symbolically sanctioned governing principle, brings with it concepts of sexual identity (homosexual), liberation politics (gay), and deliberate transgression of normative behaviors (queer) that are alien to seventeenth-century court culture, and might only be glimpsed in fictional literature or imagined situations. Ironically, it is only in the ostensibly transhistorical vocabulary of psychoanalytic "desire" and "pleasure" that we can begin to trace what really makes Monsieur *not* so very queer.

Several times in *L'Éthique de la psychanalyse*, Lacan reminds us that a patient suffers because of the guilt pursuant to "avoir cédé sur son désir" [having given in (or up) where desire is concerned or, perhaps, given up on his or her desire]:[12]

> *Je propose que la seule chose dont on puisse être coupable, au moins dans la perspective analytique, c'est d'avoir cédé sur son désir.*
>
> *Cette proposition, recevable ou non dans telle ou telle éthique, exprime assez bien ce que nous constatons dans notre expérience. Au dernier terme, ce dont le sujet se sent effectivement coupable quand il fait de la culpabilité, de façon recevable ou non pour le directeur de conscience, c'est toujours, à la racine, pour autant qu'il a cédé sur son désir.* (368)

[I propose that the only thing that one can be guilty of, at least in the analytic perspective, is having given up on one's desire. (Official translation: "given ground relative to desire"; Lacan 321)

This proposition, whether or not it is acceptable in this or that ethical system, expresses quite aptly what we do observe in our experience. When all is said, what the subject effectively feels guilty of when he experiences (fait) guilt, whether or not it is acceptable for the director of conscience, is always, at the root, inasmuch as he has given up on his desire.][13]

Clearly, Lacan is referring here to what he sees as a very common phenomenon, not a rare occurrence. The primary and secondary processes described by Freud in *The Interpretation of Dreams* have to do with fantasizing, postponing, or channeling, even foregoing the gratification of desire (V: 588 ff). If the dream-work (Freud IV: 277–338) may be read as producing scenarios of gratification, i.e., pleasure, in a nonactual universe, so does, typically, tragedy. As a student of tragedy, I always found Lacan's analysis of *Antigone* most insightful. True tragic figures/ heroes, as opposed to the common human being, have not "cédé sur leur désir." And Lacan's reliance on the archetypal figure of Antigone makes plain that this desire involves death. It is a desire to die, after, through, and as a consequence of a transgressive act that must pit the individual against social authority—Antigone vs. Creon. Again, Lacan phrases things most vividly: "Nous n'avons pas été assez emmerdés sur cette terre avec le désir, il faut qu'une partie de l'éternité s'emploie à faire, de tout cela, les comptes (366)." ["We haven't been bugged enough on this earth with desire, part of eternity must be used to settle, of all that, the account."] In other words, the eschatological constructs of religions such as Christianity are instrumental in getting mere humans to give ground relative to desire—and the analyst sees through them. Psychoanalysis transforms the Christian *memento mori*. Freud himself, in the early twentieth century, had warned, "*Si vis vitam, para mortem*" (Freud "Thoughts" 300).[14] And Lacan is quick to point out that tragic heroes aim at a death free of all reckoning: true nonexistence, or heavenly peace, at least. That is tragedy. And this, *céder sur son désir*, is real life. It is a social imperative: "Continuons à travailler, et pour le désir vous repasserez" (367). ["Let us go on working; and as for desire, better luck next time.]

How does this opposition between those who give up on their desire and those who do not illuminate the representation of such notorious sodomites as Monsieur in the culture of Ancien Régime France? If pleasure stems from the gratification of desire, then the view one takes of pleasure is significant, and we can identify at least two conceptions of pleasure at the time, which, ultimately, we might characterize as *the King's pleasure* and *Monsieur's pleasure*.

By the King's pleasure, I mean the prevalent view of pleasure, which finds its most striking expression at court. In a deeply Christian culture, pleasure is looked on with great suspicion. In the courtly and *mondain* circles, pleasure is a Master Signifier.[15] What is characteristic, however, is the connection of pleasure with power. At the King's court, power is an integral part of pleasure, and the celebrants of the King's glory are well aware of it. Take, for instance, the following amplification of the care Louis XIV took not to interrupt, despite his illness,[16] the pleasures he provided to his entourage in the true kingly spirit of magnificence:

> The King did not even want that, during his illness, the amusements of the Court be interrupted. He opened his magnificent rooms, where are gathered all the games and the pleasures that can charm the mind without corrupting it. It is a perpetual fête, that his magnificence and his wisdom invented in order to teach courtiers to gamble in moderation, to amuse themselves innocently, and also in order to know their inclinations and their behavior, by means that be the surest and the most worthy of the Royal Majesty. (Barbier d'Aucour, *Discours sur le rétablissement de la santé du Roy* (1687), [Zoberman *Panégyriques* 230])

The pleasures the King affords his entourage are clearly viewed as a refinement in the art of government. At the same time, the passage focuses on the other, most significant aspect of pleasure. What we have here is the *normal*, or rather the *normative* conception of pleasure. The potentially threatening nature of pleasure is circumvented linguistically by qualifying it: "pleasures that can charm the mind *without corrupting* it," "teach courtiers how to gamble *in moderation*," and "to amuse themselves *innocently*." So much denegation points to the received version of pleasure as something to be wary of. Even the King's pleasures are justified as well-deserved recreation from the labors he constantly undertakes for the State, whose weight rests always on his shoulders. The corollary is that the King is never so absorbed in pleasure as to be oblivious to his royal duties—the King provides the ultimate model for the social imperative. *Continuons de travailler* . . . Apostolidès sees in the mise-en-scène of the "Plaisirs de l'Île enchantée"[17] an allegory of the need to transcend worldly pleasures. "The 1664 fête is organized around a double theme: the quest for pleasure and the necessity to move beyond it." (Apostolidès 98).

Seventeenth-century discourse on pleasure, however, is not univocal. Beside satiric literature, where notorious sodomites are lampooned and reviled,[18] we are confronted with a *mondain* literature that hints at a category of people who have not *cédé sur leur désir*. By this, I do not mean simply that they have come to terms with and acted upon their homoerotic sexual urges. If anything, the complacency with which the nobility claimed that every one amongst them engaged in same-sex intercourse (what we might call the aristocratic topos of sodomy)[19] could be interpreted as a claim that they embraced pleasure. But the general perception that, for a certain group, pleasure rules can be read as a suggestion that they are both viewed and view themselves as not having given in where desire is concerned. This is where what I referred to as "Monsieur's pleasure" takes on its full significance. Because of his position in the social hierarchy, Louis XIV's brother was the subject of numerous accounts.[20] Texts about Monsieur bring into relief his total dedication to pleasure—a freer kind of pleasure than those the King provides to the courtly elite.

Arguably, Monsieur's position might also have made it easier not to give up where desire was concerned.[21] At Monsieur's court, pleasure seems to be divorced from power. Though he is quite aware of rank, he manages to bring pure enjoyment to his guests. According to Saint-Simon, he animates the life of the court: "He it was who animated it with amusements, soul, pleasures, and, when he left it, everything seemed lifeless and motionless" (Saint-Simon II: 13). This sentence comments on the sorry state of the court after Monsieur's death. It is also characteristic, however, of an apparently irrepressible connection between Monsieur and pleasure in contemporary discourse. I will take up presently the implied link with death ("lifeless," "motionless")—as though commentators could not escape, when talking about Monsieur, a sense of a death-wish, or death-urge, at the root of his pursuit of pleasure. It is clear, at any rate, that any account of Monsieur is saturated with references to pleasure. Obviously, neither the *Mercure* nor Saint-Simon[22] could be said to be Lacanian, nor can they be expected to be rigorous in their associations. Viewing the available documentation from today's perspective, however, one is struck by the sheer bulk of texts linking Monsieur to pleasure.

Nothing epitomized Monsieur's quest for pleasure as well as Saint-Cloud, a residence he embellished year in and year out, so that it embodied the topos of the *locus amœnus*, both in the enclosed space of the house and in the beautiful gardens. On this point, contemporary sources are unanimous, from the favorable monthly *Mercure*, largely subsidized by the Crown, to the usually venomous Saint-Simon, both well acquainted with quite a few beautiful places. For the memoirist: "The pleasures of all sorts of amusements, of the singular beauty of the place, that countless carriages made easy to explore for even the laziest ladies, of music, of good food, rendered it a house of delights steeped in grandeur and magnificence" (Saint-Simon II: 13). This echoes the *Mercure galant*, which had offered its imagined reader—a *dame* of peculiar refinement and education, one therefore who can appreciate the *"propreté"* evidenced by all of Monsieur's fêtes—several accounts of lavish entertainment. Thus, in May 1680:

> If countless splendid occasions had not taught you, along with the whole kingdom of France, that Monsieur is a Prince as gallant as he is magnificent, you would no doubt believe the detailed account I must give you of the latest Fête at Saint-Cloud to be an exaggerated tale; but, my Lady, you know better than I how natural these two qualities are to His Royal Highness, and it is enough for me to name Saint-Cloud when I talk about a Fête to make you picture all that is worthy of a brother to Louis le Grand.[23] (*Mercure galant*, May 1680, 295–98)

These and similar passages are quite explicit about Monsieur's charmed life, and yet, paradoxically, challenging in their very explicitness. The lexicon used by Saint-Simon and Donneau de Visé (the *Mercure's* editor) helps to bring to the fore the major difficulty in reading such representations analytically. Such terms as "grandeur" and "magnificence" or "magnificent" inscribe Monsieur's pleasures in a social context of hierarchical eminence. Magnificence is the princely, even kingly, social virtue par excellence. Yet, the recurring clues of exceptionality ("singular" in Saint-Simon's text quoted above, as in countless other accounts, or the rhetorical energy devoted by the *Mercure's* editor to forestalling disbelief in his seemingly fabulous account) signal that even in his position, the King's brother promotes his (and, by contiguity his entourage's) pleasure to a degree and in a way worthy of special notice. What I want to emphasize here is that, if we take such characterization as a suggestion that some might have found the Prince's pleasure-oriented life threatening, or "queer," this need not imply that Monsieur himself *was* queer. I am not using the term "queer" here simply as a synonym for *gay*. What is at stake is not, or is not simply, sexual orientation. "Queer" refers to all that calls into question or threatens the heteronormative order. For the purpose of this discussion, therefore, I propose that even if some sodomites in seventeenth-century France may come close to what we mean today by *gay*—and that, in itself, is interesting—they did not necessarily appear *queer* to their contemporaries, in the broadly political sense I have just stipulated. This is what texts about Monsieur allow us to argue. After all, he married twice and had children who are the forebears of today's reigning monarchs in Europe, thus fulfilling, rather than subverting, his role as a prince of the blood, the second-highest ranking personage in the kingdom. If we consider, however, statements that sodomitic "inclinations" may be inborn,[24] we are at least in a position to suggest that something like a gay subculture was developing. And this is where Monsieur's talents as a party-giver may be most relevant.

Monsieur entertains in the most lavish fashion. I have commented elsewhere on his "taste for ceremony" and parties (see "A Taste for Ceremony"). Pleasure is so prevalent that, though the *Mercure galant* mentions that the fêtes it chronicles are given in honor of the King and other members of the royal family, the accounts take on a revealing autonomy—they're interesting and pleasurable for their own sake, not as one more facet added to the celebration of the King. But the difference between the programs (symbolic-political) underlying the King's elaborate spectacles as well as all the ceremonial proceedings, and Monsieur's festive outputs is unmistakable.

Quite remarkable as well is the cast of characters involved: lots of high-ranking people, but also much more dubious characters. Monsieur's *régals* (parties organized as a treat to an honored guest, comprising supper and entertainment) often culminated in improvised balls. Contemporary sources regularly emphasize the presence of the best dancers in courtly and *mondain* milieus. Actually, dancing seems to epitomize the kind of dedication to pleasure chronicled in the accounts of Monsieur's fêtes.

> Those who danced afterwards were, on the men's side, Messieurs the Princes de Conty and de la Roche-sur-Yon, M^{rs} the Counts de Armagnac and de Brionne, M^r the Chevalier de Lorraine, M^{rs} the Dukes de la Trémoüille and de Gramont, M^r the Marquis de Biran, M^r the Count de Tonnerre, M^r the marquis de Gondran, and M^r the Chevalier de Chastillon. On the ladies' side, Mesdames the Duchesses de Foix, de la Tremoüille and de Mortemar, Madame the Marchioness de Segnelay, Madame de Grancé, and Mesdemoiselles de Laval, Chasteautiers, Potier, & Clisson.[25] (*Mercure galant*, 1680, 300–301)

The lists of male dancers at Monsieur's fêtes intersect quite significantly with those of sodomites in contemporary memoirs (see for instance Sourches)[26] or satiric texts (though the latter must be taken with some circumspection) such as *La France devenue italienne* (inserted in Bussy-Rabutin's *Histoire amoureuse des Gaules*). But I will argue that their accomplishments in the domain of worldly pleasure are even more relevant here.

Some of them were, indeed, well known for their talent at dancing—and for little else, as Saint-Simon attests; the account of the death of the comte de Brionne, son of Monsieur le Grand, the Chevalier de Lorraine's brother, is a case in point:

> There died at the same time a man of a better house, but whose merit would have been limited to hams, if he had been born to a father who sold them: it was the Count of Brionne, over-whelmed by a long series of apoplexias. He was a Knight of the Order of 1688, and the best dancer of his time, though only of an average height, and rather fat. [27]

Dancing became the paradigm of pleasure seeking. What I am suggesting is not that a special talent for dancing was in itself a marker of same-sex desire, especially given the role dance had played in court entertainment and the popularity it had enjoyed,[28] but that it epitomizes the pursuit of pleasure that is chronicled in all the *Mercure*'s accounts.[29] I am suggesting, moreover, that it is unlikely that readers of the *Mercure*—aware, as many memoirs attest, of the court's various intrigues and affairs—would have set aside their specific knowingness just when confronted with accounts of Monsieur's fêtes; on the contrary, they would most likely have associated the instances of pursuit of pleasure they were treated to with same-sex desire, and have been inclined by the pleasure these accounts afforded to find such knowledge neither threatening nor particularly upsetting (though they may have felt a thrill at the account of the boundless pleasures Monsieur and his entourage indulged in).[30]

In a description to which I shall return presently, the *Mercure* characterizes the setting of Monsieur's pleasures, the beautiful house of Saint-Cloud, as "magnificent" and "singular," a conjunction I commented upon earlier, when dealing with Saint-Simon's description of the house. In texts that combine representation and edification, for instance in funeral orations, worldly pleasures have to be excused, underemphasized, or otherwise dealt with as impediments to a Christian life.[31] The *Mercure*, on the other hand, slipping toward the margin of the *royal text*, provides a worldly, positive image of a pleasure-bound microcosm, where rank is not forgotten (which may be a reason to be cautious, and suggest that being "queer" in Monsieur's case, may have had more to do with *being seen* as "queer," in other words that it may have had more to do with *representation* than *being*), but where, as opposed to the King's court, pleasure is not used as an instrument of government—and where pleasure finds in itself its own justification, and does not need to be qualified, even linguistically, as well-deserved or innocent. Interestingly, this function of the pursuit of pleasure—in Western society traditionally a topos of negative representations of homosexuals and various "marginals" through the vilification of promiscuity—finds echoes in modern gay studies with the rather romanticized suggestion that same-sex desire bridges class divides.[32]

Monsieur's pleasure, therefore, can be said to have impressed his contemporaries as exceptional both for the intensity with which it was pursued and for its apparently unrelenting, uncompromising, unashamed, undisguised nature. This, I would claim, is the operator that transforms portraits of homosexuals (individuals we know to have been homosexual) into homosexual portraits (encoding a characterization of individuals *as* homosexuals): the embracing of pleasure for its own sake.[33] The significance of this pleasure, I will argue, exceeds the requirement of free expenditure that characterizes, in Jean-Marie Apostolidès's perspective, the aristocracy of the Ancien Régime, particularly in its attempt to keep the bourgeoisie from achieving total assimilation into the elite. Thus, at the end of the chapter devoted to "Les Plaisirs de l'Île enchantée," he remarks: "The elite invited to Versailles thus shares the State secret, but the King alone dilapidates riches produced for its sole enjoyment. He offers them to his guests only because he gets, as a return, an increase of power" (Aposotolidès 104).[34]

This leads me to a two-tiered argument with regard to the fecundity and limits of the notion of pleasure as a key characteristic of the ubiquitous textual figure of Monsieur as the *singularly magnificent sodomite*. Developing this argument will mean exploring the possibility of a *gay* subculture, and, even more interestingly, the representation of a *queer* culture in a paradoxical marginality that lies close to the very center of Ancien Régime power.

On the one hand, the case for pleasure as a marker of "queerness" is convincing, and more examples could be adduced to support it. Though this article aims at setting up hypotheses more than at giving definitive conclusions, I can already deal with some objections. The first has to do with the difficulty of distinguishing between potentially *queer* pleasure and "heteronormative" pleasure. As my brief foray into lexical commentary (about "magnificence" and "singularity") suggests, the discussion of pleasure brings to mind the difficulty that arises when one has to trace fine distinctions within characteristics that seem to be largely shared by the elite. To make this point clearer, we might draw a parallel with the curious status of fictional characters such as Mademoiselle de Chartres and the Duc de Nemours in Madame de La Fayette's *La Princesse de Clèves*. They are especially beautiful and extraordinary characters among courtiers whose main characteristic is that they are beautiful and extraordinary. And with a dearth of detail, we have to understand that, in a milieu defined by its distinction and superiority with regard to an outer world, they are superiorly superior. I lay no claim to originality here,[35] I simply point out that, while portraits may have been a fashion,[36] they were fraught with some basic difficulties. Yet, that the Princesse de Clèves was actually "an unlikely princess" is attested by the controversies the *nouvelle* spurred in the late 1670s as well as modern criticism and scholarship.[37] The parallel is not as idle as it may seem, and may, as I shall demonstrate later, suggest directions to explore in order to distinguish between *gay* and *queer*. But I am currently concerned with the problematic distinction among pleasures. As I was developing my argument on pleasure, I happened to visit, in Bath, the Pump Room and the Assembly Rooms, two venues where the gentry and other visitors taking the waters could find an array of diversions, gaming, tea, dancing—especially dancing, which had become a major, mainstream activity, judging from the seven-foot-long caricature by William Dickinson, entitled *The Long Minuet As Danced At Bath in 1787* then on loan at the Holborne museum.[38] But these were not free pleasures, as in Monsieur's court, nor were they considered as such; they were public ones; moreover, there were social stakes. Though we cannot take literature as a pure and simple reproduction of reality, the kind of negotiations and transactions (marriage arrangements and financial dispositions) that are said to take place in those venues of entertainment in Jane Austen's novels warn against underestimating those stakes. Even in France, under the rule of the Regent, when Louis XIV died in 1715 while his great-grandson and heir to the throne, Louis XV, was still a child, there was a definite departure from the austerity that had characterized the latest part of the Sun-king's reign; pleasure might be said to have played a particularly important role. One might respond to the objection in jest, by recalling that the Regent was Monsieur's son, the very same Duc de Chartres whose marriage with Mademoiselle de Blois so chagrined Madame and Saint-Simon—the latter saw in the match the symptom of a far-reaching corruption. It should come as no surprise that the Regent knew about pleasure. Moreover, Monsieur meant to give him as *gouverneur*, again to Madame's chagrin, one of his own favorites, the marquis d'Effiat—a notorious sodomite . . .[39] On a less flippant level, I will suggest the possibility that even though a certain kind of pleasure and a remorseless dedication to pleasure can be considered revealing across time, what is seen as comprising this revealing pleasure changes over times—without this admission invalidating the hypothesis. The same pleasure-giving activities may be potential markers of a gay subculture (and may even point to queerness) at one point in history and be viewed, earlier or later, as much more mainstream, with other "pleasures," on the other hand, taking on a queer connotation. Ballet had been a mainstay of court entertainment. As a staple of Monsieur's fêtes, however, dancing seemed to have become emblematic of the absolute quest for pleasure, and perhaps of the quest for absolute pleasure, but it moved to more public scenes.[40] The economic logic was transformed. It does not mean that pleasure should be ruled out as a criterion from then on, simply that what constituted revealing pleasure may have evolved.

The second objection that needs to be taken up and that is pregnant with much more weighty theoretical consequences, has to do with what may be understood, in a given society, by "queer." Until now, I have apparently moved back and forth between *gay* and *queer* as two related but not clearly circumscribed notions. The current discussion may yield some helpful pointers. Even if the case for the carefree pursuit of pleasure can be made for seventeenth-century texts, it may turn out to be, in a way, too powerful, or too inclusive. For other *marginal* figures (even if, as is the case with Monsieur, the marginality lies at the center), or at least individuals viewed as potentially threatening to the social fabric, may be characterized in the same way, and peculiarly, the libertine.[41] This is where the more political, and certainly more controversial notion of "queer," meant to characterize the very practice of questioning and controverting *order*, might be illuminating. The question would then have to be raised whether all these "marginal" figures are actually analogous or whether the dominant culture considered them equally exotic or dangerous—and, ultimately, perhaps equally *queer*.[42] Bringing together accounts of Monsieur's life and times, the figure of the libertine, and even such controversial characters as the Princesse de Clèves, is, I contend, the best way to clarify Monsieur's status and to adduce some propositions as to queerness in the Ancien Régime and as to the distinction between gay and queer.

Again, Lacan's work in the wake of Freud's *Beyond the Pleasure Principle* will be our starting point. We are, apparently, poised for an analytically founded queering of our past culture, through pleasure. As I noted from the outset, however, Lacan's warning about "not giving up on one's desire" should not be trivialized, no more than Antigone's death should be taken as an ordinary death. Monsieur dazzled his contemporaries with his magnificence and his dedication to pleasure. But, to play on words, can we go beyond that? What lies *beyond* Monsieur's pleasure principle? Has his quest for pleasure really Lacan's sublime object for its aim; is it determined by "*das*

Ding," as sketched in *L'Éthique de la psychanalyse?*[43] Not only was Monsieur seen as "singular"; when reading texts of the period, there is an uncanny connection between his singular brand of pleasure and death. I mentioned Monsieur's grand, magnificent, and singular residence of Saint-Cloud, a place that came to embody pleasure. Texts of the period give fascinating clues to both the potential for and the limits to an interpretation of Monsieur's pleasure-drive as an unswerving pursuit of *das Ding*, translating into a pure death-drive.

Most telling is the obituary the *Mercure* published in June 1701. Although the gazetteer, dealing with a royal death, is naturally obliged to use a tone of national mourning, the beauty of the house and gardens and the irrepressible ability of the residence to produce pleasure impose themselves on him in the midst of an account of Monsieur's foreboding. He narrates an exchange between Monsieur and his long-time favorite, the Chevalier de Lorraine, without anybody in the intended readership probably batting an eye at the distribution of roles:

> As for the foreboding about his death, one can judge from what follows. A few days before it happened, this Prince being in one of his galleries at Saint-Cloud, sitting by himself and lost in thought, Mr. the Chevalier de Lorraine walked by him without Monsieur coming out of his reverie. This Chevalier came near this Prince a second time, and seeing that he was still deep in thought, he could not help addressing him thus, *Monsieur is quite absorbed in his thoughts.* To which His Highness replied: *I am thinking about the beauty of this place, that I created it, and that I soon will have to leave it.* It must be observed that from that place, one could see two beautiful galleries separated by a magnificent salon; that one of these galleries served as an orangery; that one sees at the end and on a level with it a walking path of the garden with several fountains, and that this path, these two galleries, and the salon make up a perspective where the variety of the painting, the gilding, the furniture, and the greenery, forms an ensemble as magnificent as it is singular. (*Mercure*, June 1701, 287–89)

Such an account is, precisely, an analyst's dream. Even in the face of death, Monsieur is confronted with the problem of pleasure—the beauty of this locus of pleasure—but, more significantly, even when dealing with the death of such a high-ranking figure in the kingdom, the columnist cannot avoid mentioning the extraordinary nature of the place ("it must be observed"). In Freudian–Lacanian terms, it might be tempting to say that while Saint-Cloud itself might be linked to the reality principle as much as to the pleasure principle (since it is simply more than a fantasized *jouissance*), Monsieur is contemplating something *beyond* the pleasure principle. And beyond the pleasure principle, obviously, lies death. What is interesting, here, is the convergence of Monsieur's alleged portentous words, linking the pleasure of beauty to impending death, and the comment they triggered on the gazetteer's part. More than Monsieur's own take on his near-death situation, I mean to emphasize both the fact that it seems impossible in contemporary representations not to incorporate pleasure and the linkage of this pleasure to death, the former somehow leading to the latter—albeit in a somewhat muddled way—in the chronicler's consciousness.

Here, however, may lie the key to understanding queerness in Ancien Régime France—and the limit of Monsieur's queerness. This neat analytical view of Philippe of Orléans's situation, with its emphasis on the gratification of desire, on the endorsement of (free) pleasure, and on the relationship between pleasure and death, rests on a total split from the concrete, material conditions in which this distinctive pleasure could be indulged in with such apparent abandon. When replaced in the real political world of an ever-strengthening absolutist monarchy, it becomes at once less glamorous and less easy to account for in purely Lacanian terms. Most revealing is the social inscription of such pleasure. The pursuit of pleasure for its own sake, and with no qualification, might serve as a clue for the identification of gay subtexts in the culture of the Ancien Régime in France. Whether it in fact produces an identity that can be termed "homosexual" or even a more inclusive category of marginality such as "queer," it is clearly an effective textual operator. Accounts of Monsieur's life and times spin a yarn of pleasures seen as free and unfettered by ethical-religious strictures. But Monsieur's pleasures are also, literally, expensive. They have to be paid for. If we consider the paradigm of the Duke of Orléans's pleasure, his splendid residence of Saint-Cloud, its "magnificent" and "singular" layout is dependent on the purchase of costly artifacts and on the labor of highly skilled craftsmen.[44] Though the *Mercure* complacently presents Monsieur as the most magnificent prince in Europe (in the technical sense of the word mentioned earlier, as the paradigmatic princely virtue), his *taste* for ceremony and fêtes goes beyond his grasp on his duty of magnificence. More to the point, here, only the King is really entitled and able to spend freely.[45] Even Monsieur, who spent his life improving his financial situation and amassed a large fortune,[46] depends on the "kindness" of the King. To keep up with the cost of Saint-Cloud entails a kind of caving in—a way of giving ground, to quote from the translation of Lacan's *Ethics*. Saint-Simon's *Mémoires* can help us illuminate this point. The King had promised Monsieur the governorship of Brittany for his son the Duc de Chartres when the latter agreed to marry Mademoiselle de Blois. The King manages not to keep his part of the bargain by forcing the current governor to swap governorships with the Comte de Toulouse, another of Louis XIV's bastard children. Not only does the King renege on his word; he promotes his illegitimate children at the expense of a legitimate prince of the blood. Once more, Saint-Simon emphasizes the role Monsieur's favorite plays in securing the latter's eventual acquiescence to this breach of dynastic propriety:

> The King bore Monsieur's ill temper as long as he wanted: he knew well the way to appease him. The chevalier de Lorraine acted in his usual capacity, and some money for gambling and for the embellishment of Saint-Cloud soon erased the discontent about the government of Brittany. (Saint-Simon I: 219)

Saint-Simon has an axe to grind, here, and his desperate attachment to the "traditional" aristocratic order may stem from basic insecurities (arising from the awareness that his own position is relatively recent, and mostly due to the favor his father enjoyed in the eyes of Louis XIII, the previous King, and Monsieur's father). But it does not invalidate his account. To put it bluntly, Monsieur's pleasures, just like those of most courtiers, are, to a large extent, paid for by the King. In other words, Monsieur's supposedly free pleasures entangle him in the King's economy.

This realization, in turn, may cause us to soft-pedal the claim of queerness where Monsieur is concerned. There may be a hint of gayness, but it is difficult to reconcile the entanglement in royal gratifications with the splendid quest for a sublime object. It is as though there were a parallel to be drawn between the traditional characterization of the court, in religious discourse, as a most dangerous center of temptations and the difficulty of escaping the recurring seductions of material objects, with their cycle of satisfaction and pain, when one sits in the lap of luxury. If anything, Monsieur was nearer to the throne and in a more central position in courtly life than anybody; yet, he was constantly praised for his piety. Beyond the laudatory topos, however, and judging from the above interpretation of the consequence of Monsieur's passion for Saint-Cloud, he seems to have remained caught in the cycle of desire and gratification, need and satisfaction, characteristic, in analytic terms, of ordinary human experience. This has an important bearing on our analysis of gayness and queerness in terms of desire. I suggested earlier that the libertine might have enjoyed a similar reputation of not giving up on his or her desire. Were we to radicalize our definition of free pleasure and of the exigency of desire, we might find that in the seventeenth century, fictional characters are perhaps the only (imaginary) embodiments of the possibility of reaching beyond the cycle of desire and gratification.[47] This is where the limit of sexual identity in the characterization of social queerness might best be delineated.

One character that challenged the reading public at the apogee of Louis XIV's reign, the Princesse de Clèves, will illustrate the (useful) inclusiveness of the category of queer. Like Antigone and Monsieur, she is an extraordinary and singular character. What, to parody Foucault, we might term "care of the self" leads her to refuse Monsieur de Nemours and renounce life at court. She is represented as explicitly stating that she chooses a path that will protect her from suffering. Suffering would come, inevitably, from the fact that passion is not everlasting; or, to phrase it differently, that, in life, one does not possess and enjoy the object of one's desire forever, with the inevitable consequence that desire recurs and suffering arises. Moreover, Madame de Clèves's decision, a decision that completely baffled Madame de Lafayette's readers at the time—as it still does today— leads to an early death, made memorable, however, by "inimitable" acts of virtue.[48] Withdrawal from court, and from society, the choice of foregoing the fulfillment of desire in life in order to comply with one's idea of oneself (and the character is given several passages where she explains her motives): she declares her love because she feels she will get pleasure out of the experience (Lafayette 171)—but goes on to refuse the logic of fulfillment *in the world* as fleeting and as leading to more suffering (Lafayette 172–73). That her short and exemplary life should be encoded in terms of Christian virtue should not mislead us and certainly did little to diminish the perplexity of Madame de Lafayette's contemporaries. If the point was to make the heroine exemplary, Christian asceticism and virtues served the purpose without lessening the transgressive aspect of both her refusal of Nemours and her self-removal from the court. Her choice has consistently been seen as singular, and the character keeps claiming her singularity, as when she confesses to her husband her love for another man or when she does not scruple to admit to loving Nemours to his face; she always sets herself apart from all the protagonists of the court's many love affairs as the (only) one who does not simply surrender to the ephemeral seduction of extramarital affairs. If we bring together the desire for absolute and definitive gratification, and the refusal to settle for less,[49] as well as the unrelenting pursuit of her unprecedented course to death, it is tempting to conclude, even provisionally, that if there is, indeed, a seventeenth-century version of "queer," and if Lacan's analytic model may be instrumental in circumscribing it, the Princess of Clèves's self-imposed withdrawal and eventual quick demise is it. In other words, the character's actions, transgressive in the context of both the sixteenth-century court featured in the text and the late seventeenth-century court that the *nouvelle*'s readers could look to for a frame of reference, question the social, heteronormative order that governs both. She does not cede on her desire, and her uncompromising pursuit of the sublime object goes beyond the pleasure principle while fulfilling its absolute promise. She may not be gay, but she is certainly queer, and in the end confirms the usefulness of the category of *queer* as distinct from, and much more inclusive than, that of *sexual difference*;[50] for that reason, too, *queerness* is much more unsettling.

We might have to consider, then, the possibility that, in actual high circles, the ethical indifference predicated upon the pleasure of highly visible marginals may be a rhetorical fallacy—an ideological construct—carrying for the outside world both condemnation and admiration. We might also use this as a paradigmatic reminder that cultural-ideological phenomena cannot be completely elucidated along the lines of an individual analysis, or, in other words, from the perspective of an individual analysand who might correct his or her error in perspective through analysis. This perhaps is the danger underlying the phrase that serves as the title for the current volume, "the desire of the analysts." The substitution of libidinal economy for political and socioeconomic factors when one attempts to account for the status of homosexuality in seventeenth-century France may seem innocuous enough (despite the fact that it may have serious consequences both on current representations of homosexuality and the lives of individuals in today's societies and on the models that might be derived from it). But the stakes of such an interpretive shift may take on their true significance when it is observed in other areas. For instance, when Žižek, in *Enjoy Your Symptom!*, states that the Nazi mistakenly believes that by expelling the Jew he will restore the (mythical) harmony of German society, that the Nazi is in fact dealing with *objet a*, and that, as a consequence, the source of the disharmony he perceives is *already within him*, he is certainly making an interesting observation *from the perspective of the analyst* confronted with a suffering individual. But, as Žižek himself points out, the *instance de la lettre* through (empty) Master Signifiers is still effective, and people die for the *Fatherland*. And, to follow on a Lacanian path, the letter always reaches its destination. It means, if we go back to the Nazi, that he may (or may not) believe erroneously that he might solve his problem if only he could get rid of the Jews.[51] When we shift our focus to society, it does not really matter whether there is an authentic (though erroneous) belief—there is, in fact, as the text points out, no *error*, or, at least, no lack of efficacy.[52] The letter in fact does always arrive at its destination.

This line of argument leads me back to the function of pleasure in the representation of homosexuality and the heuristic fecundity of Lacan's formulations in distinguishing between *gay* and truly *queer*—i.e., culturally or even politically threatening—figures and behaviors, in past historical contexts. We are returned, however, to the initial perception of the nature of *queer* as more on the side of innovative questions than on that of definitive answers. At the same time as we can ascertain that there is no contradiction, in the end, between historical contextualization and the usefulness of (Lacanian) analysis, we are also confronted by the limits of purely analytic descriptions—or, rather, the necessity to account for the way such apparently ahistorical notions of desire and pleasure are actualized in historically specific circumstances. It may well be that contemporary observers and chroniclers of the revels of the elite simultaneously envied individuals who seemed not to give ground as to their desire and shuddered at the realization. The fact, however, that we are dealing with *discursive* strategies, with representations, should not be underemphasized. Not only do *judgments* vary with the social circles to which sodomites belong, in both purely moral and judicial, even criminal, terms; even those whose position allows them to escape explicit censure or legal prosecution fulfill their desires and find their pleasures in the concrete economy of the period—a reminder that we might generalize as a sobering word of caution.

NOTES

1. Philippe of Orleans, brother to the Sun-King, was called simply "Monsieur."

2. This might even explain Monsieur's celebrated piety.

3. "The Desire of the Analysts" was the title of the 2003 conference of the Comparative Literature Program at the University of South Carolina. The present article stems from a paper I presented there as well as from an earlier one I read at the 2002 conference of the Society for Seventeenth-Century French Studies, which met in Bath. In its current form, this chapter owes a lot to conversations with and suggestions or queries from colleagues and friends, most notably Peter Bayley, Gary Ferguson, and Paul Allen Miller.

4. Even though I am interested here in *representations* of homosexuality in the Ancien Régime, such representations cannot be viewed in total isolation from "facts" such as legal background, repression, social attitudes, and economic data. The legal

aspect, in particular, is well documented in Didier Godard's *Le Goût de Monsieur* as well as in Maurice Lever's *Les Bûchers de Sodome*, whose interpretation Godard mercilessly criticizes. Whatever Godard's reservations may be, or mine for that matter, on the *interpretation* of the available data, I think I can refer the reader to the bibliography for the facts themselves, in order to make my own text less cumbersome.

5. A comprehensive account of the contradictions would exceed the scope of this article. I will simply mention two examples. On the one hand, the author claims that "sodomites" are not viewed as different from others, and are, indeed, no different; on the other hand, he remarks several times on the fact that high-ranking sodomites were, as a rule, more tolerant, especially in matters of religion, or that Monsieur, like most generals known to be sodomites, tends to be more concerned with the lives of his soldiers. Similarly, though the author repeatedly asserts that it would make no sense to talk of "homosexuality" as a nature or an identity-defining trait, he concludes that Monsieur was truly a homosexual, in today's sense of the word, engaging in heterosexual intercourse only out of duty in the context of marriage, and with exclusively homosexual desires. Hence the book's title, *Le Goût de Monsieur*—Monsieur's taste, or leanings.

6. I call *royal text* a complex network of texts (panegyrics, official memoirs, histories and parahistorical writings) as well as pictorial and sculptural representations (portraits, statues, ephemeral architectures, and ceremonial decors or fireworks and bonfires) or mixed representations, such as *devises*, all linked intertextually, and revolving around a limited number of themes, models, and myths, that orchestrate the celebration of the King, under the auspices and for a large part, but not exclusively, at the initiative of the monarchic administration. On this concept, see Zoberman, "Eloquence and Ideology" and "Public Discourse."

7. In his memoirs, spanning half a century (1691–1743), Saint-Simon, as a privileged observer very attached to the aristocratic order, chronicles the lives and times of all the "movers and shakers" of his time. He sees Louis XIV's regime as a time of bastardization and ineluctable erosion of social distinction. In this sense, Proust's chronicle of the desegregation of the Faubourg Saint-Germain in *À la recherche du temps perdu* is reminiscent of Saint-Simon's memoirs. It is not surprising, therefore, that Proust's characters should refer to the memoirist so consistently and that the intertextual connection should be so strong between the two texts.

8. The richest source in this context is the *Mercure galant* (which was to become the *Mercure de France*). It started publication in 1672, and, after it was interrupted in 1674, it was published very regularly as a monthly periodical from 1677 on. Largely subsidized by the crown and sold in the provinces as well as in Paris, it reported on the major events in the lives of the King and the royal family and high-ranking figures, on life at court, on war, and on the latest fashions; it included accounts of ceremonies, short stories, and enigmas. When Madame de Lafayette's *Princesse de Clèves* was first published, the *Mercure* conducted a poll among its readers to assess the reaction of the social elite to the behavior of the main character (see below, n.37).

9. The lexicon of effeminacy routinely appears in contemporary debates about rhetoric or language, as the negative counterpart of manly eloquence, or, as

in the case of Italian, as a contrastive marker to enhance the superior value of the French language.

10. Saint-Simon links Monsieur's homoeroticism to a reversal of the *natural* social hierarchy. From the outset, Monsieur is said to be "governed" by the Chevalier. "Monsieur's taste did not lean toward women, and he did not even hide it. This taste had made the chevalier de Lorraine his master" (Saint-Simon I: 33).

11. See in particular I, ii and II, ii (442–44 and 466–67).

12. Žižek translates this phrase as "give way as to one's desire" (75).

13. Unless otherwise specified, all translations are mine.

14. Interestingly, "Our Attitude Toward Death" is one of the texts in which Freud takes up, almost in passing, the role of fiction in human life: we "seek in literature and in the theater what has been lost in life. There we still find people who know how to die—who, indeed, even manage to kill someone else" (Freud, "Thoughts for the Time on War and Death" 291).

15. Kathryn Hoffmann captures it in the title of her book, which she borrows from a remark by Pellisson, associated with the writing of the King's memoirs: *Society of Pleasures*.

16. In November 1686, Louis XIV underwent surgery for a fistula on one of his buttocks. The successful operation and the King's recovery were at the origin of an incredible array of celebrations and speeches that lasted well into 1687. Afterwards, the King's deportment during and after his illness becomes a topos for his incense-bearers.

17. In his edition of the complete works of Molière, Georges Couton characterizes the "Pleasures of the Enchanted Isle" as a kind of inauguration for Versailles, which was to become the King's residence. Molière played an important role in organizing the sequence of dazzling fêtes over three days. Among other things, he contributed to the *Princesse d'Élide* ("comédie mêlée de danse et de musique") and *Tartuffe* (Couton 739 ff).

18. Maurice Lever quotes the following:

> *Philippe est mort la bouteille à la main,*
> *Le proverbe est fort incertain*
> *Qui dit que l'homme meurt comme il vit d'ordinaire;*
> *Il nous montre bien le contraire,*
> *Car s'il fût mort comme il avait vécu,*
> *Il serait mort le vit au cul.* (109)

This oft-quoted song was translated by Lewis Seifert, who curiously reads the last line as "with his cock up an ass" (Merrick 41), whereas it can only mean "with a cock up his ass." The difference matters here because all the evidence points to a fixed sexual role in Monsieur's case; this in turn might be of help in a discussion about sexual practices and identities in the seventeenth century.

19. To give just one example, Madame writes: "Only commoners like women any more" (Palatine 111).

20. This aspect is essential to my later discussion of the link between pleasure and death where Monsieur is concerned. If the only accounts we had were the obituaries, in Saint-Simon and the *Mercure galant*, in particular, then we would have to envision the possibility that the context—Monsieur's death—was actually a generative factor, as a neurosis causing symptoms to erupt at all levels of the text. As it is, we have enough alternative accounts to obviate that risk.

21. As opposed to commoners, nobles and, more generally, courtiers as a whole were de facto immune from religious-criminal prosecution for sodomy. The "Italian vice" is said in contemporary sources to have been prevalent among the nobility. Godard asserts that there is no reason to assume that nobles were, in this domain, freer than commoners (or, rather, that commoners were not as free as nobles). Though his point that any position of authority over another might be considered as also entailing sexual favors is quite illuminating the cases prosecuted do indicate a social distinction. Texts of the period actually assert that the nobility was more universally given to the "Italian vice" (Palatine 111).

22. On the *Mercure*, see note 8; on Saint-Simon, see note 7.

23. The whole account is saturated with a lexicon of luxury and refinement and is worth quoting further: "Madame the Dauphine had not yet seen this delightful house, so Monsieur formed the project to treat their Majesties to a regale ["régal"] when they brought this Princess. . . . The refinement, elegance, and magnificence of all the rooms having been admired, the King passed into the gallery" (*Mercure galant*, May 1680, 295–98).

24. See Primi Visconti, who recounts how the abbé del Carretto warned him against reviling sodomites when he complained to the latter that he had been propositioned: "Il me répondit qu'il fallait avoir de la compassion, parce que les hommes de semblable inclination naissent avec elle, comme les poètes avec la rime" (81).

25. The account of the 1678 régal, particularly where the list of dancers is concerned, is a variant of this one. In 1678:

> I would have much to tell you, if I wanted to talk of Monseigneur the Dauphin's wonderful gracefulness, or the gallant ["galant"] air of Messieurs the princes of Conty, of la Roche-sur-Yon, and of Vermandois, of Messieurs the counts of Armagnac, of Marsan, and of Brionne, of Monsieur the Marquis of Hautefort, and of the chevalier of Chastillon: but if I feel unequal to the task of expressing how much they showed themselves to advantage while dancing, what could I say that might correspond to the admiration Mademoiselle, Mademoiselle de Valois caused. (333–34)

26. I am referring here to the *Mémoires du Marquis de Sourches sur le règne de Louis XIV*. They were published in France in the late nineteenth century. Merrick and Ragan (*Homosexuality in Early Modern France*) included a translation of an entry for June 1682.

27. For Saint-Simon, dancing is Brionne's only talent. The point is driven home as the portrait unfolds. It is enough, however, to make him a relevant part of Monsieur's circle of pleasure:

> He was a civil enough ["honnête"] man, but so short and so deprived of depth that nothing was lower; he was only seen in public venues of the court, and, at home, never saw anyone; his family had no esteem for him, neither did anyone at the *grande écurie* ("the royal stable"). His father, who once had had devolutions conferred upon him, had all but forced him in the past two or three months to resign them as we have seen, his *charge* to his brother, and his government to his son. Monsieur le Grand [Brionne's father, who was the Chevalier de Lorraine's older brother, was Grand Écuyer of the King, hence his title Monsieur le Grand], who was not soft, used to say that he drank all his good wine, and he was quite displeased with it. He did not have to go through the pain of finding comfort. (Saint-Simon IV: 475–76).

28. Such a suggestion would require a very nuanced and thorough study of the relationship of the King, and of the court, with dance. According to abbé d'Olivet, Du Bois was *maître à danser* when the young duc de Guise singled him out and was so taken by him as to arrange that he be made his *gouverneur*. But, precisely, Du Bois shed his dancing persona. Périgny, who was associated with Benserade's *ballets de cour*, became part of the team that oversaw the Dauphin's education and eventually was enlisted in the writing of the King's memoirs. Again, dance is here only a transitional element. Not so, it seems, in Monsieur's circle.

29. I cannot resist here quoting from Hoffmann's introduction a passage where changes in the social reality and in the social imaginary are associated with inventing homes to gambol in:

> As a monarch dreams of being a Sun God, as bourgeois struggle with their problematic relation to the aesthetic, as religious bodies narrate imaginary scenes of forbidden pleasures or as travelers, lexicographers and historians invent worlds and words that fit their readers' desires, the real forms and changes, and the plots of the imaginary, to paraphrase a formalist expression, do not so much find "homes" as create new ones in which to gambol. (Hoffmann 7–8).

30. For an elaboration of this hypothesis, see the conclusion of the article mentioned above (Zoberman "A Taste for Ceremony"). It is important to note, however, that the *Mercure* never mentions homosexuality openly, and this is where Godard misses the rhetorical strategies with regard to homosexuality.

31. Thus, Monsieur is both praised for being a punctilious church attendee and absolved for his falls, unavoidable since he is a human being, and, moreover, a human being placed at the center of worldly temptation, at the center of the center, court—thus embodying a kind of central marginality.

32. See, for instance, Michael Bronski.

33. It should be remembered that I started out seeking for clues pointing to homosexuality, or even gayness. I am therefore arguing that certain references to a particular kind of pleasure point to more than "sodomy" as sexual acts, hence the return to a lexicon of sexual identity. The difficulty, here, comes from the fact that in my discussion I am also distinguishing between "queer" and "gay."

34. Clearly, Kathryn Hoffmann's book, *Society of Pleasures*, owes a lot to this insight, and the contrast with Monsieur is made even stronger. I will return to the suspicion pleasure is steeped in, but it is illuminating to compare the pleasures Monsieur surrounds himself with, while offering them to his guests, with the way panegyrists of the King praise the latter's use of pleasures. Characteristic of the latter is Barbier d'Aucour's praise of the King for providing harmless entertainment such as gambling—in moderation!—while gaining insight into the true character of the courtiers and of their pleasures.

35. In his discussion of the misapprehension that "classical language" is transparent, Peter Bayley takes up the introduction of both characters and the phenomenon of what he terms the "hypersuperlative." His thorough reading of La Rochefoucauld's treatment of abstract notions such as bravery or virtue is also relevant to the interpretive problems of the word "pleasure" I am emphasizing here.

36. This aspect is relatively well known, and I am not treating here in detail the technique of portraiture, though such a study would be necessary for a more developed reflection. Erica Harth discusses the evolution of the portrait and its gradual appropriation by the *bourgeoisie* ("Of Portraits," Harth 68–128). See also Jacquline Plantié, *La Mode du portrait littéraire en France, 1641–1681*.

37. I am referring, here, to the poll the *Mercure* took among *mondain* readers to settle whether the Princess's refusal to marry Nemours when she was socially free to do it was believable, as well as to such comments as Valincour's *Lettres*, for the seventeenth century. The bibliography of modern studies bringing to the fore the perplexing development of the character is too extensive to reference here. "An Unlikely Princess" is the title of the chapter Harth devotes to the curious relationship of the *nouvelle* to history (Harth 180–221). Of particular interest to my analysis here is Nancy Miller's "Emphasis Added," where she discusses the "singular" nature of both character and plot events. The suggestion that the specificity of fiction written by women resides in something like a tone or emphasis is indicative of the kind of difficulty I am pointing to as well (see Miller "Emphasis Added").

38. For reproductions of fragments of the Bunbury caricature from 1787 it was based on, see the cover of *An Election Ball* by Christopher Anstey (Turner 1997).

39. On 26 August 1689, she writes:

> I begged Monsieur to give his son another governor, and I put forward the following reasons: "it seems to me it would not be an honor for my son if one might think that he was Effiat's mistress, for it is certain there is not a greater sodomite in France and I think it would be a

bad start for a young Prince such as my son to start in life by the most horrible debaucheries." To which Monsieur replied: "I must admit that in truth Effiat was unruly and that he did love young men, but he got over that vice years ago—Yet, I told Monsieur, only a few years back, a pretty young man from Germany apologized for not coming to see me as often as he wished because d'Effiat bothered him excessively every time he came tot the Palais Royal. So, d'Effiat did not mend his ways as long ago as his friends contend. But, even supposing that he did spend a few years without partaking of this vice, since his inclination moves him towards it, I do not feel I must entrust my only son to him, to put him to the test, and to ascertain whether or not the Grand-Écuyer has given up on his squires. (Palatine 126–27)

40. On this shift and its meaning, see for instance, Georgia Cowart, "Sappho's Cythera." Apostolidès had already stressed the symbolic-political significance of court ballet during its relatively short life span (1581–1672) and the significance of its disappearance.

41. In 1998, Bradley Rubidge organized a special session at the annual meeting of the Modern Language Association (in San Francisco) on "The Homosexual and the Libertine, sixteenth–eighteenth century." Because of his premature death, I chaired the session, but I am indebted to him for the insight, as I am indeed to the three panelists, Ullrich Langer, Pierre Force, and Helena Russo. Given the fact that others have discussed the connection between the libertine and the homosexual, I will be content here with mentioning it, rather than devote myself to the case of the libertine.

42. "Queer" used to be weighted politically. The term has become fashionable and arguably less threatening than "gay" and "lesbian" in that it avoids direct reference to sexual difference, which reclaims a kind of radicalness, in the tradition of John Rechy's *The Sexual Outlaw*. The advantage of *queer*, however, is precisely its ability to encompass a wider range of situations potentially threatening to the (heteronormative) order.

43. I am indebted here to Paul Allen Miller's familiarity with Lacan's work. Without his friendly and insistent prodding, I would not have been able to put forward even these hints of a distinction between simply gay and really queer (perhaps because finding textual arguments to think of a seventeenth-century magnificent sodomite as *gay* was in itself a step toward clarifying our discourse about homosexuality).

44. In this sense, we can draw a parallel between Saint-Cloud and the fictional Abbaye de Thélème, where the otiose and pleasure-filled life of the residents is sustained by a separate production of luxury appurtenances—though the inmates only participate in this economy as nonpaying consumers (Rabelais 158).

45. Royal edicts and declarations restricting ostentatious spending (prohibiting, for instance, the use of fabrics woven with precious metals in clothing, and foreign lace, as well as regulating the kind and size of jewels permissible to people

according their conditions) stress the crown's interest in preventing courtiers from spending beyond their means.

46. On this point, see Barker (166 ff).

47. And, here, Freud's remark on the role of literature, quoted in note 14, takes on its full significance.

48. Peter Bayley points out the contradiction between exemplariness and "inimitable" acts. This paradox is not new to the seventeenth century: the King is always presented as a model for all conditions as well as an inimitable character. It should be noted that "inimitable" is not one of the laudatory epithets most often associated with Monsieur (whereas "singular" and "magnificent" are). The paradox of an inimitable exemplar (rather than example) finds an archetypal actualization in the royal text, as defined in note 6 (see, in particular, Zoberman "Généalogie d'une image").

49. In her discussion of artificial plausibility in *La Princesse de Clèves*, Nancy Miller touches on many points that are relevant to the current reflection (pleasure, and more specifically sexual pleasure, daydreaming, etc.). She remarks: "She withdraws then and confesses, not to resist possession as her mother would have wished, but to improve on it; to *rescript* possession" (42).

50. It is important to remember that the notion of sexual identity is still foreign to seventeenth-century Europe even though we have textual evidence of an inchoate awareness of homosexuality as a mark of difference, even as an innate factor.

51. "What we encounter here is the paradox of the *sacrifice* in its purest: the illusion of the sacrifice is that renunciation of the object will render accessible the intact whole. In the ideological field, this paradox finds its clearest articulation in the anti-Semitic concept of the Jew: the Nazi has to sacrifice the Jew in order to be able to maintain the illusion that it is only the 'Jewish plot' that prevents the establishment of the 'class relationship,' of society as a harmonious, organic whole. This is why, in the last pages of *Seminar XI*, Lacan is fully justified to designate the Holocaust as a 'gift of reconciliation': is not the Jew the anal object *par excellence*, i.e., the partial object-stain that disturbs the harmony of the class relationship? One is tempted, here, to paraphrase the above-quoted Jacques-Alain Miller's proposition: "The Jew is not what hinders the advent of the class relationship, as the anti-Semitic perspective error makes us believe. The Jew is on the contrary a filler, that which fills in the relationship which does not exist and bestows on it its fantasmatic consistency." In other words, what appears as the hindrance to society's full identity with itself is actually its positive condition: by transposing onto the Jew the role of the foreign body, which introduces in the social organism disintegration and antagonism, the fantasy-image of society qua consistent, harmonious whole is rendered possible" (Žižek 89–90).

52. And the consequences may be long-lasting, as is attested by the current resistance of inhabitants of Jedwabne to come to terms with the fact that the Christian population of the town effectively killed hundreds of Jews on July 10, 1941—they still hold to a double creed, on the one hand that the Jews were actually guilty of bringing the communists into Poland, and, on the other hand, that the Germans, not the Poles, killed them.

WORKS CITED

Anstey, Christopher. *An Election Ball*. 1776. Ed. Gavin Turner. Bristol: Broadcast Books, 1997.

Apostolidès, Jean-Marie. *Le Roi-machine*. Paris: Minuit, 1981.

Baker, Nancy Nichols. *Brother to the Sun-King: Philippe, Duke of Orléans*. Baltimore: Johns Hopkins UP, 1989.

Bayley, Peter. "Fixed Form and Varied Function: Reflections on the Language of French Classicism." *Seventeenth-Century French Studies* 6 (1984): 6–21.

Bronski, Michael. *The Pleasure Principle: Sex, Backlash, and the Struggle for Gay Freedom*. New York: St. Martin's, 1998.

Bussy, Roger de Rabutin, comte de. *Histoire amoureuse des Gaules*. Vol. 3. Paris: 1858. Kraus Reprints, 1972.

Couton, Georges, ed. *Molière: Œuvres complètes*. Vol. 1. Paris: Gallimard, 1971.

Cowart, Georgia. "Sappho's Cythera: The *Fête galante* vs. the *Fête monarchique*." Ed. R. Tobin. *Racine et/ou le classicisme*. Tübingen: G. Narr, 2001. 395–408.

Freud, Sigmund. *Beyond the Pleasure Principle*. *The Standard Edition of the Complete Psychological Works of Sigmund Freud*. Vol. 18. Ed. James Strachey. London: Hogarth, 1955. 7–64.

———. *The Interpretation of Dreams*. *The Standard Edition*. Vols. 4–5. London: Hogarth, 1953. 1–627.

———. "Thoughts for the Time on War and Death—I. The Disillusionment of the War." *The Standard Edition*. Vol. 14. London: Hogarth, 1953. 273–300.

Godard, Didier. *Le Goût de Monsieur*. Montblanc: H & O, 2002.

Harth, Erica. *Ideology and Culture in Seventeenth-Century France*. Ithaca: Cornell UP, 1983.

Hoffmann, Kathryn. *Society of Pleasures: Interdisciplinary Readings in Pleasure and Power during the Reign of Louis XIV*. New York: St. Martin's, 1997.

Lacan, Jacques. *The Seminar of Jacques Lacan. Book VII: The Ethics of Psychoanalysis. 1959–1960*. Trans. Dennis Porter. New York: Norton, 1992.

———. *Le Séminaire. Livre VII: L'Éthique de la psychanalyse*. Paris: Seuil, 1986.

Lafayette, Madame de. *La Princesse de Clèves*. 1678. Paris: Garnier-Flammarion, 1966.

Lever, Maurice. *Les Bûchers de Sodome: Histoire des "infâmes."* Paris: Fayard, 1985.

Marc, Daniel. *Hommes du Grand Siècle*. Paris: Arcadie, 1956.

Marlowe, Christopher. *The Complete Plays*. New York: Penguin, 1969.

Mercure galant: May 1680; October 1681; June 1701.

Merrick, Jeffrey, and Bryant T. Ragan, Jr. *Homosexuality in Early Modern France: A Documentary Collection*. New York: Oxford UP, 2001.

Miller, Nancy K. "Emphasis Added: Plots and Plausibilities in Women's Fictions." *PMLA* 96 (1981): 36–48.

Palatine, Charlotte-Élizabeth d'Orléan, princess. *Lettres de la princesse Palatine (1672–1722)*. Paris: Mercure de France, 1985.

Pellisson-Fontanier, Paul, and Abbé d'Olivet. *Histoire de l'académie françoise*. Ed. Ch.-L. Livet. Paris: Didier et Cie, 1858. 2 vols.

Plantié, Jacqueline. *La mode du portrait littéraire en France, 1641–1681*. Paris-Geneva: Champion-Slatkine, 1994.

Rabelais, François. *Gargantua and Pantagruel*. Trans. J. M. Cohen. New York: Penguin, 1955.

Rechy, John. *The Sexual Outlaw*. New York: Dell, 1977.

Saint-Simon, Duc de. *Mémoires*. Ed. Yves Coirault. Paris: Gallimard, 1983–1988 (8 vols.).

Sourches, Louis-François de Bouschet, Marquis de. *Mémoires du Marquis de Sourches sur le règne de Louis XIV*, I (September 1681–December 1686). Paris: Hachette, 1882.

Valincour, Jean Baptiste Henri du Trousset de. *Lettres à Madame la marquise *** sur le sujet de la princesse de Clèves* (1679). Paris: Garnier-Flammarion, 2001.

Zoberman, Pierre. "Eloquence and Ideology: Between Image and Propaganda." *Rhetorica* 18.3 (2000): 295–320.

———. "Généalogie d'une image: l'éloge spéculaire." *XVIIe SIECLE* 146 (1985): 79–91.

———, ed. *Les Panégyriques du Roi prononcés dans l'Académie française*. Paris: Presses de l'Université de Paris-Sorbonne, 1991.

———. "Public Discourse, Propaganda, and Personality Cult under Louis XIV." *The Public* 8 (2001): 59–71.

———. "A Taste for Ceremony: Reading Monsieur's Magnificence." *Cérémonies et rituels en France au XVIIe siècle*. Eds. Fr. Canova and D. Westel. Berlin: Weidler Buchverlag, 2002. 29–42.

Žižek, Slavoj. *Enjoy Your Symptom!: Jacques Lacan in Hollywood and Out*. Rev. ed. New York and London: Routledge, 2001.

Contributors

GREG FORTER is Associate Professor of English at the University of South Carolina. He teaches courses in American literature, politics, and culture, and is the author of *Murdering Masculinities: Fantasies of Gender and Violence in the American Crime Novel*. His current book project examines the relationships among monopoly capitalism, gender, and mourning in American modernism.

PAUL ALLEN MILLER is a Carolina Distinguished Professor in Classics and Comparative Literature at the University of South Carolina. His books include *Lyric Texts and Lyric Consciousness, Latin Erotic Elegy; Subjecting Verses;* and *Latin Verse Satire*. He has edited or co-edited eleven volumes of essays on literary theory, gender studies, and classics, including *Rethinking Sexuality: Foucault and Classical Antiquity*. He has published numerous articles on Latin, Greek, French, and English literature as well as theory.

SHARON DIANE NELL is Professor and Chair of the Department of Modern Languages and Literatures at the University of Loyola, Maryland. She publishes widely on French literature of the seventeenth and eighteenth century with special emphasis on problems of gender and sexuality. She is an editor of the journal *Intertexts* and of the series Fashioning the Eighteenth Century (Texas Tech University Press).

DENEEN SENASI received her PhD from the University of Alabama in 2004. She is currently a Lecturer in the Department of English at the University of Tennessee. Her research and teaching focus on early modern British Literature, and she has published essays in *Religion and Literature* and *The Journal of Early Modern Cultural Studies*.

KAJA SILVERMAN is Class of 1940 Professor of Rhetoric and Film in the Department of Rhetoric at UC Berkeley. She is the author of seven books, including *James Coleman, World Spectators, Male Subjectivity at the Margins;* and

The Acoustic Mirror: The Female Voice in Psychoanalysis and Cinema. Silverman is currently writing a book on photography and a book—entitled *Appropriations*—that is centrally concerned with racial, sexual, and economic difference.

HENRY SUSSMAN is Julian Park Professor of Comparative Literature at SUNY Buffalo and a Recurrent Visiting Professor in the Department of German at Yale University. Among his publications are *The Aesthetic Contract: Statutes of Art and Intellectual Work in Modernity*, *Psyche and Text: The Sublime and the Grandiose in Literature, Psychopathology, and Culture's*, and *Afterimages of Modernity*. Sussman coedited *Psychoanalysis and . . .* with Richard Feldstein and *Engagement and Indifference: Beckett and the Political* with Christopher Devenney.

DOMIETTA TORLASCO is a Harper Fellow and Assistant Professor in the Humanities Collegiate Division, University of Chicago. Her research brings together film theory, psychoanalysis, and phenomenology. She is currently completing a book entitled *The Time of the Crime: Visions from Italian Cinema* while pursuing an MFA in Film, Video, and New Media at the School of the Art Institute of Chicago.

SLAVOJ ŽIŽEK is Professor and Senior Researcher in the Faculty for Social Science at the University of Ljubljana. He is the author of numerous essays and books, including "Freud Lives"; *Tarrying with the Negative; The Fragile Absolute*; *Iraq: The Borrowed Kettle; On Belief;* and *Everything You Always Wanted to Know about Lacan (But Were Afraid to Ask Hitchcock)*. His recent work explores the relationships between Leninist revolutionary thought and Lacan's conception of the Real.

PIERRE ZOBERMAN is Professor of French at Unversité de Paris 13. He is the French translator of Walter Abish's How German Is It?. A specialist in queer studies and the history of rhetoric, he is the author *Les Panégyriques du Roi prononcés dans l'Académie française*, which won the Prix de Littérature générale de l'Académie française, and *Les Cérémonies de la parole*, which won the Prix Thiers de l'Académie française. He has also published numerous articles.

Index